Alfred Wiedemann

Religion of the Ancient Egyptians

Alfred Wiedemann

Religion of the Ancient Egyptians

ISBN/EAN: 9783337238162

Printed in Europe, USA, Canada, Australia, Japan

Cover: Foto ©ninafisch / pixelio.de

More available books at **www.hansebooks.com**

RELIGION OF THE ANCIENT EGYPTIANS.

BY

ALFRED WIEDEMANN, Ph.D.

Professor in the University of Bonn.

AUTHOR OF "AEGYPTISCHE GESCHICHTE," " HERODOT'S ZWEITES BUCH,"
"ANCIENT EGYPTIAN DOCTRINE OF IMMORTALITY," ETC.

WITH SEVENTY-THREE ILLUSTRATIONS FROM THE MONUMENTS.

LONDON:

H. GREVEL & CO.,

33, KING STREET, COVENT GARDEN, W.C.

1897.

Printed by Hazell, Watson, & Viney, Ld., London and Aylesbury.

PREFACE.

EGYPT stands pre-eminent among all the nations of antiquity as the land in which every civic and public interest was dominated by religion. The great prominence of the gods in the known texts is doubtless in part due to the fact that temples and tombs are the chief remains in the country, and that it is from these sources that most of the documents in question have come down to us. Yet even when objects which had been intended for secular use only are discovered, they generally prove to be in some way or other connected with the worship of the higher powers; and the assertion of Herodotus as to the exceptional piety of the Egyptians is fully ratified by the results of modern research. In Pagan times this singular national devoutness of a people regarded as worthy of peculiar reverence on account of their extreme antiquity moved Greek and Roman writers to devote more attention to the Egyptian religion than to that of

any other nation : hence it is that we find much
valuable information on this subject in the works of
the classical writers, although we cannot utilize it
for scientific purposes as it stands.   When the
fathers of the Church and the Christian apologists
came to write of the doctrines of the Egyptian religion, they singled out from them all that was most
foolish and repulsive, in accordance with their object
of pointing out the absurdities in which paganism
necessarily involved even the most cultured of
peoples.   The classical writers, on the other hand,
showed as little critical discrimination in this as in
most other fields of scientific inquiry : they identified
their own Greek and Roman divinities with those
which they found in the Valley of the Nile, lightly
transferred Greek doctrines into Egyptian teaching,
and ascribed to the latter systems of religious belief
really of their own, devising, although the principal
deities figuring in them were invested with Egyptian
names.   Thus it is that Plutarch's interesting work
on Isis and Osiris[1] is in fact an exposition of the
author's own conception of the universe, notwithstanding the large proportion of genuine Egyptian
material which it contains.   And though we find
the names of Egyptian gods in the works of the

---

[1] περὶ Ἴσιδος καὶ Ὀσίριδος—of which the best edition is that of
PARTHEY, Berlin, 1850.

Neo-Platonists and of the Gnostics, everything is interpreted in accordance with the new philosophy, and the Ancient Egyptian classification is entirely changed. But, in spite of these drawbacks, the information as to the Egyptian religion contained in the works of the Greek and Latin writers is both valuable and extensive,[1] and it is to these that we are indebted for the preservation of many doctrines as to which the monuments are silent, but which are nevertheless undoubtedly of Ancient Egyptian origin.

By the decipherment of the hieroglyphics materials fuller and unsophisticated were made accessible to students of the Egyptian religion, and, struck by the wealth of them, Champollion at once began to publish his *Panthéon Égyptien* (Paris, 1823-31), which, like many another work of that great scholar, was brought to a standstill by his early death. Wilkinson subsequently gave considerable attention to the same subject, and in the last volume of his *Manners and Customs* (London, 1841) we have an illustrated catalogue of Egyptian deities that is still valuable for reference, although Lanzone's *Dizionario di Mitologia egizia* (Turin, 1881-6), with

---

[1] The best collection of these references is in JABLONSKI, *Pantheon Aegyptiorum*, Frankfort, 1750-52. PRICHARD'S *Analysis of the Egyptian Mythology*, London, 1819, is less satisfactory though frequently quoted.

respect to both the number of deities figured and the specification of texts referring to them, has thrown into the shade all similar works by his predecessors.

As regards Egyptian dogma, the monotheistic, or rather henotheistic, factor has been emphasized by E. de Rougé,[1] Pierret,[2] and Le Page Renouf;[3] Tiele,[4] and, latterly, E. Meyer,[5] have endeavoured to trace the evolution of the religion, and Brugsch [6] to prove that the Egyptian religion was a coherent system of belief, corresponding somewhat to that imagined by Plutarch. But far weightier than any of these writings are the essays which Maspero has devoted to the subject, and which are now for the most part collected in his *Études de Mythologie et de Religion* (Paris, 1893). One of these essays is a criticism of Brugsch's treatise on the mythology, and is emphatically outspoken in condemnation of that distinguished scholar's point of view. A multitude of works of a more or less popular character by writers who draw all their information at second-hand need not here be noticed. If to one who knows

---

[1] See his articles on this subject in the *Revue Archéologique*, N.S., I.

[2] *Essai sur la mythologie Égyptienne*, Paris, 1879.

[3] *Lectures on the Origin and Growth of Religion*, London, 1880.

[4] *Histoire comparative des anciens religions*, Paris, 1882.

[5] *Geschichte Aegyptens*, Berlin, 1887.

[6] *Religion und Mythologie der alten Aegypter*, Leipzig, 1885-90.

the language there is imminent risk of reading his own ideas into the religious texts with which he is dealing, this danger is immeasurably increased for such as are unable to study the texts in the original, and who are thus thrown on translations for their authorities. Too easily they find statements in support of their theories when simply misled by some obscure rendering of the translator. It is especially true of Egypt that no original work in the study of the religion is possible without a knowledge of the language. Moreover many of the most important religious texts are still untranslated, or can be found only in obsolete and untrustworthy versions.

The present work is based throughout on original texts, of which the most significant passages are rendered as literally as possible in order that the reader may test the justice of the conclusions drawn from them. And since, owing to the longwindedness of Egyptian scribes, it is altogether impracticable to give translations in full, references to complete publications of the inscriptions and papyri from which they are made will be found in the footnotes. The work makes no pretence to completeness in the sense of noting every single demon among the thousands which figure in Egyptian mythology, and each local myth to which any odd reference might be found. Such a scheme would have resulted in a mere assemblage of names without connotation ; of titles with no distinguishable meaning ; of fragmentary myths of which in the present state of Egyptology no clear account can possibly be given.

Neither does the writer wish to enter into any discussion of current hypotheses as to the inner significance and origin of the Egyptian religion, nor yet to propound any views of his own on the subject : he is convinced that, however easy it may be to make assertions on these points, there is indeed little that can be proved with regard to them. His aim is a modest one : avoiding any attempt to interpret or to systematize, he has endeavoured to set before the reader the principal deities, myths, religious ideas and doctrines as they are to be found in the texts, more especially dwelling on such as have important bearings on the history of religion. The friendly reception accorded to the German edition of this book has testified to a certain demand on the part of the public for some account of Egyptian beliefs which should aim at establishing the facts of the case rather than at furnishing material in favour of any theory as to the philosophy or genesis of religion.

The book has been carefully revised and augmented for the English edition, and it is hoped that it has thereby gained throughout both in clearness and in fulness of statement. This edition has, moreover, the advantage of illustrations, and these will convey to the reader a better idea of the forms attributed by the Egyptians to their gods than any mere description can do. Finally, the addition of a full Index will facilitate reference, especially as regards such deities as may have received but isolated or incidental notice in the following pages.

In conclusion, I would here express my warmest thanks to my translator—who also recently placed before the English public my little treatise on *The Ancient Egyptian Doctrine of the Immortality of the Soul*—for the care and pains ungrudgingly bestowed upon the work.

ALFRED WIEDEMANN.

CONTENTS.

xv

RELIGION OF THE ANCIENT EGYPTIANS.

CHAPTER I.

INTRODUCTION.

THE attempt has often been made to hit off a national characteristic in some apt epithet ; the Romans have been denominated "brave," the Israelites "religious," the Assyrians "cruel." In like manner the Egyptians might be called "conservative" in the first and strictest sense of the word. While such appellations are only conditionally applicable to other nationalities, here we have a characteristic which the inhabitants of the Nile Valley invariably exhibit. The Egyptian people could never bring themselves to recognize any form of language, script, government, manners and customs as antiquated, and they steadfastly retained their hold upon every stage of their development during the whole course of a national history which lasted for thousands of years. Obviously there could be no denying that progress was made and that new views were attained to, either as the outcome of reflection or in consequence of foreign influence ; but, although the Egyptians could not hold aloof from change, their acceptance of it involved no casting off of the old and cherished ideas, which were retained and allowed to subsist on equal footing with the new modes of thought. This explains why the Egyptians, after having attained to an alphabetic system of writing, went on using the signs for words and syllables in which their script had originated. Hence also it came about that when the Egyptian monarchy had become absolute, titles and offices which prevailed in the feudal period, when the king was reckoned only as first among his peers, still continued to exist in connexion with the court and with official life. Innumerable incongruities were the natural result: titles did not correspond to offices, nor words to meanings. The Egyptian aversion to allowing anything to be lost of what had formed the possessions and institutions of their forefathers—of never losing connexion with the past, so that all might remain as it had been "since the times of the god Râ"—outweighed all practical considerations in their minds.

In the natural course of things this sentiment must have received some modification from the changing aspects of civic life; for though names and forms might be steadfastly retained, it could not be so with the substance when any change of circumstances had become general. But it was otherwise in the domain of the spiritual; there contemplation and thought were governed by feeling alone, and no rude truth was permitted to disturb a system. It was pre-eminently in his religion that the Egyptian allowed full play to his conservative nature. The natural phenomena, the few general truths upon which that religion was based, could be so variously explained and transformed that no abandonment of old opinions for the sake of new—however desirable according to our ideas—was in the least necessary in Egyptian opinion. The national bent of the people towards mysticism helped them easily over such paradoxes as might arise ; and where these might seem insoluble to earthly reason their interpretation could be regarded as a profound mystery whose nature the godhead would reveal to the blessed in the life to come.

On this account the Ancient Egyptian religion is of the deepest interest. Not only does it contain the simplest forms under which the nation on the banks of the Nile conceived of its gods, and the ceremonies with which it worshipped them in the days when very restricted means were at its disposal for the adornment of divine service; but side by side with these are the beliefs of later times, a constantly increasing number of divinities, a cult growing continually more refined and ornate, new modes of worship, and divinities of foreign origin. All the different systems of thought which grew out of Egyptian religious belief in the course of centuries are found together in the texts ; the earlier forms as well as those which succeeded them have all alike been retained. Hence it was inevitable that contradictions of all kinds should abound, but they did not disturb the Egyptian, for he never attempted to systematize his conceptions of the different divinities into a homogeneous religion. It is open to us to speak of the religious ideas of the Egyptians, but not of an Egyptian religion ; and we must carefully bear in mind this fact, which cannot fail to obtrude itself upon every one who examines the texts without prejudice, and which the reader will perceive clearly from such extracts as will be brought to his notice in the following pages. , Again and again has the attempt been made to formulate the Egyptian religion into a consistent system, and thus to credit the nation with what never was theirs.   All such performances, however brilliant in themselves, are now regarded as failures by scientific men ; they are based upon an arbitrary choice of passages in the texts which the writer has selected to support a preconceived view, while taking no account of the far greater number of passages which do not agree with it.

Besides the impossibility of formulating any comprehensive system of this kind, there is that of deciding as to which was the oldest form of the Egyptian religion, and of demonstrating whether this was monotheistic—as on general grounds it has often been assumed—or whether, as others assert, it was based upon pantheism, polytheism, ancestor worship, worship of vegetable or animal life and their reproductive powers, belief in the divine power of the sun, or other religious ideas.   All these forms of belief are to be found more or less clearly represented in Egyptian religion, but it cannot be proved historically which are the earlier and which the later.· Set forth side by side in single sentences or at length, they are all extant in the oldest of the longer religious texts which have come down to us—namely, the Pyramid inscriptions of the Vth and VIth dynasties.   As far as our knowledge of Ancient Egypt has hitherto extended, research has determined nothing indisputable as to the origins of their national religion, their form of government, their writing, or their racial descent. On the contrary, the more material is made accessible and the more thoroughly it is studied, the more obscure do these questions of origin become. One theory is disproved after another without being supplanted by any demonstrable truth. In Egypt, as in other countries, history, in the widest sense of the word, knows nothing of its own beginnings. In the present state of our knowledge, all that the science of religion can do as regards Egypt is to follow the same course once traversed by the Egyptians, but in the reverse direction. Where they combined we must isolate. By study of the texts we must seek to disentangle the intermingled doctrines, to sort out the separate pieces composing that motley mosaic presented by the Egyptian belief in higher powers. In this way we shall find that we can obtain a series of separate and distinct doctrines, each of which comprises an independent sphere of thought ; the combination of these doctrines, however, though attempted by the Egyptians, could never be logical.

Before proceeding to consider the most important of these circles of ideas, which partly centre round certain forms of deity and partly round some one fundamental idea, we must briefly examine into the origin of the Egyptian state. Many important points of her religious doctrine can thus be elucidated, as is always the case where religion and government are so closely coincident as they were in the Valley of the Nile.

The Ancient Egyptian state was formed by the union of many smaller states which occupied the Nile Valley in some prehistoric period. These states were not merged at that unification of the kingdom which legend ascribes to the first human monarch of Egypt, Menes. In a certain sense they continued to exist, for they remained in possession of their own religious, political, and military administrations, acknowledging the king as their liege lord only so far as to assign him in most cases the part of confirming the princes in their rank, the post of commander in chief in case of war, the bestowal of posts of honour and of titles, and the receipt of certain taxes. It is doubtful whether he could by right depose the subordinate princes. As a matter of fact he did depose them, but only after overcoming them in war, and thus used the right of a conqueror rather than that of a Pharaoh. Nevertheless he was apparently not permitted to retain land so obtained as his private property, but was obliged to bestow it upon some one who entered upon the rights and duties of the deposed prince and could bequeath the province to his own successors. It was owing to this invariable transmission of the fief that the ancient territorial divisions lasted down to the latest times. Changes rarely occurred, but occasionally two provinces would be united by inheritance, or two which had been united would be again separated. From the Pyramid period until the times of the Ptolemies and of the Roman emperors certain districts are specified by the texts as substantially unchanged. The Ancient Egyptian name for these provinces was *ḥesp*.[1] The

---

[1] In the transliterations of Egyptian words *ḥ* is a hard h. *kh*, *sh*, *th*, each represent a single alphabetic sign in the original. The signs rendered *a*, *ā*, *ă*, *i*, *u*, more nearly approach to the Semitic semi-vowels than to our vowels, but they are used as vowel signs in the rendering of foreign, and sometimes even in Egyptian words. Generally the Egyptian, like the Semite, did not write the vowels;

Greeks called them nomes (νόμοι), a designation retained
by the Romans, under whose rule they enjoyed so much
independence as to be allowed to issue a coinage of their
own. Each nome consisted of four subdivisions : the
capital, which was the seat of authority and the residence
of the nomarch and of the principal deity ; the regularly
tilled arable land ; the marshes, which were mostly used
as pasture and for the cultivation of water plants ; and
lastly the canals, which were in charge of special officials.
The control of the canals was necessarily far more
centralized than that of the rest of the country, for the
regular irrigation of Egypt can only be secured when
directed by a single authority which opposes in the common interest any attempt to cut off and divert the water
for the gratification of private ends. Such an attempt was
regarded in Egyptian morals as a serious crime, which
the godhead itself would punish in the life to come ;[1] but
the need for such a threat testifies to the readiness with
which an Egyptian gave himself to the practice.

The effects of this division into nomes on the condition

hence, where a vowel is to be inserted on phonetic or other grounds,
it is here denoted generally by *e*, which may thus correspond to
the most various vowel sounds in the ancient language. The true
vocalization of the words is, as a rule, unknown, and in the following pages the Greek transcriptions (but not the names of Greek
deities identified with the Egyptian) are generally employed when
such are to be found, Ammón, however, being given in the usual
English form of " Amen." These correspond to the pronunciation
more accurately than a mere transliteration of the Egyptian signs,
which will be given once only in the case of proper names for which
there is an adequate Greek equivalent.

á stands throughout for the Egyptian radical ⌁ = *y*. *ú* simply
indicates that the *u* is to be pronounced as in " rule."

[1] *Book of the Dead*, cxxv., l. 28.

and development of Egypt, as well as on its religion, were so important that a list of them is here given in tabular form, together with certain particulars.

UPPER EGYPT.

	NOME.	CAPITAL.	DEITY.
1	Ta-Kens	Ab (Elephantine), later Nûb-t (Ombos)	Khnûm
2	Tes-Hor	Deb (Apollinopolis magna, Edfû)	Hor - behûdet
3	Ten	Nekheb (Eileithyia), later Sene (Latopolis, Esneh)	Nekheb
4	Ûs-t	Ûs-t (Thebes), later An-res (Hermonthis)	Amen Râ, later Ment
5	Hor-ûi	Kebti (Koptos)	Khem
6	Aa-dû	Ta - en- terer (Tentyris, Denderah)	Hat-hor
7	Sekhem	Ha (Diospolis parva)	Hat-hor
8	Abd	Abdû (Abydos), Teni (This)	Anher
9	Khem	Apû (Panopolis)	Khem
10	Ûazt	Debû (Aphroditopolis)	Hat-hor
	Neter-ûi	Dû-ka (Antaeopolis)	Hor (Horus)
11	Set	Shas-hetep (Hypsele)	Khnûm
12	Dû-f	Nû-ent-bak (Antaeopolis)	Hor (Horus)
13	Atef-khent	Saû-t (Lycopolis, Siût)	Ap-ûat
14	Atef-peh, later Antinoïtes	Kesi (Kusae)	Hat-hor
15	Ûn	Khemennû (Hermopolis)	Thoth
16	Meh-mahez	Hebennû (Hipponon)	Hor (Horus)
17	Anûp	Ka-sa (Kynopolis)	Anûp (Anubis)
18	Sep	Ha-sûten (Alabastronpolis)	Anûp (Anubis)
19	Ûab	Pa-mazet (Oxyrynkhos)	Set
20	Atef-khent	Khenen-sû (Heracleopolis magna)	Hor-shef (Arsaphes)
21	Atef-peh	Semen-Hor	Khnûm
	Ta-she	Ta-shed (Krokodilopolis in the Fayûm)	Sebek
22	Mâten	Tep-ah (Aphroditopolis)	Hat-hor

LOWER EGYPT.

	NOME.	CAPITAL.	DEITY.
1	Anûb hez (white wall)	Men-nefer (Memphis)	Ptah
2	Aâ	Sekhem (Letopolis)	Hor-ûr
3	Ament (the West)	Nû-ent-Hâpi (Apis)	Hat-hor
4	Sepi-res	Zekâ	Amen Râ
5	Sepi-em-het	Saû (Sais)	Neith
6	Ka-set	Khasûû (Xois)	Amen Râ
7	. . . . . ament	Sent-nefer	Hû
8	. . . . . abd	Thûkot (Sukot)	Tûm
9	Athi	Pa-Asiri (Busiris)	Osiris
10	Ka-kem	Ha-her-ab (Athribis)	Hor (Horus)
11	Ka-hebes	Ka-hebes (Kabasos)	Isis
12	Ka-theb	Theb-neter (Sebennytos)	Anher
13	Hek-ad	An-û (Heliopolis)	Râ
14	Khent-abd	Zân (Tanis)	Hor (Horus)
15	Tehût	Pa-Tehûti (Hermopolis)	Thoth
16	Khar	Pa-ba-neb-ded (Mendes)	Ba-neb-ded (Osiris)
17	Sam-hût	Pa-khen-en-Amen (Diospolis)	Amen Râ
18	Am-khent	Pa-Bast (Bubastis)	Bast
19	Am-peh	Pa-Ûaz (Bûto)	Ûaz (Bûto)
20	Sepd	Kesem (Gosen, Phakussa)	Sepd

A glance at the above list shows that each nome had its own god. In its capital stood his principal temple, and there the college of priests vowed to the service of the nome god exercised their functions. The Egyptian priests bore the titles of *âb*, "the pure," *hen neter*, "servant of the god"—the latter title being translated by the Greeks as "prophet," though the official in question had nothing to do with prediction—and others of a similar nature. At the head of each college was a high priest with a specific title ; at Memphis he was " Chief of the Artificers," at Mendes " Director of the Soldiers," at Heliopolis the " Great Seer," [1] at Thebes in earlier times the " First Prophet of Amen," and later " Opener of the Gate of Heaven." In the later period a high priestess generally took rank beside the chief priest, who was surrounded by a staff of permanent officials, the number varying with the size and wealth of the temple. This staff was not so large as we might expect ; at Siût, for example, it consisted of ten and at Abydos of only five persons. To these, however, must be added many minor officials of the temple, and many personages of the city who performed priestly functions at stated times and in addition to their other functions. The priests of each nome were independent and subject to no higher jurisdiction. If occasionally the idea arose of appointing a high priest for all Egypt who, living at court and being under its influence, should rule the priesthood in a sense friendly to the government, the attempt invariably failed, owing to the jealous independence of the different colleges. The kings were obliged to be content with appointing their own relations or men devoted to their interests as chief priests of the more important shrines, and thus to gain an indirect influence over the priesthood. But it was not only in regard to government that the independence of the various colleges was preserved ; it maintained itself also in religious matters. Each nome had its own religion which it developed regardless of neighbouring faiths, and

---

[1] This must be understood in the physical sense. The literal translation of the title is " Great One of Seeings."

which in almost every case became henotheistic from time
to time. The god of a nome was within it held to be
Ruler of the Gods, Creator of the World, Giver of all
good things, and it mattered little to his adherents that
another deity played a precisely similar part in some
adjacent nome where their own god was relegated to a
subordinate place.

Quarrels between the nomes could not fail to arise
from such isolation of interests. Some gods were
enemies of others, according to the myths; and one
deity being honoured in one province while his enemy
was worshipped in another, their worshippers also took
sides against one another. Even in Roman times this
state of antagonism occasionally led to sanguinary con-
flicts between the inhabitants of different districts. Moreover, in the course of history, owing to the independent
growth of local religions, divinities once the same in character and origin took different shape in different nomes,
and became at length entirely distinct; while other gods
which eventually appear identical in name and nature
were originally and radically different. In historical times
Horus of Edfû no longer corresponded to the Horus of
Letopolis. The former is the keen sighted god of the
bright sun, and the latter a blind deity whose manifestation
was in solar eclipse. Hence, in treating of any one god
we cannot indiscriminately apply all references to him
without running the risk of acquiring false notions; we
must carefully examine whether they originated in the
same place and arose out of the same fundamental ideas.

Occasionally indeed this isolation was intruded upon.

This would often happen on a small scale when an inhabitant of one nome had established himself in another, bringing with him his own gods, to whom he proceeded to erect shrines, after obtaining the necessary official permission. If such a shrine was richly endowed and magnificent festivals were solemnized there, it was only natural—especially in a place where the chief temple was poor—that more and more adherents should flock to the new deity, and gradually give him precedence over the original god. At Abydos, for instance, in course of time, Anher, god of the city and of the Thinite nome, was almost entirely displaced by Osiris. Such events transpired quietly and were of local importance only, but the religious revolution which the assumption of power by a new dynasty involved had far wider issues. The new dynasty always believed that it owed the crown to the god of its native nome ; hence it considered the worship of its tutelary deity of primary importance, and endeavoured to spread the cult over the whole kingdom. In this endeavour their sovereign was willingly met half-way by the people. To them the elevation of the king over the other nomarchs implied the exaltation of his god over all the other divinities, and to this god all henceforth made their offerings and addressed their prayers. It was to such considerations and to royal influence that the worship of Ptah and that of Amen Râ were indebted for their extension. Again, other gods were raised to power as the result of certain tendencies of thought. From the Hyksos period onwards the origin of all forms of religion was sought in sun worship ; nearly all the principal deities

were thenceforth amalgamated with the Sun god, and
hence arose composite forms like Amen Râ, Khnûm
Râ, and many others of the same kind. And although
the train of ideas connected with the Osirian religion—
to take only one example—could not logically be brought
into harmony with the new doctrine, yet the solar bias
which characterized Ancient Egyptian mythology from
the beginning of the New Kingdom ultimately and inevitably turned the whole scheme of faith into pantheism.

CHAPTER II.

SUN WORSHIP.

R Â is the name by which the Sun god is generally mentioned in the texts. Attempts have repeatedly been made to draw from his name far reaching conclusions as to the nature of his divinity, and it has been conjectured that since " to give " and also occasionally " to order, to regulate " are among the meanings of the word *râ*, the god was so called as the being who created, ordered, and regulated all things, especially as, according to certain inscriptions, he was older than the firmament, and maker of gods and men. But this explanation is too far fetched. As a matter of fact, the name of the god has nothing to do with the word meaning " to give," but is derived from *râ*, the oldest and most common designation of the sun, afterwards extended to the god in whose figure the animating spirit of the sun was supposed to be embodied. Creative activity was of course ascribed to this being : the existence of life without the cooperation of the sun was inconceivable ; apart from its agency all would have remained lifeless. The sun, and light with it, must needs have been formed before any creatures could come into existence ; once it had been personified there was but a step from the accepted

idea of its prior existence to the belief that it was
the sun which had called all things into being.

Originally the sun was considered to be male; and not
until a comparatively late period did the idea occur to the
Egyptians of resolving it into
a masculine and a feminine
being.   The latter received
the name RÂ.T, or RÂ.T TAÛI,
" Râ.t of the Two Lands," a
name the late origin of which
is indicated in its artificial
formation by the addition of
a feminine suffix to the primitive word.[1]   It was not easy,
however, to assign any particular function to the goddess.
Often she is called the Lady
of Heliopolis ; but she was
also supposed to dwell in
other places—*e.g.* in the Sinaitic Peninsula—and to be
included in the divine triad
of Erment along with Month
and Harpokrates.   Nowhere
did she attain to any standing of her own.   Her functions were those of Isis, and

FIG. I.

RÂ. (T) TAÛI.   (L. D. III. 188.)

Great temple of Rameses II. at Abû
Simbel.

she is even represented as bearing the cow horns of that
goddess.   But she is never represented as hawk headed,

[1] This feminine suffix, which often forms part of the names of

and this would not have been the case had she been one of the genuine solar deities of the olden time.

Sun worship existed in Egypt from prehistoric times, and it held its place in popular favour until the latest period of Egyptian history. The obelisks which stood at the entrance of temples were dedicated to the sun, as were also the little votive objects of like form which were placed in tombs, particularly during the period of the Old Kingdom.   During the New Kingdom the latter were superseded by small pyramids.   These did not represent the sepulchral pyramids of the Old Kingdom (which were no more than geometrically formed tumuli of masonry, without any deep symbolical meaning), but are to be considered as representing the obelisks, the pointed tops of which are of the same form.[1]   Sometimes these votive pyramids are very small, and then are commonly flattened at the tops and furnished with a ring so as to be worn as amulets.   A third kind of monument takes a place midway between these two forms.[2]   This consists of a pyramid base without apex, thus producing the form of the so called " mastabas," the private tombs of the Old Kingdom ; from the flat upper surface an obelisk

Egyptian goddesses, has been conjecturally vocalized as *it*.   In later times the pronunciation of the *t* was dropped, and such names of goddesses were pronounced, as the Greek transcriptions testify, Isi(s), Athyri, Anuki, etc.

[1] For an account and confutation of the numerous false hypotheses based on the form and size of the sepulchral pyramids, and especially of the great Pyramid of Gizeh, cf. WIEDEMANN, *Globus*, 1893, lxiii., pp. 217, 242.

[2] See SETHE, *Aeg. Zeit.*, 1889, pp. 111 *et seq.* ; SCHIAPARELLI, *Il Significato Simbolico delle piramide*, Rome, 1884.

rises, generally surmounted by the solar disk. During the Vth Dynasty these were much in favour, and in the neighbourhood of Memphis several kings set up great monumental erections on this model, with temples in connexion with them, to which various orders of priests were attached. These edifices were dedicated to Râ, or to Râ Harmakhis; occasionally also Horus and Hathor were worshipped in them. As to their sites, plans, and so forth, we have no positive data, but probably there was some connexion between them and the sepulchral pyramids; at least this is suggested by the fact that the same priests who served the pyramids as "prophets" occupied also official positions in these sanctuaries of Râ.

The place round which the solar worship centred was *An*, Hebrew On. It was also called by the Egyptians *Pa Râ*, "the house of Râ," Bethshemesh by the Hebrews, and by the Greeks Heliopolis. The history of the city in detail cannot indeed be carried back very far. In texts of the Old Kingdom it is named but seldom, and the foundation of the great temple of Râ, so zealously adorned by later Pharaohs, dates only from the XIIth Dynasty (before 2500 B.C.), as is related in a poetically embellished description of the event written on leather and preserved at Berlin.[1] This, however, was not the first sanctuary built in the city: the same manuscript mentions that on the occasion of the new foundation the great house of Tûm in Heliopolis was enlarged. Of the temple of Tûm nothing remains, and only the peribolus and a single obelisk

---

[1] Published and discussed by STERN, *Aeg. Zeit.*, 1874, pp. 85 *et seq.*

with the names of King Usertesen I., that stands near the little village of Matarieh, bear witness to the XIIth Dynasty foundation. The work of destruction was begun in ancient times. Under Rameses III. (*circa* 1200 B.C.) the temple was at the height of its power; 12,963 persons are said to have been then engaged in its service.[1] But, later, Herodotus can testify only to the learning and wisdom of its priesthood, and not to the splendour of its buildings; and in Strabo's time[2] the place was almost entirely forsaken, although still visited frequently by travellers, both on account of the temple and of the college of learning connected with it. In Arab times the ruins were still extant; the fall of the fellow obelisk to the one still standing took place only in the thirteenth century, and a magnificent statue of a deity was destroyed in the vicinity by Ahmed ibn Tûlûn (868—883 A.D.). Excavations on the site have produced little or nothing, but it must be admitted that none have been carried out systematically as yet.

The sacred spring of the god Râ has lasted longer than his monuments. About 730 B.C., when King Piankhi of Ethiopia arrived at Heliopolis on his triumphal march through Egypt, he washed his face, as he himself relates,[3] in the pool of fresh water in which Râ was wont to lave his divine countenance. The Arabs still call it "The Spring of the Sun"; and here, as the ancient legend tells, the mother of our Lord washed her child's swaddling

---

[1] *Great Harris Papyrus*, pl. 31, l. 8.

[2] xvii. 805.

[3] *Piankhi Stela*, l. 102, translated by BRUGSCH, *Gesch. Aeg.*, pp. 682 *et seq.* ; WIEDEMANN, *Gesch. Aeg.*, pp. 564 *et seq.*

FIG. 2.— OBELISK OF USERTESEN I. AT MATARIEH (HELIOPOLIS).

clothes after reaching Egypt in the flight from Herod, and from the water falling on the ground there sprang up a balsam shrub, which, according to Maqrizi's account, grows nowhere else in the world. Even to this day the traveller is shown the sycomore in the shade of which the Holy Family is said to have rested, and, although itself but a few centuries old, it is the latest successor of one which may have existed in the time of Christ. The site is still held sacred by Arabs and Copts alike.

The Ancient Egyptian text to which we have already referred gives an account of the ritual observed by a Pharaoh who visited Heliopolis in person. After performing his ablutions Piankhi went in ceremonial procession to the sandhill at Heliopolis, and there offered a great offering of white cattle, milk, balsam, incense, and all manner of sweet smelling woods before the god Râ at his rising. On his return to the temple of the Sun he was extolled by the chief of the temple ; the temple lector recited the formula warding off the king's enemies ; the ceremony of the " House of Stars " (a room in the temple) was completed ; and the king assumed the sacred band. He then purified himself with fresh incense ; there were given unto him flowers of the Hat Benben—*i.e.* those borne by the celebrant in this part of the temple when appearing before the god. " He bore the flowers, he ascended the steps to the great chamber (the Holy of Holies) to behold Râ in the Hat Benben, he the king himself. There stood the prince alone ; he loosed the bolts, he opened the doors, he beheld his father Râ in the sacred Hat Benben, the Mâd or Mâdet bark of Râ and the Sekti bark of Tûm.

Then he closed the doors, placed sealing clay upon them,
and sealed it with the royal seal. Then spake he and
commanded the priests : ' I have impressed the seal ; no
man of the other kings (*i.e.* of his vassal princes) shall enter

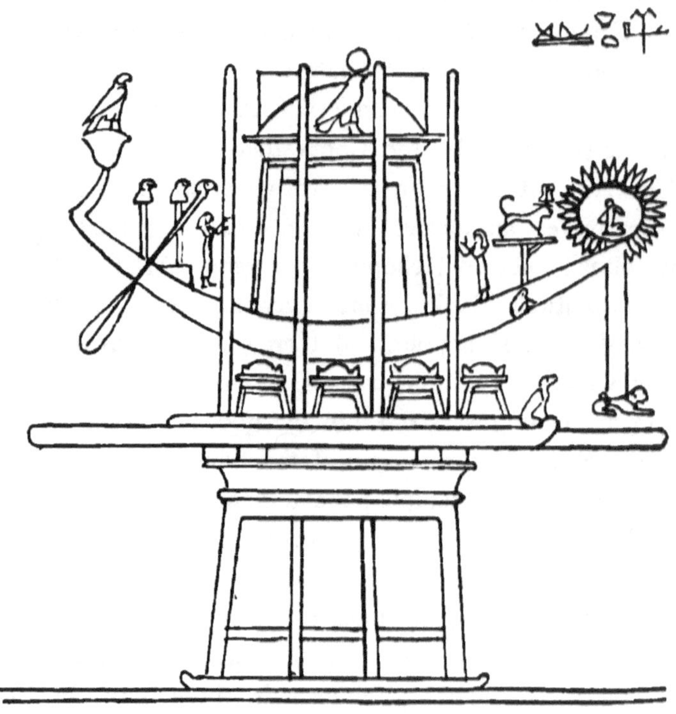

FIG. 3.—MÂDET BOAT. (MAR., "DENDERAH," IV., PL. 64.)
Upper chamber of temple of Denderah. Roman Period.

into it (the sanctuary).' He stood, but they cast themselves
down upon their bellies before his majesty and said : ' May
he endure and increase and never be destroyed, Horus who
loveth Heliopolis !' (*i.e.* the king himself). Then Piankhi
returned to the temple of Tûm, and with him was brought

the image of his father Tûm Khepera, prince of Heliopolis."
After this the king left the city.

The chief relics of the sanctuary visited by Piankhi were
two barks. These were for the use of the Sun god in his
daily course through the sky ; for, according to Egyptian

FIG. 4.—SEKTI BOAT. (MAR., "DENDERAH," IV., PL. 64.)

ideas, the movement of the heavenly bodies consisted in
a navigation, either on the waters which were supposed
to form the firmament, or else on the celestial Nile which
was supposed to run through a sky of metal—according
as either idea of the heavens prevailed. It was commonly

understood that the Sun had two barks at his disposal :
the Mâd or Mâdet boat for the morning, and the Sekti
boat for the afternoon.   But there was another theory that
the number of the barks was far larger, and that one
was provided for every hour of the day.   These barks were
made on the model of the ordinary Nile boat : amidships
was a cabin in which the god Râ installed himself; fore
and aft were his attendant deities to fight his foes and
navigate the boat, the watch being relieved hourly.   Tûm
and Khepera, cognate forms of Râ himself, were generally
represented as accompanying him.

FIG. 5.—BARK OF RÂ.   (LEPS., "TODT.," CAP. 16.)
Book of the Dead.   Ptolemaic?

Within the temple was also treasured a divine symbol
in the form of a small obelisk, called *benben*, probably of
stone, from which the whole temple had received its name
of *Hat Benben*, "House of the Obelisk," or rather of the
"pyramidion of the obelisk," a name more especially employed in religious and magical texts.   This *benben* was
held to be an embodiment of Râ himself.   The choice of
an inanimate object for such a purpose may be traced to
the influence of Asiatic ideas, as will be shown later.   It
is noteworthy that in Heliopolis not only is this mode
of worship found even in the earliest period, but it continued throughout the whole duration of Egyptian history.

This is the more remarkable since the worship of the phoenix as a second embodiment of Râ also prevailed at Heliopolis, and this was a purely Egyptian conception. A close connexion between Heliopolis and Asia seems to have existed even in prehistoric times, and the tradition of it long survived : Greek writers and travellers were aware of it, and erroneously concluded that Heliopolis was of Arabian foundation,[1] though as a matter of fact the only foundation made there by the Semites was that of a certain form of worship.

The fact that in Heliopolis it was thought incumbent to worship two embodiments of the Sun god shows that this deity was not considered as one and indivisible, but could be resolved into separate parts, to each of which an independent existence might be ascribed. Originally each form of the deity would have its own separate sphere of activity, but gradually one encroached upon the domain of the other to such an extent that, though the ideal significance of each was still radically different, in other respects their natures and functions were almost identical. The following are the more important of these forms :—

Râ himself, whom the inscriptions designate as god of Heliopolis, of Xoïs, of Apollinopolis Magna, and of the Hermopolite nome in Upper Egypt. He is almost invariably represented as a hawk headed man holding in one hand the sign of life, and in the other the symbol of sovereignty, the kingly sceptre *ñas*. Upon his head is the solar disk in the coil of the uraeus, that serpent being symbolic of power over life and death. It is the charac-

---

[1] *Juba*, in *Pliny*, vi. 26.

teristic sign of all solar deities that they are hawk headed, many being supposed, according to Egyptian belief, to become incarnate in hawks; when any god is so represented his solar nature may be confidently assumed. In times when it was sought to turn the whole Ancient Egyptian religion into a solar cult, the figure of the sparrow hawk proper was equivalent to the sign for *neter*, "god," and was also its determinative, in the same way as the figure of the uraeus serpent was employed with regard to *neter.t*, "goddess." We have no information as to how the hawk came to be associated with the sun. *Bak*, the Egyptian name of the bird, has no philological connexion with the heavenly body. Probably this bird of prey—which now hovering high in air seems to disappear into the blue heaven and to merge itself in the sun, and anon shoots down suddenly to earth like a ray of light—was regarded as the messenger and even as part of the Sun god, and hence it was concluded that he himself bore the form of a sparrow hawk. Even the Neo Platonists thought they had found a close connexion between the two; Porphyrius giving as the reason for it that the hawk is formed of blood and spirit ($\pi\nu\epsilon\hat{\upsilon}\mu\alpha$). We must needs admit that such conclusions are natural when we remember that races

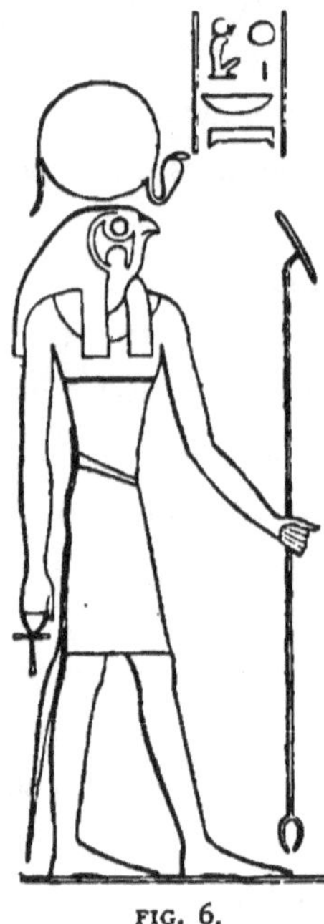

FIG. 6.

RÂ. (L. D. III. 138°.)

Stela of Seti I. at Redesiyeh.

having no connexion with the Egyptian have associated sun and sparrow hawk. Homer, for instance, *Od.* xv. 525, calls the hawk the "swift messenger of Phœbus." In pursuance of this train of thought divine honours were accorded in the Valley of the Nile to various kinds of hawks; the birds were kept in sacred groves, and after death their bodies were embalmed.

HORUS, *Her.*—By the name of Horus at least two entirely distinct deities were originally denoted—Horus the son of Isis, and Horus the sun god. The attempted blending of the two divinities was a subsequent development: so also was the likening of the war which Horus the sun god waged against the powers of darkness to the prolonged combat of Horus the son of Isis with Set the murderer of his father. The primary significance of Horus the sun god, whom the Greeks identified with their Apollo, has nothing in common with that of the son of Isis. Generally speaking, the sun god may be distinguished from his namesake by the possession of certain cognomens varying with the nomes or cities in which he was worshipped. In course of time each of the different forms became an independent divinity, and we frequently find several such worshipped contemporaneously as distinct deities in the later periods of Egyptian history. Among these forms of Horus the sun god the following are especially important :—

HER-ÛR, "Horus the Elder," the Greek Aroëris, who was particularly worshipped at Letopolis in the neighbourhood of Memphis, his birthplace being supposed to be Apollinopolis Parva, and his mother an Hathor. An extensive temple was also dedicated to him at Ombos in Upper Egypt. He was represented as a hawk headed man, or simply as a hawk. It is characteristic of the religious medley of later times that he then appears as Her-ûr-Shû, the son of Râ, although he himself and Shû and Râ were originally independent solar deities representing similar conceptions.

Her-mer-ti, " Horus of the Two Eyes," *i.e.* sun and moon, Lord of Shedennû, a city of Lower Egypt in the nome of Pharbaethus. In later times he was identified at Panopolis with Min, the generative power of nature, and with the moon, being thus changed from a solar to a lunar deity.

Her-khent-àn-ma, " Horus Lord of Not Seeing," a Letopolitan god who was supposed to be blind and to symbolize solar eclipse.[1] Among the animals sacred to him was the shrew mouse, which, according to Plutarch,[2] received divine honours in Egypt because it was blind, and because darkness was older than light.

Her-em-khû-ti, the Harmakhis of the Greeks, " Horus on the Two Horizons," *i.e.* the horizon of the east and the horizon of the west, Horus at his rising and at his setting. Sometimes he was designated simply Her-em-khû, " Horus on the Horizon," and then represents more especially the god of the rising sun. He was easily and frequently merged with Râ, and under these circumstances he was entitled " The Great God, the Lord of Heaven, Râ

---

[1] On this point see Renouf in *Proceedings of the Society of Biblical Archæology*, vol. viii., p. 155.

[2] *Symp.*, iv. 5.

Harmakhis." In this form he appears as god of Heliopolis, occasionally bearing the additional name of Tûm, and there IÛ-S-ÂAS was accounted his wife. He played a prominent part also in the city of Tanis, in the far east of the Delta, on the Asiatic frontier. And the Great Sphinx of Gîzch,[1] a monument which the inscriptions would have us believe had been in existence at the time of King Khephren (Khafrâ), was likewise dedicated to Harmakhis.

FIG. 7.—RAMESES II. BETWEEN HARMAKHIS AND IÛ-S-ÂAS. (L. D. III. 178, a.)
Temple of Gerf Hussein.

ḤER-NÛB, "the Golden Horus," is primarily the god of the morning sun, manifesting himself in the golden glory of the dawn. Hence he may be considered as being in a certain sense the counterpart of the Golden Hathor. The Golden Hathor had no connexion with the Golden Aphrodite of the Greeks, but was goddess of the western

[1] See pp. 195, 197.

sky which received the dying sun in the glow of sunset, and hence was supposed likewise to receive the dead on their decease. In the latter capacity she was usually represented as emerging from the Mountain of the West. From of old the Pharaohs, who always sought to pose as the Sun on earth, greatly affected this title of "the Golden Horus," and their public appearances are commonly described as the breaking forth of light by the use of the word *khâ*, which also denotes the sunrise.

ḤER-ḤEKENNÛ, a hawk headed deity, known in Denderah as the husband of the goddess Bast, and of whom we find it often stated : "he shines in the sun disk."

ḤER-BEHÛDTI corresponds to ḤER-DEMA, and plays the chief part in a solar myth of which more will be said anon.

ḤER-KA, "Horus the Bull," is the planet Saturn ; ḤER-DESHER, "the Red Horus," is the planet Mars ; and ḤER-AP-SHETA, "Horus the Opener of that which is Secret," is the planet Jupiter. Hence it would seem that the three planets were regarded as emanations of the sun.

ḤER.T, the feminine form of *Her*, is a goddess of purely grammatical origin. Under this name Hathor was worshipped at Sebennytos, being there accounted the daughter of Râ and the mother of ÁNḤER, and in later times identified under her lioness form with Tefnût and also with Nephthys, goddesses with whom she had originally nothing but her sex in common. It is easy to understand how there would be no natural place in the myths for this product of priestly speculations, any more than for Rât ; the titles and attributes with which Hert was endowed, the story of her birth in Denderah, and the like were all transferred from other divinities.

KHEPERÀ, "he who is (in process of) becoming," strictly the god of the rising sun. In a Turin papyrus[1] it is said, "I am Khepera in the morning, Râ at noon, Tûm in the evening." But this distinction was not thoroughly carried out, and occasionally Khepera may indicate the sun in general. The god is usually represented as a man with a scarabaeus on his head or in place of his head, the creature serving as an

FIG. 8.—KHEPERÀ.
(LEPS., "TODT.," CAP. 17.)
Book of the Dead.
Ptolemaic?

ideogram both for the divine name and for the word denoting the god's chief attribute, viz. *kheper*, "to become."

TÛM, ÀTÛM, the Tomos of the Greeks, is properly the evening sun, in contradistinction to Khepera. He became a chief object of worship at Heliopolis as Lord of the World and the great Creator. In the Book of the Dead he is called "Creator of heaven, maker of beings, procreator of all that is; who gave birth to the gods, self-created, Lord of Life, he who grants new strength to the gods." He himself came forth from Nû, the primeval waters, and his worship was intimately connected with the Egyptian doctrine of immortality. But as regards this life also he appears as a beneficent being : from before him went the north wind bringing cool airs to the people of the land during the hot Egyptian summer, and "to breathe its sweet breath" was reckoned one of the passionate desires of their dead. Besides Heliopolis, another centre

[1] Cf. p. 57.

of the worship of Tûm was *Pa Tûm*, "the House of Tûm,"
the Pithom of the Old Testament, the ruins of which were
discovered by M. Naville in 1883, at Tell el Maskhûtah,
east of the Delta.[1] Tûm was generally represented as a
man wearing the crowns of Upper and Lower Egypt, and
when associated with other solar deities he is usually
placed after Râ Harmakhis, but preceding Khepera.[2]
Originally he was not accompanied by any divine consort ;
it is only in one of the later texts, from Denderah, that we
find mention of the goddess TÛM.T, the feminine of Tûm.
The texts assert that she was worshipped at Bubastis.

SHÛ, called Sos, Sosos, Sosis, by the Greeks, is the
first-born son of Râ and Hathor,[3] and the twin brother
of the lioness headed goddess Tefnût. He stands third
in the divine dynasties both of Thebes and of Memphis.[4]
A text from the tombs of the kings at Thebes, speaking

[1] *The Store City of Pithom*, NAVILLE, First Memoir of Egypt
Exploration Fund, London, 1885.

[2] Cf. illustration on p. 24, and for Tûm see illustration on p. 156.

[3] According to a remarkable cosmogonical myth, at the beginning
of the creation, after heaven and earth were uplifted from out the
primeval waters, Râ produced his children Shû and Tefnût of his
own body alone, without the cooperation of any goddess. From Shû
and Tefnût were born Seb and Nût, and from these Osiris, Her-
khent-an-ma (who here appears in the place of Aroëris), Set, Isis,
and Nephthys. This account is most completely preserved in the
copy of a papyrus dating B.C. 306—305 (*Nesi Amsû*, BUDGE,
Archæologia, lii., Col. 26 *et seq.*; Col. 28 *et seq.*), but its main
point is alluded to in texts of the Old Kingdom (Pyr. Pepi I.,
ll. 465 *et seq.*=Merenrâ, ll. 528 *et seq.*; Pepi II., l. 663), and of the
beginning of the New Kingdom (MARIETTE, *Abydos*, i., p. 51,
pl. 47*b*; NAVILLE, *Todtenbuch*, ii., p. 39. Cf. also *Ibid.*, Turin text,
chap. xvii., l. 9; BRUGSCH, *Thesaurus*, p. 634, ll. 25-6 (time of
Darius), *Dict. Géog.*, p. 1387 (Ptolemaic period).

[4] For an account of the divine dynasties, see p. 107.

of him in his composite form of Khûnsû-nefer-ḥetep-
Shû, says: "He has divided the heaven from the
earth ; he has uplifted the heaven in eternity above the
earth." Other texts ascribe to him the uplifting of the
primeval waters (Nû), the pillars of heaven, and the like.
He is represented as a man wearing a feather on his head,

but frequently also as a lion when
portrayed along with Tefnût. Among
the centres of his worship were the
island of Biggeh near Philae, Latopolis, Denderah, and Memphis. The
radical meaning of his name can
scarcely be other than "the Uplifter,"
corresponding to the root *shû*, "to
uplift, to uplift oneself," and expresses
the belief that he was the supporter
of the heavens, or the divinity who
had once uplifted them and thus separated them from the earth. In later
texts he becomes the representative
of the glowing heat of the sun, or
the hot wind. This is a misplaced
identification, doubtless brought about
by the accidental assonance of the
above-mentioned root *shû*, with the

FIG. 9.

SHÛ. (L. D. III. 124, *a*.)
Karnak, Hypostyle Hall,
Rameses I.

roots signifying "to be hot, to be parched up," and "wind."

In the Book of the Dead TEFNÛT, the divine consort of
Shû, is classed together with him and with Tûm as a ruler
of Heliopolis. In Philae she was designated the daughter
of Râ, in Nubia she was considered the mother of Thoth,

and in Elephantine she was identified with ISIS SOTHIS;
later texts transfer both Shû and Tefnût to the zodiac
as the Twins. It is clear that the goddess was very
differently apprehended in the different localities which

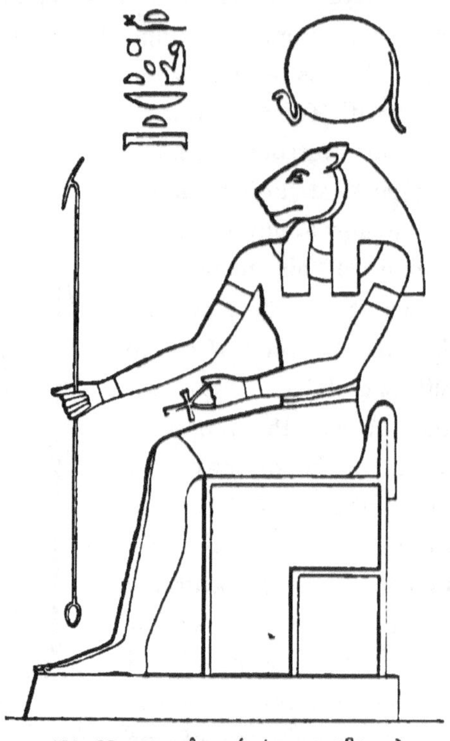

FIG. 10.—TEFNÛT. (L. D. III. 182, c.)
Temple of Rameses II. at Wady Sebûah.

were centres of her cult. To these, besides the above,
belong Memphis, Lycopolis in Lower Egypt, Denderah,
Eileithyia, etc. She is generally represented as lioness
headed and wearing the sun disk, more rarely as human
headed or simply as a lioness. In origin she was

undoubtedly a solar deity or goddess of the sky, but ultimately she became as vague and shadowy a personality as most of the Egyptian goddesses.

ÁTEN primarily denotes the solar disk. There is no ground other than a certain assonance for the comparison of the word Aten either with the Semitic Adonai or with Adonis, the meaning of each of these names being radically distinct from that of Aten. Generally speaking, Aten is named only in connexion with Râ, who is then called " Râ in his Aten " and the like ; yet occasionally, though rarely, worship seems to have been accorded to the Aten itself, even down to a comparatively late epoch. Such a cult apparently prevailed for some time in Heliopolis, where stood an Aten temple to which structural additions were made by kings of the XVIIIth and XIXth Dynasties. During one short period of Egyptian history the worship of the Aten became the religion of the state. This took place under King Amenophis IV. (about 1450 B.C.), a monarch distinguished from other Egyptians by striking bodily peculiarities—the sharp advancing chin, the disproportionate length of limb, and the rolls of fat about the waist. The fact that his contemporaries are pictured in like fashion is no proof that they resembled him, but is due to the Egyptian artistic convention of representing the men of any period after the model of the reigning Pharaoh and as endowed with his characteristic features. Attempts have repeatedly been made to prove an Asiatic descent for this king, and thus to explain his idiosyncrasies, but no evidence of any weight has ever yet been advanced in favour of the theory. On the other

hand, many things in this royal Reformation rather
indicate a deep seated working of Libyan influences,
although no proof is forthcoming that there was any
Libyan blood in the king's veins. So far as may be
gathered from the inscriptions, his predecessor, Amenophis III., was an adherent of the old Egyptian customs
and cult, and the temples raised by him were chiefly
in honour of Amen Râ of Thebes. At his death the
old conditions remained, for a time, unchanged; the
new king also bore a name compounded with that of
Amen, and in the earliest of his monuments his likeness
still resembles that of his predecessor. But about the
fourth year of his reign his views changed; he assumed
a new name, *Khû-en-âten*, "Glory of the Aten," and
resolved to introduce the cult of the Aten throughout
Egypt. The worship of the Aten was to be henotheistic,
and, henceforth, of the other gods, only solar deities were
to be acknowledged whose nature easily allowed of their
being merged in the Aten. In this sense, that is, as parts
of the one godhead; Horus, Râ, Tûm, and also Amenophis III. under his prenomen of *Râ-neb-maâ*, " Râ, the
Lord of Truth," appear in the inscriptions of this time.
The change would seem to have been somewhat sudden.
There is still preserved in Thebes a tomb begun in the
first years of the king's reign, one part of it representing
him as a follower of Amen, while another makes mention
of the Aten, and the unfinished sepulchral chamber bears
reference to the third stage in the evolution of this religious
reformation.[1] Thus it appears that the king was desirous

---

[1] Cf. WIEDEMANN, *Aeg. Gesch.*, p. 397, Suppl. p. 46.

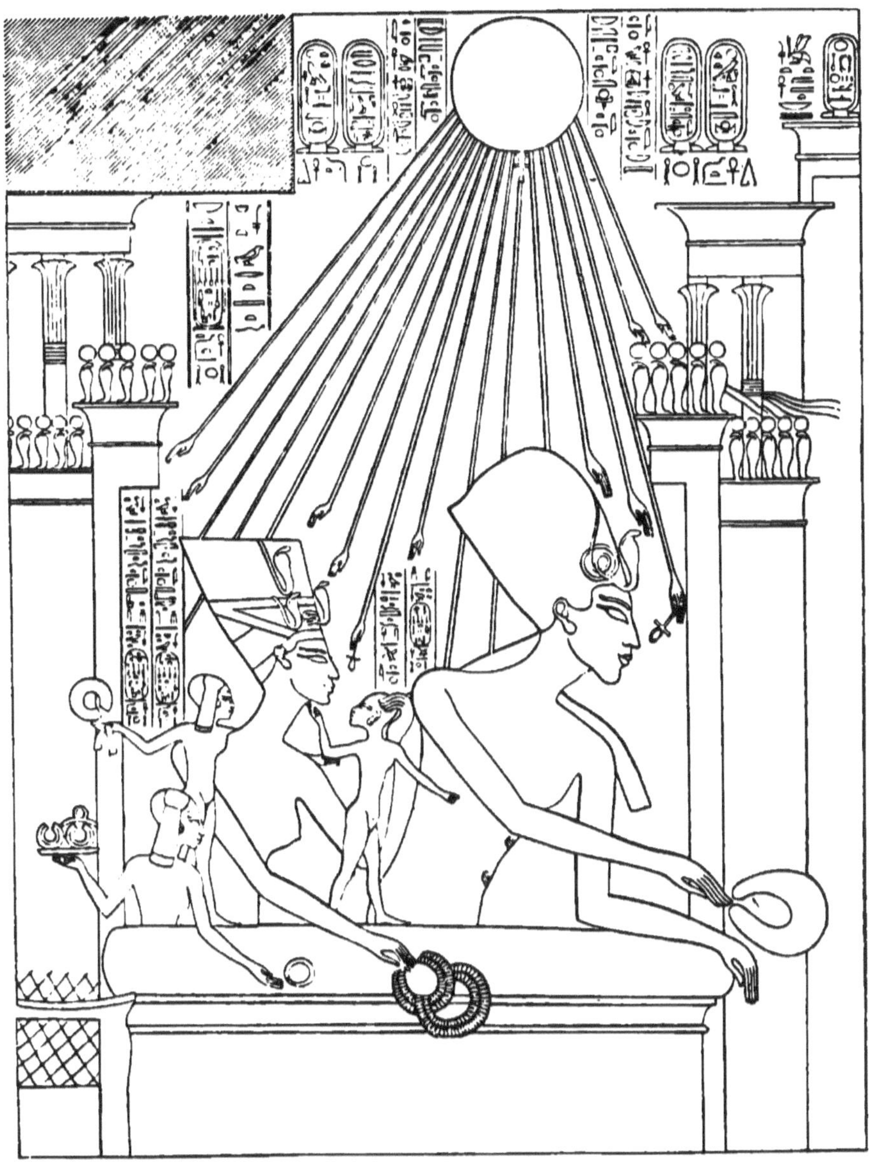

FIG. 11.—KING KHÛENATEN AND HIS FAMILY DISPENSING REWARDS FROM A BALCONY: THE ATEN EXTENDING ITS RAYS OVER THEM. (L. D. III. 103.)

Tomb of Aï, Tell el Amarna.

at first of following the example of his predecessors, and took up his residence in Thebes, where he intended to raise a great temple to Râ Harmakhis Aten, a Benben— that is to say, an obelisk with its appropriate sacred buildings. But the opposition of the Theban priesthood prevailed ; the king forsook the city, accompanied by all his court, and on the site of Tell el Amarna in Middle Egypt he founded a new capital wholly dedicated to the worship of the Sun. Thither were carried the national archives, and it is from among these that we have recovered the famous cuneiform inscriptions of the Tell el Amarna tablets. There also are the tombs of the king's followers, the inscriptions and reliefs of which, together with the ruins of the temple and palaces,[1] have furnished all the scanty data which we possess concerning the worship of the Aten.

The god was always represented under the form of the solar disk, with rays downspread towards earth and severally terminating in hands. These hands are often depicted as presenting to the king, or shedding abroad upon the world, the symbols of life, power, or other blessings. The Aten is never represented as anthropomorphic. In this as in other Egyptian cults religious worship chiefly consisted in solemn processions, in which the king and his family took part, and the singing in whole or part of a hymn, which is in this case remarkable for the beauty of its style. One of the most characteristic and poetical versions is preserved in the tomb of Aï, a

---

[1] See chiefly PETRIE, *Tell el Amarna*, London, 1894.

very exalted official of the time, at El Amarna.[1] With a
few unimportant omissions the hymn runs as follows :—

HYMN TO THE ATEN.

Beauteous is thy resplendent appearing on the horizon of heaven,
O Aten, who livest and art the beginning of life!
When thou risest on the horizon of the east thou fillest every
   land with thy beauties;
Fair shining art thou, great and radiant, high above the earth,
Thy beams encompass the lands to the measure of all that thou
   hast made ;
Thou art the sun, thou bringest what is needful to them by thy
   love ;
Thou stretchest out thy beams to the earth.
When thou art above [the earth] day follows thy steps ;
When thou settest on the western horizon then is the earth in
   darkness like unto one that is dead;
They (men) repose in their dwellings, their heads are covered,
   none seeing his fellow,
They are robbed of all the things beneath their heads and they
   know it not ;
Every lion cometh forth out of his cave, all snakes bite;
Night darkens (?), earth becomes silent, their maker hath set on
   his horizon.
Light is the earth when thou risest on the horizon and shinest
   as Aten by day; darkness flees ;
Thou sendest forth thy rays and the world is full of joy day by
   day.
They (men) awake, standing on their feet ;
They purify their limbs, they take their garments
And uplift their hands in adoration, because thou illuminatest
   the whole earth. They perform their labours.
All cattle rest in their pastures, the trees and the plants grow
   green ;

---

[1] Published by BOURIANT in the *Mémoires de la Mission au
Caire*, i., pp. 2 *et seq.* ; also with translation and commentary by
J. H. BREASTED, *De Hymnis in Solem sub rege Amenophide IV.
conceptis*, Berlin, 1894.

The birds fly out of their nests, their outspread wings praise thee.
All flocks leap on their feet, birds and all fowl live; thou risest
 for them.
Barks go up and down stream, thy road (the Nile) is opened at
 thy rising;
The fish in the river rise to the surface towards thy face, and
 thy rays penetrate the great waters;
They cause women to be fruitful and men to beget,
They quicken the child within the body of its mother.
Thou soothest it that it cry not,
Thou dost nourish it within the body of its mother,
Thou givest breath to give life to all its functions.
It cometh forth from the body of its mother . . . on the day of
 its birth;
Thou openest its mouth that it may speak.
The chick is in its egg, cheeping within its shell,
Thou givest it breath therein that it may live;
Thou makest it complete (fully developed) that it may break out
 of the egg;
It cometh forth from the egg to cheep, to be made complete;
It runneth on its feet when it cometh forth [from the egg].

.   .   .   .   .   .

Thou createdst the earth according to thy will when thou wast
 alone:
Men, herds, all flocks,
All that is upon earth and goeth upon feet,
All that is on high and flieth with wings,
The lands of Syria, of Kush, and of Egypt;
Thou settest each in its right place;
Thou providest each with that which pertaineth to it. . . .
Thou measurest (?) to them the duration of their lives,
Their tongues are loosened that they speak, their forms are
 according to the complexions of their skins:
Ordaining them, thou hast ordained the inhabitants of the lands.

Thou makest the Nile in the Underworld (Dûat), thou conductest
 it hither at thy pleasure,
That it may give life to men whom thou hast made for thyself,
 Lord of All!
Thou givest the Nile in heaven that it descendeth to them

It causeth its waters to rise upon the rocks like the sea; it
    watereth their fields in their districts.
So are thy methods accomplished, O Lord of Eternity! thou who
    art thyself the celestial Nile;
Thou art the King of the inhabitants of the lands.
And of the cattle going upon their feet in every land, which go
    upon feet.
The Nile cometh out of the Underworld to Egypt.

Thy [rays] nourish every field, thou risest and they live for thee.
Thou makest the seasons of the year that they may bring into
    existence all that thou hast made:
The winter to refresh them, the heat [to warm them].
Thou createdst the heaven which is outspread that thou mightest
    rise in it,
That thou mightest see all which thou didst create.

Thou art the Only One, when thou risest in thy form as the living
    Aten, splendid, radiant, fair-shining.
Thou createdst [the forms] of the beings who are in thee.
Thou art the Only One [in respect of] cities, fields, roads, water-
    ways [of the Nile].
All behold thee in their midst, for thou art the Aten of day
    above the earth. . . .
At thy rising all live: at thy setting they die by thee;
But the duration of thy life is the life that is in thee.
Eyes shine brightly until thou settest; ceaseth all labour when
    thou settest in the west. . . .
Thou ordainest since thou createdst the earth, and raisedst them
    up (*i.e.* its inhabitants),
For thy son who came forth from thy body, the King of Upper
    and Lower Egypt,
Who liveth by truth, the lord of the two lands, Khûenaten;
And the great royal wife, whom he loveth,
The lady of the two lands, Nefer-aiti-Nefer-neferû.

As king of the world, the Aten was even invested with
a cartouche, and is styled in the inscription " Râ Harmakhis, who rejoiceth on the horizon in his name of Shû,
who is in the Aten "; and the expressions " Lord of

heaven," "Lord of earth," "He who giveth life for ever," "He who illuminateth the earth," "He who reigneth in Truth," frequently appear among his titles.

Khûenaten seems to have tried to carry out his reform at first in a friendly spirit; the opposition which he encountered turned him into a fanatic. The name of Amen, in whom he recognized the chief rival of the Aten, was erased from the monuments and even in the tombs ; it was likewise sought out on smaller objects such as funerary stelae, and diligently effaced even when occurring in proper names. In spite of these violent measures the king did not succeed in attaining his end. His faith, though held by one or two of his immediate successors, was subsequently allowed to drop, and Aten worship was persecuted in its turn. The capital of the Sun king was abandoned, never again to be inhabited ; the temples of the Aten were destroyed ; the names of god and king alike were consistently effaced, and any mention of this particular form of solar deity was thereafter extremely rare. Heliopolis seems to have been the one spot in which an Aten sanctuary survived ; throughout the rest of the land the other solar gods again represented the Sun. But henceforth, even as it had been from the beginning of the New Kingdom up to the time of Khûenaten, the old solar deities seldom appeared singly and in their simple forms : they were generally fused with others, and became Amen Râ, Khnûm Râ, etc. Of the more important gods Ptah was almost the only one to escape the common lot of fusion with the Sun, and this simply because he was already practically merged in Osiris, god and ruler of the realm of the dead, who stood in a certain contrast to Râ, god of the world of the living.

The cult of the Sun god in no way differed from that of the other deities. Food and drink were offered to him ; vegetable offerings and animal sacrifices were alike presented. The assertion that blood and wine were not acceptable to him is based on error. In one thing only can the rites of his worship be said to differ from those of the other gods : more hymns were sung to Râ and longer prayers were addressed to him than to any other deity. In the nature of things it was easier to extol and set forth the beneficent might of an activity so obvious to all as that of a deified power of nature, than to do the like by deities more ethical, who could not lay claim to such tangible results of their energy. Hence it is that poetical works dedicated to Râ and to his equivalents Harmakhis, Khepera, Tûm, etc., are found in abundance on both stone and papyrus, dating from the earliest times down to the rule of the Roman emperors. Especially numerous are the hymns from funerary texts which repeat with wearisome iteration the same reflexions on the creative and gladdening power of the sun and the blessings hoped for from it by the deceased. A good illustration is afforded by the following, which is preserved in many slightly varied forms : it is here translated from Chapter XV. in the Turin copy of the Book of the Dead.

" Speech of the Osiris N. (name of the deceased) : ' Hail to Râ, Lord of Rays, who shineth above the Osiris N. ! He extolleth thee in the morning, he doeth homage to thee at evening ; his soul goeth forth to thee in heaven, journeying in the Mâdet bark, arriving in the Sekti bark, it entereth among the never resting stars in heaven.'

"The Osiris N. saith, praising the Lord of Eternity: ' Hail to thee, Râ Harmakhis, Khepera who art self-begotten! Twice beautiful! When thou ascendest on the horizon, Egypt is enlightened by thy rays. All the gods rejoice when they behold the King of Heaven. The uraeus is erect upon thy head, and the crown of the South and the crown of the North are upright upon thy forehead ; they have prepared a seat for themselves on thy brow. Hail to the beneficent one who is at the prow of the bark,[1] because he destroyeth for thee all thine enemies who tarry in Dûat (the Underworld), he goeth forth defending thy majesty that he may see thy beauteous form.

"' I come unto thee, I am with thee to see thy disk (*âten*) every day. Let me not be imprisoned, let me not be repulsed, for I renew my limbs at the sight of thy beauty, as do all who praise thee, because I am one of these thy devoted ones upon earth. I reach the Land of Eternity, I unite myself with the Land of Everlasting, with thee. Behold ! there shineth upon me Râ with all the gods !'

"The Osiris N. saith : ' Hail to thee when thou ascendest by day on the horizon ! Thou traversest the heavens in peace to cause trueness of voice.[2] All men rejoice at sight of thy coming, extolling thee (?) with the hand. Every morning thou causest growth and movement beneath thy

[1] Shû is here meant ; he is often represented as standing in the prow of the solar bark, armed with a lance and ready to strike the foes of the Sun god.

[2] *Mâă kher*. The meaning of this expression will be more fully considered later.

majesty. Thy rays are upon men. As none may tell the splendour of *asem* (an alloy of silver and gold), so cannot thy splendour be told. The lands of the gods see all the colours of Pûnt when thou dispersest the darkness which is over them. Thou alone art the creator when thou createst thine own forms there on Nû (the primeval waters).

"' May I advance as thou advancest. May I, even as thy majesty, O Râ, find no end. There is no prince so great that he passeth through endless water in one short moment.

FIG. 12.—SUN GOD UPLIFTING THE DISK : CYNOCEPHALI ADORING.
(LEPS., "TODT.," CAP. 16.)
Book of the Dead. Ptolemaic ?

Thou doest it. Thou settest, thou completest the hours— otherwise said :[1] In like manner hast thou measured out day and night, thou completest them as thou hast ordained. —As the sun (Râ) thou enlightenest the earth with thy arms when thou risest on the horizon !' (This refers to the representations of the Sun god as a man uplifting the sun disk on high with both arms.)

" The Osiris N. saith as he adoreth thee in the morning

[1] This phrase introduces an alternative formula.

when thou shinest; he speaketh praises unto thee at thy rising : ' Thou who exaltest thy forms shining—otherwise said : Great in this thy beauty!—Thou beatest out and fashionest thy limbs (as a goldsmith). Thou bringest forth thyself without birth ; on the horizon thou ascendest on the high heaven. Let me attain unto the high heaven of eternity, unto the places of those who extol thee. I unite myself with the venerable, perfect, luminous spirits of the Underworld ; I go forth with them to see thy beauties at thy going forth at evening when thou traversest thy mother Nût (the goddess of heaven); and when thou turnest thy face to the West, my arms are uplifted in adoration of thy setting in the Land of Life (the Under-world). Yea, thou didst create eternity ; thou art extolled at thy setting in Nû (the primeval waters). Thou hast established thyself in my heart without ceasing. Thou rejuvenatest (*neter*) thyself more than all the gods (*neterû*).'

"The Osiris N. saith : ' Hail to thee when thou risest in the primeval waters enlightening the earth on the day of thy birth, when thy mother brought thee forth upon her hands. Thou art radiant, thou rejuvenatest thyself. Thou shinest as the Great One of Sunrise in the primeval waters. The dwellers thereby deck themselves as they hasten towards thee ; festivals are solemnized in thine honour by the nomes, by all cities and temples which are illumined by thy beauties. Gifts are offered unto thee in abundance and excess. Valiant one! Exalted form of the exalted forms, who protectest all thy abodes against Evil! Great one of glory in the Sekti bark, great one of that which is desired in the Mâdet bark! Thou givest splendour unto the Osiris N. in the Underworld; thou grantest him to tarry in the West as lord over Wrong, protected against Evil. Place him among the venerable ones who have devoted themselves unto thee; let him unite himself with the souls (*ba.û*) in the Underworld; after a joyful journey may he roam in the fields of Aalû.'

"The Osiris N. saith: 'I go forth unto the heaven, I traverse the iron of the sky, my body is in the midst of the stars. Salutations are made unto me in the bark, I am invoked in the Mâdet bark; I behold Râ within his sanctuary when I pray daily unto his solar disk (*aten*). I see the Phagros fish when it riseth on the stream and emergeth from the green surface; I see the turtle and its particles (?). If any wicked person appeareth he falleth to the ground before the proclamation of Râ; I hack him in pieces, cutting along his backbone. I open unto thee thy path, O Râ, when there is a favourable wind; the Sekti boat reduceth her speed; the crew of Râ rejoice when they behold him, the Lord of Life, whose heart is refreshed, for all his enemies are overthrown. Behold! I see Horus at the helm (?), and Thoth with Truth upon his hands. All the gods rejoice to see him who cometh in peace. The hearts of the glorified ones (*khû*) are made luminous (*khû*); the Osiris N. is with them in the West, his heart is refreshed.'

"Saith the Osiris N. :—

"' Hail to thee! thou who comest as Tûm, thou who wast when thou createdst the Ennead of the gods.

Hail to thee! thou who comest as spirit (*ba*) of the spirits ruling in the West.

Hail to thee! chief of the gods, who illuminatest the Dûat with thy beauties.

Hail to thee! thou who comest as glorified one (*khû*), journeying in thy solar disk (*âten*).

Hail to thee! thou who art greater than all the gods, who shinest in heaven, who rulest in Dûat.

Thou givest sweet breath of the north wind to the Osiris N.

Hail to thee! thou who openest up Dûat, thou who showest all doors.

Hail to thee in the midst of the gods! thou who weighest words in the Underworld.

Hail to thee in thy cradle! thou who creating createst Dûat by thy glory.

Hail to the great and mighty One! thine enemies are flung down in the hall of execution.

Hail to thee who destroyest thy foes and annihilatest the Âpep serpent (darkness).

Thou givest sweet breath of the north wind to the Osiris N.

"'Aroëris openeth the door (of the Underworld), he the great opener of the great Land of Rest in the mountain of the Underworld. The Dûat is illumined by thy glory. The souls (*ba.û*) in their secret dwellings are illuminated in their caverns. Thou annihilatest Evil in dashing down and annihilating the foes.'

"The Osiris N. saith, in adoring Râ Harmakhis at his setting in the Land of Life: 'Hail to thee, Râ! Hail to thee, Tûm, at thine arrival! Beautiful, radiant, exalted One! Thou passest along the heaven, thou traversest the earth, thou unitest thyself with the upper heaven in incense.[1] The dwellers in the two halves of Egypt bow themselves before thee, they give adoration unto thee; the gods and the dwellers in the Underworld rejoice over thy beauties, the dwellers in secret places extol thee. The princes whom thou hast created upon earth make offering unto thee. They who tarry on the horizon convey thee, and those who are in the Sekti bark guide thy wandering. They extol thee because of the victory of thy majesty, saying: 'Come! come! approach in peace!' To thee belongeth joyful acclamation, Lord of Heaven, Ruler of the Underworld. Thy mother Nût embraceth thee. She seeth in thee her son who is the fearful and the terrible One, who setteth in the Land of Life at the gloaming. Then uplifteth thee thy father Tanen (in this connexion the earth); he putteth his arms behind thee (to protect thee). There ensueth thy rejuvenation on the earth. Tanen placeth thee among the honoured before Osiris. The deceased N. is in peace, in peace; he is Râ himself.'

"These are the words to be spoken before Râ when he setteth in the Land of Life; both arms of the speaker must hang downwards.

"The Osiris N. saith, extolling Tûm at his setting in the Land of Life, in the splendour of Dûat (in Dûat which he fills with splendour): 'Hail to thee! thou who settest in the Land of Life, thou father of the gods; thou unitest thyself with thy mother in the Land of the West; her arms enfold thee daily. Thy majesty hath part in the abode of

---

[1] A metaphor derived from the story of the self immolation of the phoenix by fire at Heliopolis, on an incense strewn pyre.

Sokaris.[1]   Rejoiced art thou at the love which is borne thee. The gates upon the horizon are opened unto thee, thou settest in the Mountain of the West.   Thy rays traverse the earth to enlighten the lands of the dwellers in the Under-world.   They who are in the Underworld and the acclaiming spirits are stirred in excitement at the sight of thee every day.   Give peace to the gods upon earth, namely unto them which follow thee ; I am of those who follow in thy train.   Exalted spirit (*ba*) who didst beget the gods, who didst equip them with his attributes, over whom no judgment is held (?)!   Prince! thou who art great in secret things!   May thy beauteous face be gracious unto the Osiris N.   Khepera, father of the gods!

" ' There is no destruction (for the deceased) to all eternity, because of (the existence of) this book ; I am established thereby.   He who recites it or copies it is thereby in peace. Abundance was given unto me ; mine arms are full of food and drink (literally, bread and beer).   I united myself with this book after my lifetime.   It was written to great comfort of heart.' "

It will be seen that the last sentences assure the reciter of the chapter (including any one who should have it copied for his use) that he should be united with the book, take it with him into the life beyond, and so attain to everlasting bliss.   This assurance is often given in similar words in other religious, and more especially in magical texts.

---

[1] A division of the nether world: cf. p. 92.

CHAPTER III.

SOLAR MYTHS.

R A was regarded by the Egyptians, not only as the Sun god, but also as the first King of Egypt. In early times the people seem to have held this conception with a fixity which no theological attempts of the priests to set other deities higher in the pantheon could shake. Not until later times did he yield his place in popular favour to Osiris, the archetype of Egyptian kings ; nor even then was he altogether deposed, but while Osiris was supposed to have ruled as a man over men only, the dominion of Râ was relegated to a time when gods still sojourned among men and Râ bore rule over both.

The reign of Râ was placed in remotest antiquity. "The like has not happened since the time of Râ," was a common phrase in reference to any event such as had never been known within the memory of man. The god was regarded by the Egyptian people as purely anthropomorphic. We find him appearing in popular tales, and—as in "The Story of the Two Brothers"[1]—walking upon earth along with other gods, conversing with mortals, granting to his favoured ones gifts which did not always

---

[1] *Pap. d'Orbincy*, p. 9 : cf. MASPERO, *Contes populaires*, second edition, pp. 18 *et seq.* ; PETRIE, *Egyptian Tales*, ii., pp. 36 *et seq.*

minister to their permanent happiness, and imagined as a kindly old man. There is nothing remarkable in this; parallel ideas can be adduced from the popular tales of the most diverse races and religions. But in Egypt this anthropomorphic and somewhat low conception of divinity prevailed even among the cultured classes. The king was held to be as literally the son of Râ as of the queen, materially begotten; the preceding monarch, therefore, was but his reputed father. This belief was directly expressed in popular tales such as " The Story of King Khûfû," in which it is told how Râ was father of the first kings of the Vth Dynasty.[1] We find the same belief still current in the tradition that Alexander the Great was born of the union of Zeus Ammon and Olympias, a tradition which Alexander himself favoured, but which was afterwards interpreted to the effect that his father was not indeed a god but the magician Nectanebus, the last native King of Egypt, who had assumed this disguise. The same idea is expressed repeatedly in official inscriptions: from the time of the Vth Dynasty the king systematically refers to himself as "Son of Râ," and there are also texts in which the god boasts of this paternal relation in no equivocal terms.[2] This anthropomorphic presentation of Râ also runs through the surviving myths concerning him, myths which usually relate to the time

[1] *Westcar Papyrus*, Berlin, published and commented upon by ERMAN, *Die Märchen des Papyrus Westcar*, Berlin, 1890. Cf. MASPERO, *Contes populaires*, 2nd Ed., pp. 74 *et seq.*; PETRIE, *Egyptian Tales*, vol. i., pp. 9 *et seq.*, especially p. 32.

[2] Cf. WIEDEMANN, *Le Roi dans l'ancienne Égypte. Le Muséon*, xiii., p. 372.

when, owing to his extreme old age, the reins of government began to fall from his hands, and gods and men became disobedient and rebelled against their lord. The three most important of these legends are: 1. The Legend of Râ and Isis, preserved in a Turin papyrus dating from the XXth Dynasty; 2. The Legend of the Destruction of Mankind, inscribed on the walls of the tombs of Seti I. and Rameses III.; 3. The Legend of the Winged Sun Disk, of which the text covers a wall of the Ptolemaic temple of Edfû. These texts are of profound significance as regards Egyptian thought and conceptions of deity, and hence it is desirable to give an approximately literal translation of them in their main portions.

The Legend of Râ and Isis.[1]

"Chapter of the divine god who created himself, maker of heaven and earth, of the breath of life, of the gods, of men, of the wild beasts, of cattle, of creeping things, of fowl and fish; king of men and gods, to whom the centuries are years, who hath many names, whom none knoweth, whom even the gods know not.

"Isis was a woman, mighty of word; her heart was tired of men, she preferred the gods. Then she thought in her heart whether she might not possess the world in heaven and upon earth even as Râ did, by means of the name

---

[1] PLEYTE AND ROSSI, *Pap. de Turin*, pls. 31, 77, 131-8; LEFÉBURE, *Aeg. Zeitschrift*, 1883, pp. 27 *et seq.*; ERMAN, *Aegypten*, pp. 359 *et seq.*; MASPERO, *Les Origines*, pp. 162-4; BUDGE, *First Steps in Egyptian*, pp. 241 *et seq.*

of the august god "—*i.e.* the secret name of Râ, which no man knoweth, and to knowledge of which the god himself owed his power over gods and men.

"The god Râ came daily at the head of his companions to sit upon his throne; he had grown old, his mouth ran and the drivelling flowed to earth, his spittle fell upon the ground. And Isis with her hand kneaded it together with the earth that was there; she made thereof a sacred serpent unto which she gave the form of a spear. She wound it not about her face (as goddesses wore the uræus coiled about the head), but cast it on the way which the great god traversed in his Double Kingdom whenever he would.

"The venerable god advanced, the gods who served him as their Pharaoh followed him, he went forth as on every day. Then the sacred serpent bit him. The divine god opened his mouth, and his cry reached unto heaven. His cycle of gods cried, 'What is it?' and his gods cried, 'Behold!' He could not answer; his jaws chattered, his limbs trembled; the poison seized on his flesh even as the Nile covers its domain (at the inundation).

"When the great god had quieted his heart he cried unto his following: 'Come unto me, ye children of my body, ye gods who went forth from me! Let Khepera know it. A painful thing hath injured me; my heart feeleth it, but mine eyes see it not, my hand did it not. I know not who hath done it to me; never felt I pain like unto this, no evil is worse than it.

"'I am a prince, son of a prince, the seed (*mû*) of a god; I am the Great One, son of the Great One, my father excogitated my name; I am he of many names, of many forms; my form is in every god. I called forth Tûm, Horus, the gods who give praise. My name was pronounced by my father and by my mother, then it was hidden in me that no magician might arise who should use magic arts against me (which might be done by one knowing the secret name of the god).

"'I had come forth to look upon that which I had made, I was walking in the two lands which I had formed, when something which I knew not stung me. Fire it is not, water it is not. My heart is burning, my limbs tremble, my members shudder. Let the children of the gods be brought unto me, with magic words, with an understanding mouth, whose might reaches unto heaven.'

"The children of all the gods came full of mourning. Isis came with her magic arts, she whose mouth is full of breath of life, whose formulas destroy sufferings, whose word animateth the dead. She said, 'What is it, divine father? what is it? A serpent hath spread this evil in thee, one of thy creatures hath lifted up his head against thee. Verily it shall fall by mighty incantations; I will cause it to recede at the sight of thy rays.'

"The venerable god opened his mouth: 'I went upon the way, I walked in the two lands of mine earth, it was the desire of my heart to see that which I formed; then was I bitten of a serpent which I saw not. Fire it is not, water it is not. I am colder than water, I am hotter than fire; all my members sweat, I tremble, mine eye hath no power, I see not the heaven, and water runneth from my face as in the season of summer.'

"Isis said unto Râ : ' Oh tell me thy name, divine father for he shall live who is delivered from the ill by his own name.' Then spake Râ : ' I have made the heaven and the earth, I have ordered the mountains and formed all that is thereon. I am he who made the water, creating the inundation. I created the husband of his mother (a title bestowed upon various deities [p. 104] ; in this instance it is probably Amen Râ who is meant). I made the heaven and the secret of both horizons, and I placed the soul (*ba*) of the gods within them. I am he who at the opening of his eyes createth all light ; when he closeth his eyes he createth darkness. The water of the Nile riseth at his command ; the gods know not his name. I make the hours and create the days ; I send the festival of the New Year and form the river ; I make the living fire in order to regulate the tasks in the dwellings. I am Khepera in the morning, Râ at noon, and Tûm in the evening.'

"The poison was not turned in its course, the great god was not healed. Isis spake unto Râ : ' Thy name was not mentioned in thy speech. Tell it unto me, that the poison may go hence, for he shall live whose name is repeated ' (in the incantation).

"The poison burned with burning, stronger was it than the flame of fire. The god Râ said : ' I grant that Isis search me, that my name pass from my bosom into her bosom.' The god hid himself from the gods, the bark of eternity was empty (*i.e.* the bark in which the Sun god traversed the heavens). When the moment had come for the going forth from his heart, then said Isis to her son Horus : ' He shall bind himself with a sacred oath to give up his eyes ' (Sun and Moon, the visible signs of the Sun's power).

" The great god's name was taken from him, and Isis, the great enchantress, said : ' Flee, poison ! go forth from Râ ! Eye of Horus,[1] depart out of the god, and flow forth glittering out of his mouth ! I it is who work ; I cause the vanquished poison to fall upon earth, for the name of the great god was taken from him. Let Râ live, but let the poison die ! ' So spake Isis the Great One, the mistress of the gods, she who knoweth Râ and his name itself."

The concluding words of this text go on to say that it .s an excellent charm against snake poison to recite this story over an image of Tûm, or Horus, or Isis ; or, having written it down, to dissolve the writing and drink the concoction ; or to inscribe it on a piece of linen and wear it suspended from the neck.

THE DESTRUCTION OF MANKIND.[2]

" Râ is the god who created himself, and was king over gods and men alike. 'Mankind took counsel against his majesty and spake : ' Behold, his majesty the god Râ is grown old ; his bones are become silver, his limbs gold, and his hair pure lapis lazuli.' His majesty heard the words which men spake concerning him. His majesty

[1] An expression denoting any god sent gift and here referring to the poison of which Isis was the cause.

[2] LEFÉBURE, *Tombeau de Seti I.*, part iv., pls. 15-18 ; *Tombeau de Ramses III.*, pls. 2-5 : see also BERGMANN, *Hieroglyphische Inschriften*, pls. 75-82 ; NAVILLE, *Trans. Soc. Bib. Arch.*, iv., pp. 1 *et seq.* ; viii., pp. 412 *et seq.* ; BRUGSCH, *Die neue Weltordnung*, Berlin, 1881, and *Religion der Alten Aegypter*, pp. 436-7 ; MASPERO, *Les Origines*, pp. 164-9.

spake to those who were in his train : 'Call unto me mine eye (the goddess Hathor Sekhet), and the god Shû and the goddess Tefnût, the god Seb and the goddess Nût, and the fathers and the mothers who were with me when I was in Nû (the primeval waters), and also Nû (the god of the primeval waters). Let him bring his companions with him ; let him bring them in all secrecy, that men may not see them and flee. Let him go with them to the great temple (the temple of Heliopolis), that they may give counsel, for I will go forth out of the primeval waters to the place at which I shall be : let these gods be brought to me.'

"Now when these gods came to the place at which Râ was, they cast themselves down to earth before his majesty, and he spake before Nû, the father of the oldest gods, he who created mankind, he who was king of the spirits that know. They spake before his majesty : 'Speak unto us that we may hear thy words.' And Râ spake unto Nû : 'O thou eldest god by whom I first had my being, and ye ancestral gods ! behold, mankind, who had their being from mine eye, hold counsel against me. Tell me what ye would do in face of this. Take ye counsel for me. I will not slay them until I have heard what ye say concerning it.'

"Then spake the majesty of the god Nû : 'O my son Râ, thou the god who art greater than his creator (Nû himself), and than those who formed him ! Thy throne standeth fast, great is the fear of thee. Turn thine eye against those who conspire against thee.' The god Râ spake : 'Behold, men flee unto the hills ; their heart is full of fear because of that which they said.' Then spake the gods before his majesty (Râ the king): ' Send forth thine eye; let it destroy for thee the people which imagined wicked plots against thee. There is no eye among mankind which can withstand thine eye when it descendeth in the form of the goddess Hathor.'

"Then went forth this goddess, and she slew mankind upon the hills. Then spake the majesty of this god: ' Approach in peace, Hathor! Never will I be parted (?) from thee.' Then spake the goddess: ' Mayst thou live for me! When I took possession of mankind, then was my heart rejoiced.' Then spake the majesty of the god Râ: ' I will take possession of. mankind as their king, and destroy (?) them.' And it came to pass that for several nights Sekhet waded in the blood of men, beginning at Heracleopolis Magna.

"Then spake Râ: ' Call unto me swift messengers; let them run like a blast of wind.' The messengers were forthwith brought. The majesty of this god spake: ' Let them run to Elephantine; let them bring me many mandrakes''[1] (?). These mandrakes (?) were brought to him. They were given to the god SEKTI (the grinder), who dwells in Heliopolis, that he should grind these mandrakes. Behold, when the women slaves had crushed corn for beer, then these mandrakes were put in the jars [in which was the beer and also] human blood. Seven thousand beer jars of this were made.

[1] See BRUGSCH, *Aeg. Zeitschrift*, 1891, pp. 31 *et seq.*, on the name of this plant; his translation, however, can be accepted only as an hypothesis.

" When the majesty of Râ, King of Upper and Lower
Egypt, came with the gods to see this beer, and day
dawned, after this goddess had been slaughtering men as
she went up stream, then spake the majesty of this god :
' This is excellent. I shall protect mankind against
her.'

" Râ spake : ' Let these jars be carried and brought (?)
to the place at which men are being slaughtered.' The
majesty of Râ, King of Upper and Lower Egypt, commanded that this soporific drink should be poured forth
during the fine night. The fields on all four sides were
overflowed, as the majesty of this god had commanded.

" And the goddess Sekhet came in the morning ; she
found the fields inundated, she was rejoiced thereat, she
drank thereof, her heart was rejoiced, she went about
drunken and took no more cognisance of men. Then
spake the majesty of Râ to this goddess : ' Approach in
peace, thou charming goddess ' (*ámi.t*). From this the
pleasant damsels in Amû have their origin (*i.e.* because Râ
had called Sekhet *ámi.t*, " charming," attractive damsels
were installed as priestesses in the city of Amû in the
western Delta, a city called Apis by the Greek writers)·
And the majesty of Râ spake to this goddess : ' Soporific
drinks shall be prepared for thee at every New Year's
feast, and verily their number (*i.e.* the number of the jars
containing the drink) shall correspond to that of my handmaidens.' Therefore from that day soporific drinks are
made by all men at the feast of Hathor, according to the
number of the handmaidens.[1]

[1] The feasts of Hathor were festivals at which drink flowed freely

" And the majesty of Râ spake to this goddess : ' I suffer from a burning pain ; whence is this pain (?) ? ' The majesty of Râ spake : ' Truly I am alive, but my heart is weary of being together with men ; I have not destroyed them, they are not destroyed as befits my might.' Then spake the gods who were of his following : ' Let thy weariness alone ; thy might is according to thy desire.' But the majesty of this god spake unto the majesty of Nû (the god of the primeval waters) : ' For the first time my limbs ail ; I will not wait until this weakness seizeth me a second time.' "

Here the narrative is broken by considerable lacunae, and of the sequel only detached portions of sentences can be deciphered. According to these it would seem that Nû commanded Shû, and the goddess Nût under her form of the celestial cow, to help Râ in his pain, in order that he might again feel inclined to reign ; and after somewhat long discussion Nût took the god Râ upon her back. At this juncture men once more ventured to show themselves upon earth, and seeing Râ upon the back of Nût were seized with repentance for what they had done, and prayed Râ that he would slay his enemies, *i.e.* those who had conspired against him. Meanwhile Râ was carried onward until he came to the Abode of the Cow (a temple in the Libyan nome), and the men went with him. " He reached it while it was still night. But when the earth grew light and it was morning, the men went forth with

and much intoxication prevailed ; the inscriptions even make mention of a certain festival known as the Intoxication Festival held in her honour and celebrated at Denderah in the month of Thoth.

their bows and marched to battle against the enemies of the god Râ. Then spake the majesty of this god : ' Your crime is forgiven you ; the slaughter (which ye have executed for me) atoneth for the slaughter (which the rebels had purposed against me).' And this god spake unto the goddess Nût: ' I have determined to cause myself to be uplifted into the sky ' " (*i.e.* to join the blessed gods and to renounce his rule of the world). His desire was fulfilled, and having reached the upper regions he inspected the territory which he had there chosen for his own, declared his purpose of gathering many men about him in it, and created for their future accommodation the various divisions of the heavenly world. " His majesty—to whom Life! Prosperity! Health![1]—spake: ' Let there be set (*hetep*) a great field,' and there appeared the Field of Rest (*hetep*) ; ' I will gather (*aarad*) plants in it,' and there appeared the Field of *Aarû* (*Aalû*) ; ' Therein do I gather as its inhabitants things which hang from heaven, even the stars.' Then Nût trembled exceedingly (*i.e.* the vault of heaven shook so that the stars were dislodged and fell, as Râ had commanded, into the land which he had made). And the majesty of the god Râ spake: ' I excogitated millions of beings that they may extol me.' And there appeared millions. And the majesty of Râ spake : ' O my son Shû, do thou unite thyself with my daughter Nût, and there watch for me over the millions of millions who are there, who there tarry in darkness ' "—*i.e.* Shû is

---

[1] Compare this common Egyptian formula, used after naming the king, with " in health and wealth long to live " in Prayer for the Sovereign, *Book of Common Prayer*. (TRANS.)

appointed by Râ to be a light to men upon earth : he is installed by the old Sun as the new.

At this point in the narrative there follows a long text describing the celestial cow in very obscure terms of which the difficulty is enhanced by clerical errors. According to one scheme · of Egyptian cosmography, this cow was supposed to form the celestial vault, and the sun to travel over the surface of its body, which was supported in its standing position above the earth by various divinities, and more especially by the god Shû. Sometimes the cow was identified with Hathor, and sometimes with Nût. It was upon her back that Râ abode after his retirement, and there he ruled the upper heaven, which, as the text relates, he had himself created, together with all its fields wherein the Egyptian hoped to find a dwelling place after death as one of the millions who there give praise unto the god who made them.

After this reorganization of the heavens and the earth Râ remembered that he was leaving existent upon earth creatures dangerous ·even to himself, and whose sting had brought about the first detriment to his strength. So before altogether relinquishing the kingly office he gave command concerning these creatures and constituted serpent charmers special favourites of the godhead. " The majesty of this god spake unto Thoth : ' Call unto me the majesty of the god Seb and say unto him : Come thou forthwith.' When the majesty of Seb came to him, then spake the majesty of the god Râ : 'Complaint is made of the reptiles which are in thee ; may they be afraid of me as I now am ! When thou hast learned their purpose

FIG. 13.—THE CELESTIAL COW. (LEFÉBURE, "TOMBEAU DE SETI I.," IV., PL. 17.)

against me, then hasten to the place where my father
Nû is and say unto him, 'Watch thou the reptiles of the
earth and of the water, and make also writings for every
hole in which the reptiles find place, saying: Beware
of harming anything. Let them know that I go hence,
but I shall shine upon them. Their father shall keep
watch on them : thou art their father upon earth eternally.
Let heed be taken to these creatures. They who know
magic formulas shall charm them, armed with my peculiar
magic formulas. I will give away mine own formulas,
I will commend their possessors to thy son Osiris ; their
children shall be protected ; they shall prosper ; they shall
deal as they will with the whole earth, for they charm those
who are in their holes.'

"The majesty of the god Râ spake : 'Let Thoth be
called unto me.' He was forthwith brought. The majesty
of this god spake unto Thoth : ' Let us go, leaving heaven
and my dwelling, for I will make something shining and
resplendent in Dûat and in the Land of the Deep. There
shalt thou register those who did wicked deeds as inhabitants, and there shalt thou imprison them, . . . and
the servants whom my heart hateth. But thou art in my
place, the dweller in my place ; thou shalt be called Thoth,
the Resident (representative) of Râ. I give unto thee
power to send forth thy messengers ' (*hab*)—thereupon the
ibis (*habi*) of Thoth came into being. ' I cause thee to
uplift thine hand before the great Enneads of the gods :
good is the deed (*khen*) which thou accomplishest'—
thereupon the sacred bird (*tekhni*) of Thoth came into
being. ' I cause thee to embrace (*anh*) the two heavens

(the day and the night sky) with thy beauties'—thereupon the moon (*àâḥ*) of Thoth came into being. ' I cause thee to turn (*ânân*) to the people of the North '—thereupon the cynocephalus (*ânân*) of Thoth, who shall be my (*i.e.* Râ's) representative, came into being. ' Thou, Thoth, dost now possess my place in the sight of all who turn themselves towards thee ; all creatures extol thee as a god.'" Thus, whenever throughout this speech Râ pronounces the word which phonetically corresponds to the name of a sacred animal, that moment the animal comes into being.

After these words, in which Râ designated the god of wisdom and of lawful order as his representative, and at the same time created for him his sacred animals, there follows a short notice quite irrelevant to the narrative, and concerned rather with the manner in which the myth must be recited in order to bring about magical results. " When a person pronounces these words for himself he shall rub himself with oil and unguent ; an incense burner full of incense shall be on his hands ; behind his two ears (?) shall be natron, sweet smelling unguent upon his lips. He shall be clothed with two new garments, he shall be purified with water of the inundation, he shall wear white (?) shoes upon his feet, the figure of truth shall be painted upon his tongue with green paint. When the heart of Thoth desires to recite this book for Râ, then shall he purify himself seven times in three days : priests and men shall do the like."

The Legend of the Winged Sun Disk.[1]

"In the year 363 of the reign of Râ Harmakhis, the ever living. Râ was in the land of Nubia with his warriors, but foes conspired (*ûû*) against him, and therefore to this day that country bears the name of Conspirators' Land (*Ûaûa*). Then the god Râ went on his way in his bark together with his following, and landed in the nome of Edfû. Here the god Horbehûdti[2] was in the bark of Râ, and spake unto his father: 'O Harmakhis! I see how foes conspire against their lord.' Then spake the majesty of the god Harmakhis to the person of Horbehûdti: 'Thou son of Râ, Exalted One who didst come forth from me, slay the enemy who is before thee speedily.' Horbehûdti flew up to the sun[3] as a great winged disk; therefore was he henceforth called the Great God, the Lord of Heaven. From heaven he saw the foe, he pursued them as a great winged disk. Because of the fierce onset of his face against them their eyes no longer saw, their ears no longer heard; each man slew his neighbour speedily, not a head remained by which they could live. But Horbehûdti came in the bark of Râ Harmakhis in a many coloured form as a great winged disk. Then spake Thoth to Râ: 'Lord of the gods! there came the god of Behûdet (Edfû) in the

---

[1] Published by NAVILLE, *Mythe d'Horus*, pls. 12-19; translated by BRUGSCH in *Abh. der Göttinger Akad.*, xiv. (1870).

[2] For the reading of this name designating Horus as a sparrow hawk cf. WIEDEMANN, *Pro. Soc. Bibl. Arch.*, xvii., pp. 196 *et seq.*

[3] In this case it is evident that Râ is supposed to be dwelling upon earth rather than in the sun.

form of a great winged disk. From this day forth he shall be called Horbehûdti' (Horus of Edfû). And (Thoth) spake: 'From this day forth the city of Edfû shall be called the city of Horbehûdti.' And Râ embraced the form of Horus and spake to Horbehûdti: 'Thou didst put grapes in the water which cometh forth from Edfû (*i.e.* thou didst cause the red blood of the enemy to flow into it), and thereat thy heart rejoiceth.' This water of Edfû is called [Water of Grapes] from that day forth.

"And Horbehûdti spake: 'Advance, Râ, that thou mayest see thine enemies lying beneath thee in this land.' Now when the majesty of Râ had traversed the way, and with him the goddess Astarte, then saw he the foe lying upon the earth, each lay stretched out like a prisoner. Then spake Râ to Horbehûdti: 'That is a pleasant life.' Therefore from that day forth the place of Horbehûdti is called Pleasant Life. The god Thoth spake: 'This was a stabbing (*deb*) of my foes.' The nome of Edfû is called Stabbing (*deb*) from that day. Thoth spake to Horbehûdti: 'Thou art a great protector' (*mâk âa*). From that day the sacred bark of Horus is called Great of Protection (*âa mâk*).

"Râ spake unto the gods who were in his following: 'Let us voyage (*khen*) in our ship to the Nile; we are glad, for our enemies lie upon the ground.' The [canal] in which the great god was is called Navigable Water (*pe khen*) from that day.

"Thereupon the enemies of Râ went into the water; they were changed into crocodiles and hippopotami. But Harmakhis sailed along on the water in his bark. Now when the crocodiles and hippopotami had reached him, then they opened their jaws with intent to harm the majesty of the god Harmakhis. Then came hither Horbehûdti ; his servants were in his following as workers with weapons of metal (*mesen*) ;[1] each had an iron lance and a chain in his hand ; then they smote the crocodiles and the hippopotami. There were brought in on the spot three hundred and eighty-one enemies who had been slain before the city of Edfû.

" Then spake Harmakhis to Horbehûdti : 'Let mine image be in the south land, for that is a place where there was victory' (*nekht âh*). The abode of Horbehûdti is called the Victorious (*nekht âh*) Abode from that day. Thoth spake after he saw the enemies lying upon the earth : ' Joyful is your heart, ye gods of heaven ! Joyful is your heart, ye gods of earth ! The young Horus cometh in peace ; he hath performed wonders in his expedition, wherein he did according to the Book of Slaying the Hippopotamus.'[2] And from that day there have been metal (*mesen*) statues of Horbehûdti.[3]

" Horbehûdti changed his form into that of a winged sun disk, that which rests over the prow of the bark of Râ. He took with him Nekhebit, the goddess of the South, and Ûazit, the goddess of the North, in the form of two serpents,

[1] With regard to these *meseniu*, which are in the first place smiths and in the second place the armed companions of Horus, cf. MASPERO, *Les Forgerons d' Horus*, *Études de Mythologie*, ii., pp. 313 *et seq*.

[2] *I.e.* Horbehûdti, when on this expedition, had duly made use of the magic formulas contained in that book and had thereby obtained his victory.

[3] As a matter of fact Horus is very commonly represented in metal, and especially in bronze.

that they might destroy the enemies in their bodily forms
of crocodiles and hippopotami at each place to which he
came in the South Land and in the North Land.

"Then his enemies turned from before him; they turned
their faces to the south (when they were overtaken, for,
as the sequel shows, they had already set out northward
in retreat); their courage had failed them for fear of him.
But Horbehûdti was behind them in the bark of Râ; a
lance of iron and a chain were in his hand. With him
was his following equipped with weapons and chains.
Then he beheld the enemies on a plain to the south east
of Thebes." And so on. Of course the foes were conquered on this and successive occasions. They had
already been driven back to the nineteenth nome of Upper
Egypt and there beaten, when the leader and instigator
of the rebellion decided to go out in person against
Horbehûdti.

"Behold, Set went forth and cried out horribly (*neha*)
as he flung forth curses for that which Horbehûdti had
done when he slew the foes. Then spake Râ to Thoth:
'The horrible one (*nehaha*) cries out aloud at that which
Horbehûdti hath done against him.' Then spake Thoth
to Râ: 'Therefore such cries shall be called horrible
(*nehaha*) from this day forth.' Horbehûdti fought with
Set; he threw his iron at him; he cast him down onto the
ground of this city, which is called from that day forth
Pa rehehû.[1] When Horbehûdti returned he brought Set

---

[1] *I.e.* place of the twin brethren Horus and Set, for such is the
mutual relationship attributed to these gods in a myth to which
we find frequent reference.

with him ; his spear stuck in his neck, his chain was on his hand, the club of Horus had smitten him to shut his mouth. He brought him before his father Râ.

"Râ spake unto Thoth : 'Let the companions of Set be given unto Isis and to Horus her son, that they may deal with them at their pleasure.' . . . Then Horus the son of Isis cut off the heads of Set and his confederates before his father Râ and the assembled great company of the gods. He dragged him at his heels through the land ; he put the trident on his head and back " (an allusion to representations of Horus in which he is shown standing over Set, trident in hand). After a few lines the text goes on to say, "Thus did Horbehûdti on the 7th Tybi, together with Horus the son of Isis, who had made his form like unto that of Horbehûdti, slaughter this wretched foe and his confederates." But still the issue of the conflict was indecisive. Set lived on notwithstanding his decapitation ; he changed himself into a roaring serpent that hid itself in a hole which it was forbidden to leave. The land was searched throughout, and the isolated adherents of Set were massacred. From time to time Set himself reappeared, and once it was even necessary to have recourse to the magic formulas of Isis against him. The last battle field was at the city of Thalû (Zaru) in the far east of Egypt. Here Horbehûdti "in the form of a lion slew one hundred and forty-two enemies ; with his talons he slew them, he tore out their tongues, and their blood streamed on the heights. Then the rest of the enemies fled to the sea.

"Then spake Râ to Horbehûdti : 'Stay, let us go upon

the sea to smite the enemies in their forms of crocodiles and hippopotami before the coast of Egypt.' Then spake Horbehûdti to the person of Râ: 'O Lord of the gods! the navigation is stopped because of the third part of the enemies which are still remaining and are in the sea.' Then Thoth recited the Chapter of Protecting the Ship [1] and the barks of the fighters in metal to calm the sea in the hour of its raging." The magic formulas were of course efficacious, any statement to this effect being omitted as altogether superfluous, and the enemies who stirred up the storm all disappeared. "Then spake Râ to Thoth: 'Have we not now traversed the whole land? Have we not now traversed (*seked*) the whole sea?' Thoth spake: 'From this day forth this water (the sea) shall be called Sea of Traversing (*seked*).'"

Hereupon the gods turned back by night, for they saw no more enemies. As they drew near to Nubia and the city of *Shas-her*, Horbehûdti beheld the enemies and their champions in the land Ûaûa, conspiring (*ñaña*) against Horus their lord. The god again changed himself into a winged sun disk, and in·this form he slew them.

After this last victory the gods returned to their own country. Harmakhis came in his ship and landed at the Horus Throne (*Tes Her*, Edfû). Thoth spake: "'The darter of rays who came forth from Râ, he conquered the enemies in his form [of a winged sun disk]; from this day he shall be called the Darter of Rays who emergeth from

---

[1] An analogous work is preserved containing the formulas for the protection of the bark *neshemt*, which played a great part at Abydos. Cf. CHASSINAT, *Rec. de Trav.*, xvi., pp. 105 *et seq*.

the horizon.' Harmakhis spake unto Thoth : ' Set this
sun at every place at which I tarry, at the places of the
gods in the South Land, at the places of the gods in the
North Land, [at the places of the gods] in the Underworld, that it may banish Evil from their vicinity.' Thoth
set this form at every spot, at every place, how many
soever they were, at which any gods or goddesses might
be. And this is the winged sun disk which is over the
sanctuaries of all gods and goddesses in Egypt, for their
sanctuary is also that of Horbehûdti."

This legend as given above is translated for the most

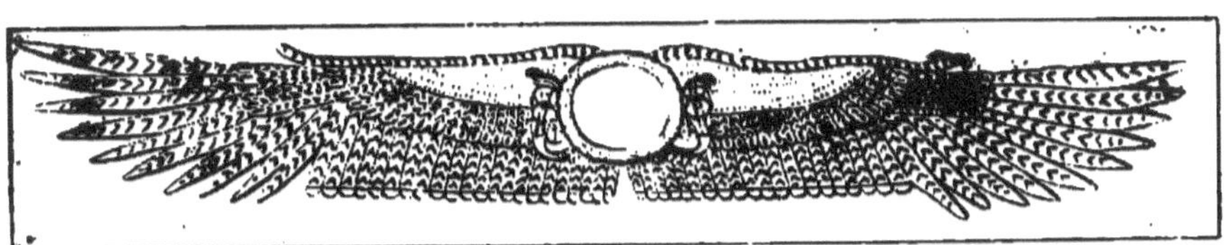

From drawing by R. E. F. PAGET.]

FIG. 14.—WINGED SUN DISK.

From door to chapel of Thothmes I. at Deir el Bahri, XVIIIth Dynasty.

part literally from the original. It is interesting in various
aspects. It strikingly exemplifies what is already noticeable in the Legend of the Destruction of Mankind : the
characteristic impulse of the Egyptians to explain the
origin of certain designations by plays upon words.[1]
Because a god pronounced a word at a given juncture,
therefore this word is said to have become the name of
some thing connected with the occasion. This was of
course an exact reversal of the real process by which these
very trivial sayings were invented ; for they were attempts

[1] Cf. *Exodus*, xvi. 15, 31.   (TRANS.)

to account for designations already existing by attributing to the gods utterances phonetically suggestive of the terms in question. Little respect was paid to grammar in the matter : as an instance, the group of signs signifying "Great Protection" is used to explain the name "Great One of Protection," *i.e.* Greatest Protector. Still less regard was given to the meaning, and of this we have a flagrant instance in a Ptolemaic inscription of Philae,[1] where the name of Isis is explained as follows: "When Isis was born, her mother Nût said on seeing her, 'Behold ! (*ás*), that is I' (*i.e.* it is my image), and therefore the name of Isis (*Ás.t*) was given to the goddess." Obviously such plays upon words have no more mythological significance than the etymologies advanced by the Greeks and Romans to account for the names of their divinities. But the prominence of such punning in these myths is a good indication of the comparative lateness of their origin, since it implies that it was thereby sought to explain the existence of sacred names which had already ceased to be comprehensible. The myths are also striking examples of the audacity of Egyptian conclusions in linguistic mythology, while yet their thoroughly prosaic form betrays a want of imagination and the absence of any sense of poetical construction. In the latter respect they present a marked contrast to the beautiful and imaginative explanations given by Greek and Roman poets in their day as to archaic terms of which the original significance had been lost. This suggested comparison of national genius is the more applicable since the Legend of the

---

[1] DÜMICHEN, *Kal. Insch.*, 50ᵇ, l. 2 : cf. *Aeg. Zeit.*, 1880, p. 42.

Winged Sun Disk was an essentially popular one. It outlived the fall of paganism and affected a series of Coptic texts which, in making use of the well known apocryphal account of Christ's journey through Egypt as a child, describe the triumphal march of the Saviour along the Valley of the Nile, and relate how He drove His foes from place to place, destroying them as He went.

Finally, this text is valuable as an instance of that deliberate mythological syncretism which often confronts the reader in earlier texts. The gist of the story is a description of the conflict of the god Râ with foes who, like mankind in the legend of their destruction, take advantage of his old age to conspire against him. Râ did not himself go forth to the conflict, but had recourse to the god Horbehûdti, as incorporate in the form of a winged sun disk. Horbehûdti also was originally a solar deity, but in the fusion of different cults he came to be represented as subordinate to Râ instead of his equivalent. To him fell the task of conquering the enemies of the Sun, and he accomplished it, traversing the whole of Egypt in company with Râ and always warding off Evil from the king of the gods. It was therefore hoped and believed that he would everywhere and at all times exercise the same beneficent power, and hence the image of the winged sun disk was placed over the entrances to the inner chambers of a temple as well as over its gates, and on stelae and other objects, as a protection against all harm and especially against destruction. It is to this practice that the concluding words of the text refer. Sometimes this emblem is simply a winged sun disk, but we also find it combined with two serpents, one on either side of the disk, which are occasionally crowned with the diadems of Upper and Lower Egypt. They represent the tutelary goddesses of the two divisions of the land, whom Horbehûdti had taken with him to the conflict, namely, Nekhebit and Ûazit, called by the Greeks Eileithyia and Bûto. Although seldom represented in the Old Kingdom, these winged disks were common in the New; and in later times a series would be placed one below the other on the same monument, in the hope that the efficacy of the sacred symbol might be strengthened by its repetition.

The above form of the myth was a local legend of Edfû, where Horbehûdti was worshipped as the nome god, and it was only gradually that it obtained acceptance over the rest of Egypt; for although similar legends of the passage of the Sun god are derived from other localities, yet these assign the part of his defender to other deities. Thus ÀNḤER, god of This, bore in Abydos the cognomen of Slayer of the Enemies, and it was his function to stand in the prow of the sun bark and strike down with his lance the creatures—especially the crocodiles and hippopotami—which impeded the progress of the boat, and therefore also that of Râ. In other places a similar part was ascribed to the god Shû.

The old myth of the conflict of Horbehûdti with the enemies of Râ, who represent the powers of darkness, is fused in the Edfû text with a second myth—namely, that of the expedition of Horus the son of Isis against Set the murderer, to avenge the death of his father Osiris. To the consideration of this second myth we shall return later. In outline it corresponds to the original form of the Horbehûdti legend, and according to it Horus traversed Egypt and everywhere conquered Set and his adherents. In this case, however, the foes are not the powers of darkness inimical to the God of Light ; they are the evil enemies of the Good Being. Hence the issue of the conflict is in both cases indecisive. In the Horbehûdti myth the enemies of Râ, after being driven northward throughout the length of Egypt, suddenly reappear in the south, and so the whole war threatens to break out afresh, because although light can indeed conquer and repulse darkness, yet it cannot do away with it. So also in the Horus myth: good wins the victory over evil, but has no power to destroy it from out the world. Hence also in the story of the Horus expedition in the Edfû myth, Set is conquered and executed, but immediately he returns to life and attacks the deity in another form. Osiris himself is not mentioned in the inscription, but his legend is presupposed, and apart from it there would be no sense in handing over the punishment of Set to Isis, upon whom, as wife and sister of the murdered god, devolved the duty of avenging his blood.[1]

There were many lesser myths relating to the god Râ besides the three chief ones which have been given in this chapter. One of them, however, is important as offering a mythological explanation of solar and lunar eclipse.[2]

---

[1] Cf. the myth on pp. 206 *et seq.*

[2] *Book of the Dead,* ch. 112 : cf. GOODWIN, *Aeg. Zeit.,* 1871, pp. 144 *et seq.* ; NAVILLE, in *Études déd. à Leemans,* pp. 75 *et seq.* ; PLUTARCH, *De Iside,* c. 55.

This tells how one day Horus desired to see all the beings which Râ had created, and at length Râ showed him a black hog, and at the same moment Horus felt a violent pain in his eye, for Set had changed himself into a hog in order to do hurt to Horus. Therefore Horus, after he was well again, would never more receive swine in offering. As related by the Greeks, the myth appears in a modified form, and states that Set injured the eye of Horus, tore it out, and swallowed it, but was afterwards compelled to restore it to Helios (Râ).

CHAPTER IV.

THE PASSAGE OF THE SUN THROUGH THE UNDERWORLD.

THE northernmost of the great Theban temples is that of Qûrnah, built on the west bank of the river by Seti I. and Rameses II. about 1350 B.C. Leaving the plain and turning to the hills a little to the north of this temple, the traveller presently reaches a narrow opening in the rocks made by a prehistoric torrent seeking outlet to the Nile. A few hundred yards farther there is a fork in this ancient watercourse, but its two branches run behind the Libyan range, roughly parallel to each other, up to the heights above the Valley of the Assassif in the midst of the Theban necropolis. Just before the branch nearer to the Nile finds its abrupt termination in a steep cliff, its sides are pierced by some three-and-twenty rock cut passages leading to tombs of New Kingdom kings, while in the second gorge only two such inscribed tombs have been discovered. Anciently many more of the royal sepulchres were still visible; Strabo[1] mentions some forty as worthy of inspection; but now the entrances are in part hidden beneath the talus which has fallen from the weathered cliffs into the valley below, and are not likely to be rediscovered, unless by accident. Indeed it was only the casual

[1] xvii. 46, 816.

observation that a rain torrent disappeared into the cliffs instead of flowing down into the valley which led to the discovery of the finest tomb among them all, that which was the resting place of the mummy of Seti I.

These tombs belong to the XVIIIth, XIXth, and XXth Dynasties. From the entrance, a passage, which is sometimes stepped, slopes downwards into the rock, occasionally widening into chambers, or having entrances to different rooms hewn in its walls, but keeping the same general direction and at length reaching the large chamber containing the royal sarcophagus. Further chambers may be connected with the sarcophagus chamber, or sometimes a blind passage only may be prolonged beyond it. The varying plans of these tombs are thus accounted for: a king began to prepare his place of sepulture on his accession by making a simple passage leading to a sepulchral chamber; but if his life was spared he carried on the passage to a second chamber, and so on, until his death put an end to the extensions. And in this way the tomb of Seti I. attained to a length of nearly two hundred feet.

The walls of the passages and chambers, the ceilings, and the sarcophagus itself were adorned with scenes and inscriptions relating exclusively to the world beyond.[1]

[1] The best publications of these scenes and inscriptions are: LEFÉBURE, *Les Hypogées royaux de Thèbes*, I. *Tombeau de Seti I.*; II. *Notices des Hypogées*; III. *Tombeau de Ramses IV.* (Mémoires de la Mission Française au Caire, ii.-iii. 2). For the contents of the text cf. MASPERO, *Les Hypogées royaux de Thèbes*, in *Rev. de l'hist. des Rel.*, 1888, also given in *Études de Mythologie*, ii., pp. 1 *et seq.* A shorter version of the text has been well edited from the Berlin and Leyden papyri, with commentary, by JEQUIER, *Le livre de ce qu'il y a dans l'Hadès*, Paris, 1894.

One of these wall texts, that of the Legend of the Destruction of Mankind, has been given already; two others, the Negative Confession and the Funeral Ritual, will call for our attention when we come to consider the Osirian doctrine of Immortality. Many others must remain unnoticed, such as the litanies to the Sun,[1] seventy-five invocations to the Sun god to be recited "at evening when Râ is made 'true of voice' (*maâ kher*) against his enemies in the Underworld," *i.e.* formulas to be used when the dying Sun, overcoming all obstacles, enters the next world as a blessed god. In these litanies the god is invoked by all manner of secret titles, incomprehensible without detailed commentary, and which represent him as all embracing and as uniting in himself the most various divine functions. Thus they testify to the strong influence of syncretism even in 1300 B.C. But more important than these litanies for the understanding of the Egyptian religion are the two extensive texts which we shall now proceed to consider: the *Book of Am Dûat*, and the *Book of the Gates*.

In certain of the tombs which we have described the text of the Book of Am Dûat, "of that which is in the Dûat (or Underworld)," is accompanied by scenes representing the divisions of the next world and its inhabitants. The text was also inscribed on sarcophagi, as on the sarcophagus of King *Nekht-Her-heb-t* (Nectanebus I., died about 369 B.C.), now preserved in London. It was written also upon papyrus, especially during the times of the XXth —XXIInd Dynasties, and in this form copies were

---

[1] NAVILLE, *La Litanie du Soleil*, Leipzig, 1875.

placed in the graves of priests and priestesses of Amen. The copies which have come down to us fall into two classes, one class consisting of those which give the complete text and all its scenes, and the other of examples, generally on papyrus, which represent the first to the seventh Hours of the Night by a short epitome, while the remaining five are given at length. It is curious that the text should appear in both the perfect and abridged forms in the tomb of Seti I.: there was no inherent advantage in so giving it, the duplication is simply owing to the indifference of Egyptian scribes, who copied out the various religious texts which might happen to be at their disposal without any regard to the contents, and hence ran the risk of giving duplicate texts on the same monument. Magnificent as was the tomb of Seti I., there is no order whatever among its inscriptions : the texts belonging to the different hours do not follow in regular progression, but have been disposed by the artist according to his convenience in the matter of space.

In these texts there were twelve divisions of Dûat, and the journey of the night Sun through each of them occupied one hour. The divisions were designated fields cities, or dwellings, and each was entered by a door. They were connected by a river running through their midst, upon which the Sun god in his bark journeyed from West to East; while upon its banks dwelt all manner of spirits and demons. The scenes relating to the river are divided into three rows, the top row representing the right bank, the middle one the stream, and the third the left bank. The demons themselves are far from homogeneous ; some

were ancient gods, while others were later personifications
endowed with forms adapted to the qualities which it was
deemed necessary to ascribe to them. For example, some
of the demons were represented as monkeys, because
it was their function to worship the setting sun : the
Egyptians having noticed how monkeys chattered together
at sunset took this to be an expression of adoration of the
Sun. Others, male and female, stabbed and rent the
wicked, and therefore carried knives and lances and bore
such names as *Denit*, " she who cuts "; *Nekit*, "she who
tears to pieces"; *Shesri*, "the piercer," etc. Others again
owe form and name entirely to the active imagination of
the Egyptians, who took a truly Oriental pleasure in
devising the impossible. A glance at the Am Dûat text
will show that almost every conceivable combination of
the animal with the human form is given ; yet to the
Egyptian all these creatures were really existent, and he
hoped, or rather feared, to meet them after death. In
these fancies the dwellers in the Nile Valley have outdone
all other nations of antiquity of which we have record.

In its shorter and more comprehensible version the work
begins with the words : " Beginning of the Opening of
Amenti (that is the West, and hence the Underworld) of
the limit of the gathered darkness "—*i.e.* of the Underworld, and of the domain into which darkness retreats and
collects during the day, and whence it threatens to break
again over the earth so soon as the power of the sun
begins to flag.

" The god (the Sun) enters from the earth, from the Compartment of the western horizon. A hundred and twenty

áterû[1] must be traversed in this Space before he comes to the gods of Dûat. *Net Râ*, Stream of Râ, is the name of the first field of Dûat. Râ allots the fields of the territory to the gods who are in his train. He begins to speak words of command, ordaining the circumstances of the gods of Dûat as regards this field. If a man represents this according to the appearance which is in the Amenti of Dûat (*i.e.* if the condition of things really existent in Dûat is duly portrayed), and knows these pictures which are the semblance of the great god himself, then shall he (who does this) be luminous upon earth, he shall be luminous in the great Dûat. *Ushemt hâtu kheftiû Râ* ('Destroyer of the forefront of the enemies of Râ') is the name of this first hour of the night which conducts this great god in this Compartment."

The illustrated version gives the same text with unimportant modifications, and also presents us with a view of the Compartment traversed by the Sun during the first hour of the night. A stream of water runs through the midst, with a bark floating upon it. In the cabin stands the Sun god, with a sceptre in one hand, and the sign of life in the other; his head is a ram's head surmounted by the solar disk. This god is *Áf Râ*, "flesh of Râ"—not Râ himself, for the Sun is dead, but his flesh and blood—for even the body of Râ is immortal. The sign of life which the figure is holding represents the life which remains to him even after death. The sceptre is the symbol of his rule over the Underworld. The ram's head serves to show that he

---

The *ater* was a linear measure. A parallel text states that this division was 309 *áterû* long by 120 wide.

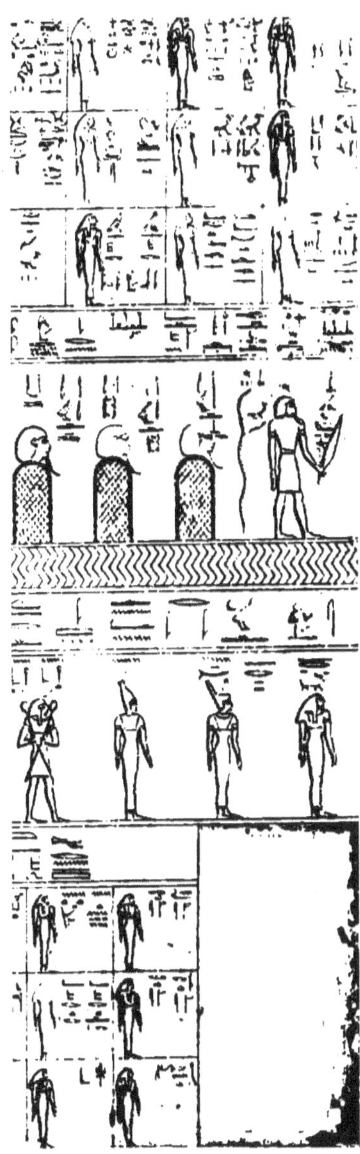

HOUR OF THE NIGHT.

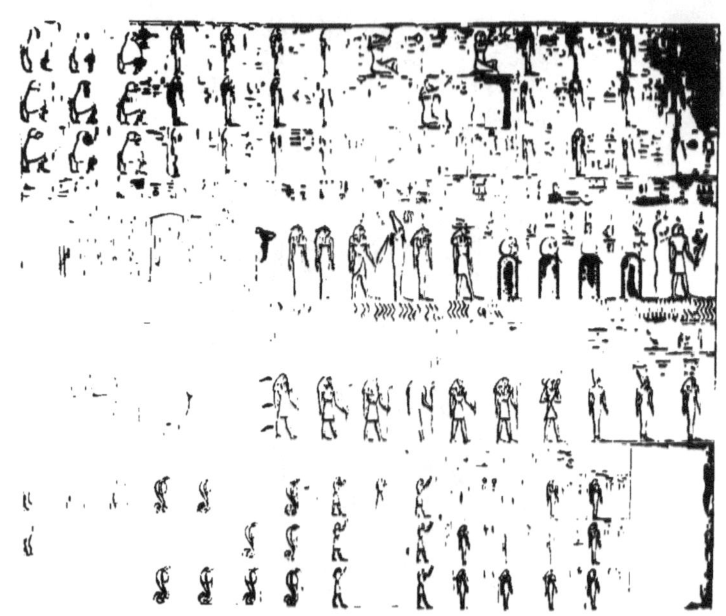

is not simply Râ the Sun god, who is always represented as hawk headed, but that he is here manifest in his Theban form of Amen Râ, whose earthly embodiment was a ram. In front of the cabin stands *Ap ûat*, "Opener of the Ways," a form of Anubis, whose office it was to introduce the soul of Râ as well as the souls of departed men into the Underworld. Next come Sa, the god of taste and knowledge, and the figure of a woman crowned with the horns of a cow and with a sun disk. She is designated Lady of the Bark. Behind the cabin stand the hawk headed god Her hekenû, who is upon this journey the representative of Râ ; the *Ka* of Shû ; *Nehes*, "the Watchman" ; *Hû*, "the Striker" (?) ; and the steersman of the ship, rudder in hand. The *Ka* of Shû, that is the *Ka* of one form of the Sun god, is thus present ; for it, no less than the human *Ka*, must descend into the Underworld with the being to whom it belongs, there to remain with him and yet to lead an independent existence.

Twelve divinities precede the bark, headed by the Watchman of the Hours with his knife in his hand. Behind them comes a serpent, and behind that are four chests, each surmounted by a human head and named respectively the Speech of Osiris, of Khepera, of Tûm, of Râ. These must therefore have been regarded as personified words of the four deities, existing independently of the gods themselves. Next is the great Illuminator, ram headed and obviously a form of the Sun god, albeit detached from him. Beyond him is the Sun's faithful companion, the lioness headed goddess Sekhet—or, as she is here called, *Sekhmet*, "she who is exalted"—followed by " Him who Dwells in Amenti," the mummiform figure of Osiris wearing the crown of Upper Egypt, by a god in human likeness armed with a knife and entitled " Cutter in pieces," and, finally, by the two goddesses of Truth— Truth and Justice. The text accompanying these scenes approximately repeats the introductory words, with only one noteworthy addition, which states that the river is Ûrnes,[1] and that the solar bark is the Sekti bark. At this point in the text the dimensions of this division of the Underworld are estimated at 220 *âteru* in width by 300 in length, a variation from the data given above which shows how little regard for consistency the Egyptians had in religious matters. It may be that these dimensions had been differently reckoned by the writers, and that the compilers of this text considered it better to place the two readings side by side rather than to run the risk of adopting the wrong measurements only.

The row below shows those who awaited the god and his companions in the Compartment of the first hour, and accompanied him through it, remaining behind, how-ever, when he passed on to the next. They consist of ten divinities, some of which bear serpents as sceptres, and of three long spotted snakes. Then follows a bark in the midst of which hovers a scarabaeus, adored as " this Râ " by two men, each of whom is called an Osiris. The scene is evidently intended to represent the adoration of the Sun by the dead. The line of inscription above runs somewhat as follows : " This god traverses this Com-

---

[1] Ûrnes has, of course, no connexion whatever with the Greek Uranos.

partment in the form of a ram. When he has traversed it, then the dead who are in his train do not rise with him (into the domains of the other hours); they remain in this Compartment. But Râ gives command (in favour of the dead, to whom he grants fields) to the gods who dwell in this Compartment." The dead to whom reference is here made are those whose souls hastened at the moment of death to the opening in the western heaven through which Râ enters into the Underworld. Thus far they had followed in the train of the god, but here their journey ended, and only those specially favoured ones who knew the Book of that which is in Dûat might enter the solar bark and proceed with the Sun god. The rest remained behind, not even Râ himself having power to take them along with him.

On the left bank of Ûrnes squatted nine cynocephali, "porters for this great soul," beings who, so soon as the Sun had reached the West, opened to him the gates of the Compartment of the first hour. Each of them is named by name: "Opener of the Earth," "Soul of the Earth," "Heart of the Earth," "Double Heart of the Earth," "He who beholdeth Râ," etc. Then come twelve goddesses, "those who extol upon earth"—that is, who offer hymns of praise to the god at the moment of his leaving earth and entering the Underworld. Their names are those of the twelve hours of the day who take leave of Râ and return to the eastern sky, there to await the new Sun. Beyond these are nine squatting gods—three human, three jackal, and three hawk headed—"the gods who adore Râ"; and with them are twelve goddesses, "they who lead the Great God." The latter are shown by their names to be the twelve hours of the night who now supersede the hours of the day in the guidance of the Sun.

On the right bank of Ûrnes are, first, other nine cynocephali, "they who speak the praises of Râ"; then come twelve uraei spitting forth fire to lighten the gloom of the Underworld. They are "the goddesses who lighten the darkness in Dûat." The nine men following them "extol the lord of the cycle of the gods," *i.e.* Râ, and the twelve goddesses who accompany them "give praises to Râ when he traverses Ûrnes."

Here ends the description of the first Compartment of the Underworld. When Râ has traversed the length of it, a door is opened at the end, and he enters into the domain of the second hour of the night, still continuing his way upon the river Ûrnes. The divinities who accompany him in his bark are, generally speaking, the same throughout the journey, but the attendant beings who are not on board, and especially the demons of both banks, change continually. It is needless to examine them one by one; the description of the first hour may serve to show after what fashion his Dûat was pictured to himself by the Egyptian. Only in one respect was there any important change as the god advanced from hour to hour: the number of the demons was hourly greater, while they were represented as more and more fantastic in appearance, and composite human and animal forms increasingly abounded. All had their names, which the deceased Egyptian was supposed to know by heart;

in case he had failed to learn them he must be provided
with a papyrus from which to read them ; unless, indeed,
he had been careful during life to have the guidebook
to Dûat inscribed upon the walls of his tomb, as was
done by Seti I.

As in the domain of the first hour, so in each division
of the Underworld, Râ left behind some of his companions
whom he had brought with him from the earth above,
making them grants of land to cultivate. In thus handing over territory to his followers as a reward for services
rendered, and as encouragement to future loyalty, Râ
only acted after the manner in which earthly kings were
wont to recompense their faithful subjects. The Pharaoh
was constrained to this course as a means of preventing
the separatist tendencies, which were never wholly subdued
among the Egyptians, from issuing in rebellion, and
also to secure for himself loyal and devoted dependents
in each of the nomes. And in the same way Râ acted
in his own interest, for although he gave light on his
way to the dwellers in the Underworld, he could not
unaided conquer the demons of darkness. To that end
he needed allies, and these he found not only in a succession of the good demons of Dûat, but also in the dead
whom he had established in the place, and who were
bound to the land even as earthly vassals to the estates
with which they were invested. Here they awaited Râ their
lord to help him against the Apep serpent, the symbol of
darkness. In some parts of the text Osiris is treated as
interchangeable with Râ ; other references show that the
two were distinguished, Osiris being regarded as the

permanent lord of the dead in Dûat. These contradictions testify to the fact that it was no longer a homogeneous doctrine that was embodied in these texts, but that in them we have a fusion of distinct theories. This is further made evident by the introduction, here and there, of yet another heterogeneous deity in the person of Sokaris, to whom were specially ascribed the domains of the fourth and fifth hours. On his journey through the last of the Compartments Râ met the scarabaeus Khepera, the god of the new morning Sun, who thereupon embarked with the dead god of the Sun of yesterday to give him escort as far as the eastern horizon, where his own reign would begin.

The sixth and seventh Compartments were especially dedicated to Osiris. In the first of them were many beings connected with the Osirian myth : Isis, the ibis; a Horus; and various manifestations of Osiris himself. Here in a large room dwelt the kings of Upper Egypt, the rich in offerings—that is, the wealthy, to whom their survivors made many offerings—the kings of Lower Egypt, and the glorified spirits. To them the god assured the possession of their fields, the continued exercise of dominion, the power to use the magic formulas which they had learned, and the personal enjoyment of the offerings made to them. In the seventh hour the serpent *Mehen*, "the Enfolder," coiled round the cabin of Râ ; and now came the sharpest part of the conflict against the Âpep serpent, which was at length overcome and pierced with knives, while at the incantations of Isis the sun bark proceeded self-impelled upon its way. Here in the seventh Compartment were

four chests partly filled with sand, but also containing the
forms of Tûm, Khepera, Râ, and Osiris. Being talismans
of extraordinary efficacy in the next world, which would
seem to have appeared to the help of Râ at his call, each
was guarded by a goddess armed with a knife. Near
by were serpents which cast forth flames against the foes
of Osiris and devoured the souls of his enemies ; stellar
divinities and gods of the hours were there also.

In the ninth Compartment twelve uraei spat out
fire to light the path of Râ so long as he might tarry
there ; as soon as he had passed on they devoured and
reabsorbed the flames, again to cast them up at the end of
twenty-three hours. Their fires struck down the enemies
of Râ, and they lived upon the blood of such as they
slew daily. The tenth Compartment chiefly contained
water, and aquatic creatures, and here the scene gives a
representation of the birth of Khepera, thus contradicting
the above mentioned assignment of his first appearance
to the fifth hour. A secret way led from the eleventh
Compartment to Sais, and was guarded by two forms of
the goddess Neith, one wearing the crown of Upper and
the other the crown of Lower Egypt. Neith of Sais being
accounted the mother of Râ, this road was doubtless
intended to provide her with the means of reaching the
Underworld from her own city and here giving birth to the
Sun god. Near by it were great fires in which the enemies
of Râ were consumed under the supervision of Horus. In
the twelfth and last Compartment the new Sun at length
appears in his earthly form ; he attains new life, and is
uplifted at the horizon by the god Shû ; and with him go

forth into the light of day those souls of the dead who had succeeded by means of their knowledge of magic formulas in remaining in the sun bark and therein traversing the whole of Dûat; henceforth they are to remain for ever with Râ, inseparable from him and yet without loss of individuality.

The idea of immortality and of the world to come presented in this text is altogether peculiar to it. The doctrine centres in the dead god Râ, yet parts of doctrines belonging to the cults of Sokaris and Osiris are blended with it. But this Osiris is not the Osiris of the Book of the Dead, whom we shall consider later; he, as also Sokaris, is here a Sun god, sometimes apprehended as a secondary form of Râ, and sometimes as ruler of a portion of the Underworld of which the whole belongs to Râ. This doctrine indeed taught that immortality was the lot of all men, but also that only the friend of Râ could look forward to possessing fields in Dûat, the produce of which should ensure him against hunger. For one hour daily would he behold the Sun, but the rest of the time he was plunged in darkness, which at best was only lightened by fire spitting serpents, or by the sea of flame in which the enemies of Râ were consumed. Shouting for joy, he greeted the light at the appearance of his god; but his joy was short: at the end of one hour the door was closed behind his lord, and he again was left in darkness. Such was the lot even of kings and of the rich and great, except that in their case it was ameliorated inasmuch as they obtained their food without labour. Few were those who remained for ever with the Sun, and they were not necessarily the great ones of the earth, nor yet the very good, but those who possessed the most minute information as to the next world and who were best versed in magic. Thus the whole doctrine is based on a belief in the power of magic : by magic only could demons be worsted and everlasting bliss be won ; the idea of attaining to it by the virtuous conduct of earthly life is altogether in the background : the one thing needful in this respect was—not to have been in life an enemy of Râ.

The second work found in the tombs of the kings dealing with the progress of the Sun through the Under-world—the Book of the Gates—in the main corresponds to the above, especially in its presentation of the life of the dead as that of dwellers in a darkness penetrated by the light of the Sun for but one hour in the twenty-four. It has, however, supplied one omission of the Am Dûat text by embodying the judgment of Osiris on the righteous and the wicked. The scene of this is a hall situate between the fifth and sixth hours, and here Osiris is seated upon his throne, upon the steps of which are the nine gods forming the Osirian cycle. In front of Osiris stand the scales in which a man is weighed against his deeds, and beyond stands Anubis, who is here present as spectator only, although, according to the Osirian rituat, it was his office to conduct the dead into the hall of judgment. The accompanying text states that all the enemies of Osiris are overthrown and destroyed, and this destruction is illustrated by a scene representing the god Thoth in a small bark as a cynocephalus armed with a stick, and driving forth from the hall and from the fellowship of the righteous a hog which is called the "Devourer of the Arm," and which stands for Set, the enemy of Osiris.

The sixth hour displays the outcome of the judgment scene : the righteous are at work in their fields, while, bound to stakes, the wicked are awaiting a punishment by fire and water which follows partially in the eighth hour. The agricultural scenes recall in many ways the Fields of Aalû of the Osirian creed ; but Aalû was flooded with light, while here there was little or none.

A similar melancholy conception of the life after death is set forth in isolated texts as well as in the Book of the Gates ; but in many ways it differs from that of the latter, and is not without affinity to Greek feeling on the subject, picturing the life of the dead as a mere shadowy existence. In the inscription on a stela dating from the time of Cleopatra, and preserved in the British Museum,[1] a dead woman thus calls upon her husband : "O my brother, my husband, cease not to drink and to eat, to be drunken, to enjoy the love of women, to make holiday. Follow thy desire by night and by day ; grant care no place in thine heart. For as for Amenti it is a land of sleep and of darkness, a dwelling wherein those who are there remain. They sleep in their mummy forms, they nevermore awake to see their fellows, they behold neither their fathers nor their mothers, their heart is careless of their wives and children. On earth each

---

[1] Published by SHARPE, *Egyptian Inscriptions*, i. 4 ; PRISSE, *Monuments*, pl. xxvi., *bis* ; LEPSIUS, *Auswahl*, pl. xvi. ; REINISCH, *Chrest.*, i., pl. 20 : cf. RENOUF, *Religion*, pp. 242 *et seq.* ; MASPERO, *Études Égyptiennes*, i., p. 187.

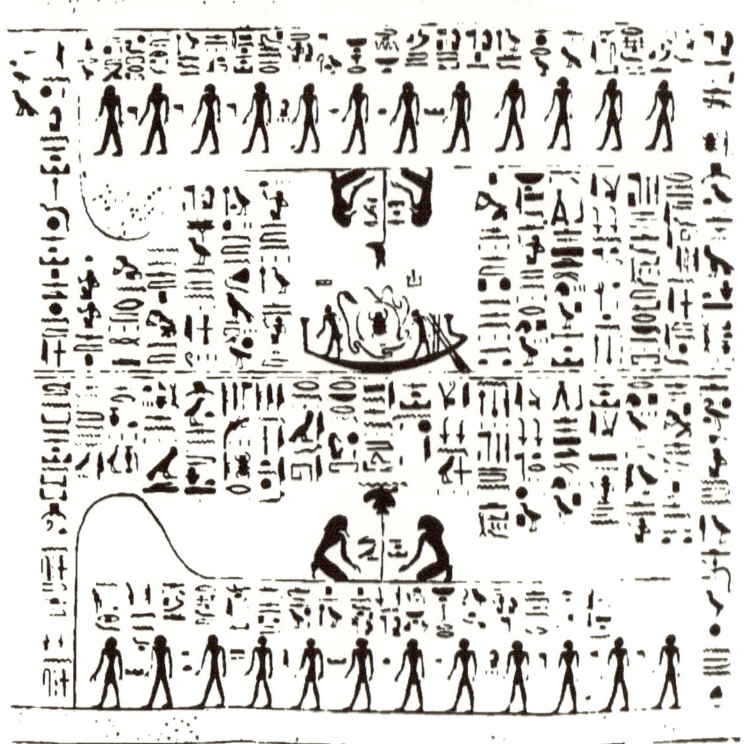

tasteth of the water of life, but I suffer thirst. Water cometh to him who is upon earth, but I thirst after the water that is by me. Since I came unto this valley I know not where I am. I long for the water that floweth by me. I desire the breeze. on the bank of the river, that it may refresh my heart in its distress. For the name of the god who ruleth here is 'Utter Death.' At his call, trembling with fear, all men come unto him. He maketh no distinction between gods and men ; before him the great are as the small. He showeth no favour to him who loveth him ; he snatcheth the child from its mother, and the old man also. None cometh to worship him, for he is not gracious unto them who adore him ; he regardeth not him who presenteth him with offerings."

The Book of the Gates begins with a description of the Sun's entrance into the Underworld. In his bark, and in the form of a disk round which a serpent is coiled, the Sun god approaches a valley bounded by two high sand-hills. On one of the banks is a standard with the head of a ram, and on the other a standard with the head of a jackal ; for in the Underworld the god will bear the head of a ram, while the jackal is symbolic of Anubis, his guide thither. Before each standard kneel two genii —the genius of Dûat, and the genius of the hills of earth, *i.e.* of the regions of which the boundaries meet at the gates of the Underworld. The valley is closed by a simple door, which at a conjuration opens to Râ, who through it enters the domain of the first hour in ram headed form. The demons are fully described here as in the other divisions, and throughout all the scenes flows the

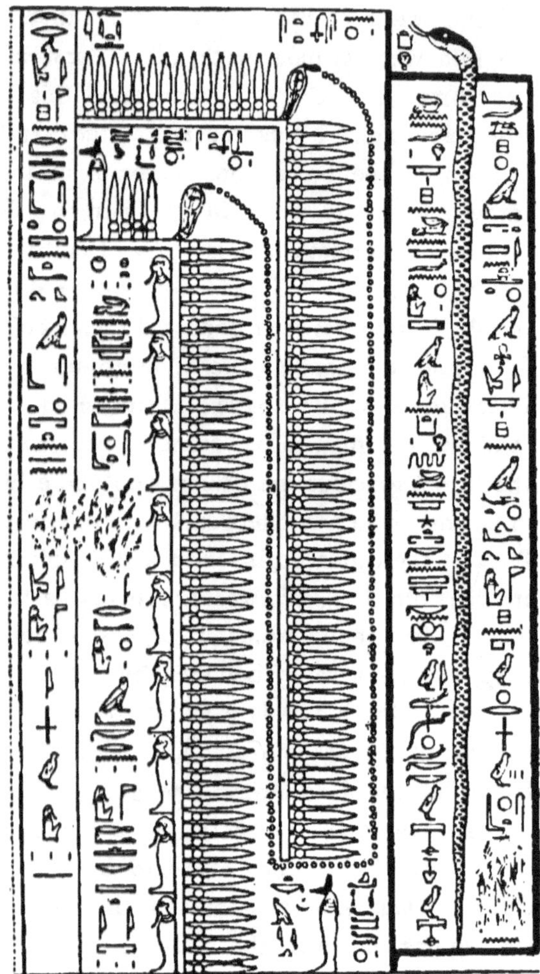

FIG. 17.—GATE IN THE UNDERWORLD.
(MASPERO, "ÉTUDES DE MYTHOLOGIE," II. 167.)
XIXth Dynasty.

same river, on which the Sun travels accompanied by his companions; while right and left upon its sandy banks stand the spirits. But although the general arrangements correspond to those of the Am Dûat text, yet details, names of demons, scenes, and texts are different throughout.   On similar foundations we have an altogether different super-structure.   Two distinct conceptions of the next world had been formed by the Egyptians, and they found it so difficult to choose between them that both were sometimes represented in the same tomb.

To begin with—the divisions between the twelve hourly spaces of the night are of a different kind.   In " Am Dûat " a simple door suffices; in the second text, except for the first hour, we have veritable fortifications.   Each division is bounded by a wall in which a single narrow opening leads into a passage between two battlemented walls, and the passage bends at a right angle in order further to increase the difficulty of forcing an entry.   This method of construction may be actually seen in Egyptian fortifications still extant.   At each end of the passage is a mummiform figure, and at the corner there hangs over from either side a serpent spitting forth flames which flow in a fiery stream along the road.   Besides these there are also nine gods standing with their backs against the wall to defend it.   Only by means of conjurations could Râ himself pass through; but when these were duly pro-nounced by his conductor the mummiform figures opened their arms to him, the serpents ceased to spit forth flames, and the great serpent keeping watch over the gate at the end of the passage gave him entrance into the next hour. Scarcely had Râ passed before the demons were again on guard as before.   Yet notwithstanding all these defensive measures the god was never in safety : everywhere enemies met him, and especially the Âpep serpent, which he was bound to conquer.

And, finally, the conclusion of this text claims attention

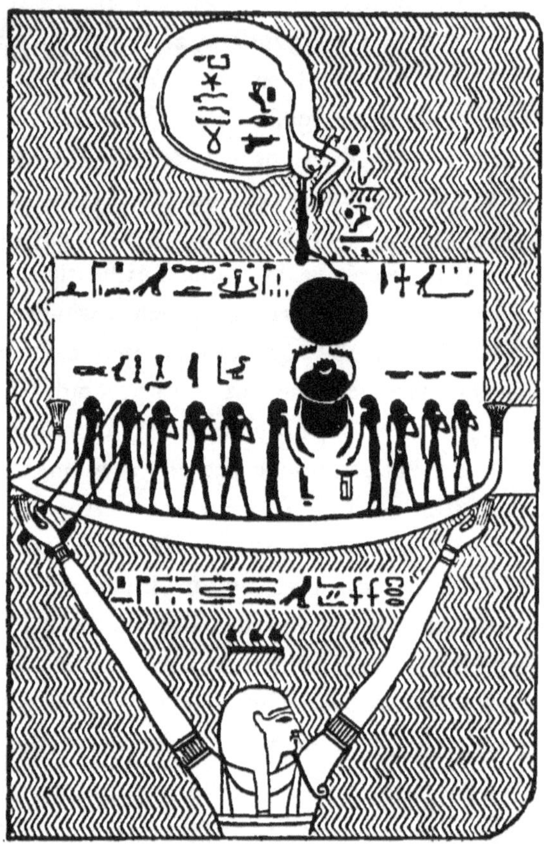

FIG. 18.—NÛ UPLIFTING THE SUN BARK AT THE END OF THE NIGHT.
(BONOMI AND SHARPE, PL. XV.)
Sarcophagus of Seti II.

as dealing with the birth of the new Sun in far more detail than does the "Am Dûat." When at the end of the twelfth hour the last door had swung to, then there was great mourning among the souls who dwell in Amenti and remain behind in darkness. But Isis and Nephthys, each in the form of a uraeus, sit by the gates to protect the young Sun god, even as they protected Horus the son of Isis. Before them stretches Nû, the primeval water, from which, as one myth tells us, all things came forth. From this Râ too must rise, and to effect his rising the god of the water uplifts him together with his Mâdet bark. Râ is in the midst of the bark, and beside him stand Isis and Nephthys as his guardians, while aft are Seb, Shû, the god HEK who knows the magic formulas, and two steersmen. Forward are the three porters who have opened the gates of day, and who will open also the various doors of the upper heaven. Nût, goddess of the day sky, reaches from the other side to receive the Sun. She stands upon a figure which by touching its head with its feet forms a circle and is designated the " Osiris who encloses Dûat," the whole arrangement signifying that the day sky is here uplifted above the night sky, the realm of Nût above that of Osiris.

As we have more than once had occasion to observe, the doctrine contained in these texts is no longer pure ; it comprises much that had been borrowed from the Osirian teaching and which was of independent origin. This influence was reciprocal. In the Book of the Dead, the text book of the Osirian faith, we are continually beset by passages and allusions which, strictly speaking, have nothing to do with the fundamental cult, and are indeed often in direct contradiction to its dogmas ; these are in many instances taken from texts relating to the passage of the Sun through the Underworld. Thus in Chapter XV. of the Book of the Dead we find reference to the Dûat which Râ enlightens, the appearance of the Âpep serpent, together with other indications of a prevalent syncretic tendency.

CHAPTER V.

THE CHIEF DEITIES.

THE Egyptian temple was dedicated, as a rule, to a
single deity, who inhabited the sanctuary in corporate
form ; to him the chief offerings were made, and in his
honour the great local festivals were celebrated. This is
clearly set forth by the inscriptions on the walls. But
these same inscriptions make it evident that the god was
not regarded as standing alone ; in almost every case
divine honours were also paid to his companion deities, the
θεοὶ σύνναοι of the Greeks. These, generally, were connected with the great god of the temple by close bonds
of relationship, and, together with him, formed a cycle of
divinities. The cycle being usually three in number the
so called triads arose, which generally consisted of two
gods and one goddess ; the goddess being the wife of the
chief god, and the third member of the triad being their
son. The son was the counterpart of the father, and
destined to replace him when he should grow old and die,
according to that law of nature to which even the gods
were subject. Thus the son became the father, and the
Egyptian texts could speak of the gods as eternal ; for so
soon as the elder god vanished he would be succeeded by

a divine personality precisely similar. In this sense also
the god was self begotten, being father to the son who
was as himself ; and he was " the husband of his mother "
in that, after the death of his father, he had entered upon
all rights as regards the goddess of the triad, and was in
his turn by her the father of the new divine son who
should one day replace him. This scheme of functions
provided not only for the unfailing continuance of the
divinity, but also for the independent existence of each of
the divine individualities by means of which it was carried
on. It is complete in all its parts except as regards the
goddess ; for, *a priori*, she also would grow old, and pass
away, and be superseded. No explanation of this omission
is given in Egyptian doctrine ; it must be accepted as
arising from the fact that the part assigned in the divine
world to the goddess of a triad is in general very insignificant. She brings forth the young god and she brings
him up, but she has no defined personality. This is the
case with almost all the Egyptian goddesses : they are, as
a rule, unnoticed in the myths and neglected in the cults ;
the inscriptions, generally speaking, simply give their
names and designate them mothers, nurses, guardians,
without adding the mention of any characteristic traits.
Isis is an exception, but she is scarcely to be classed
among the goddesses of the triads.

A triad of the kind just described was formed at Thebes,
for instance, by Amen, Mût, and Khûnsû ; at Memphis
by Ptah, Sekhet, and Imuthes ; at Kom Ombo by Sebak,
Hathor, and Khûnsû ; but in some places the triad was of
another kind. In certain temples where the chief deity

was without traditional family, it was still considered desirable to worship him in conjunction with two of the more important local divinities, even although the three formed a triad in number only and not in relationship. Thus, for example, the triad of the cataract district groups the goddesses Sati and Ânûki with the god Khnûm simply because they were two of the chief deities of that vicinity, and it was therefore expedient that they should be worshipped in its temple.

The triad appears to have been the earlier outcome of the effort after a systematic grouping of the deities. Later it was expanded into an ennead—a cycle of nine deities;[1] but the members of an ennead were united rather by reasons of state than of kinship, the chief god being lord and king, while the other deities formed his court, assisted him in the government of the world, and therefore participated in the honours that were paid him. The conception of the ennead is also very ancient, but the expression early lost its numerical significance and became generally equivalent to a cycle of gods. In the tales it is said that the god went forth with his divine nine when the statement means simply that he was accompanied by his court; and from several texts in which the ennead is specified it is clear that the members of the ennead referred to were eight only.[2]

Some of the temples had two enneads—" the great and

---

[1] On the formation of the ennead see particularly MASPERO, *Sur l'Ennéade*, in *Rev. de l'Histoire des Religions*, 1892, or *Études de Mythologie*, ii., pp. 337 *et seq.*

[2] Cf. LEPSIUS, *Ueber die Götter der vier Elemente*, in *Ab-handlungen* of the Berlin Academy, 1858, pp. 227 *et seq.*

the small," a higher and a lower—and enneads were even occasionally spoken of in the plural to denote the totality of divine beings. As a rule there is no evidence that the selection of the gods of an ennead was dictated by any profound philosophy : its members were simply the principal national deities headed by the god of the nome in question. There was perhaps one exception, however, in the ennead of Heliopolis, which occasionally influenced the formation of the ennead in other cities also. But it is difficult to determine whether the processes of thought exhibited in the Heliopolitan ennead were operative in its original constitution or imported during the course of subsequent systematizing. In Heliopolis Tûm-Râ was held to be the creator of the world, from him came forth Shû and Tefnût, and of this pair were born Seb and Nût, who were the parents of Osiris and Isis, Set and Nephthys. The chief function of Shû was to separate the heavens from the earth (Nût from Seb), in order to provide the path for the sun (Râ). When this was accomplished there appeared upon earth Nile and desert, life and death, good and evil, these contrasts being personified in Osiris and Set. The creator had no consort, and of and by himself all his acts of creation were performed ; but the other members of the Great Ennead were grouped in pairs as god and goddess, and from the first pair, Shû and Tefnût, the rest proceeded. The members of the Lesser Ennead of Heliopolis (Horus son of Isis, Thoth, Maât, and others) seem to have been specially concerned with the civil and moral organization of mankind ; but in the present state of our knowledge it is impossible to form any trustworthy conception of the way in which their several functions came to be assigned to them.

It often happened that gods of the same attributes were grouped together in the same cycle : the absurdity involved in this was avoided by the expedient of allowing them to have reigned in succession, as did the Pharaohs, attributing to each in turn the title of King of Upper and Lower Egypt. Thus, according to Heliopolitan tradition, Atmû (Tûm) was succeeded by Râ, Shû, Seb, Osiris, Set, and Horus, while in Memphis Ptah, and in Thebes Amen Râ was considered as the founder of the divine dynasty. The new dogma did not find extended approval, for this pretended succession in the supremacy left untouched the main difficulty presented by the Egyptian faith, which regarded the gods as eternally capable of exerting their several activities at any moment. Hence the dogma was confined to certain schools of the priests and never pervaded the beliefs of the people.

It is obvious that among the countless deities of the inscriptions we can here consider only those of which most frequent mention is made in the texts, and which were looked upon as chief by the Egyptians themselves ; even as regards these, only what is most salient can be noticed. An account of all the Egyptian deities and the discussion of their functions and attributes would fill volumes.

ÁMEN, MÛT, and KHÛNSÛ formed the triad of Thebes. This city, the Diospolis of the Greeks, was the capital of Egypt during nearly the whole of the period from the XIth Dynasty until far on in the times of the New Kingdom ; and from it proceeded the greatest and most warlike kings of the land. Its temples and tombs have furnished by far the greater part of the material now at the service of Egyptian research. Thus we are in possession of a long series of texts relating to the worship of the Theban deities ; but we must carefully guard against the conclusion that the abundance of these texts argues the general predominance of Amen in Egypt. The Theban Pharaohs did indeed seek to introduce the cult of their god throughout the whole realm, and in so far succeeded that he was admitted into many of the great sanctuaries ; nevertheless it was not as principal god that he was so received, and he took, usually, minor rank beside the local deities.

According to the received explanation in the time of the New Kingdom, the name of the god, *Amen*, signifies "The Hidden One." In the pure and simple form of Amen he appears but seldom in the texts, where he is rather represented as a sun god in the composite form of Amen Râ. This was scarcely his original nature, but of that the Egyptians themselves seem to have lost all tradition. His name is derived from the same root as the word *Amenti*, which designated both the West and the Underworld, and thus suggests that he may have been considered a god of the dead ; while, on the other hand, there are texts, especially those referring to Amen in combination with Min, which would lead us to regard him as having been a deity personifying the continual self renewing power of nature. When Amen is spoken of in the later texts it is always Amen Râ who is meant. In the last millennium B.C. Amen Râ became a pantheistic deity, and much mystic philosophy was evolved out of his name, " The Hidden One," first by the Egyptians themselves and afterwards by the Greeks.   He was held to be the secret, all creating, all sustaining power primarily incorporate in the Sun.   Earlier texts, and especially hymns, deriving their arguments and comparisons from the sun that warms and enlightens all, had already praised Amen Râ in almost monotheistic style as Lord and Creator of the universe, and so prepared the way for the later and pantheistic conception.

Besides such texts, many passages are found in Egyptian inscriptions and papyri where it is stated that " god "—*i.e.* " a god," the indefinite article not being generally expressed in Egyptian—is praised, "god" knows the wicked, "god" grants a field, "god" loves the obedient, etc., and from all these it has often been concluded that hereby is meant the one God who is from everlasting to everlasting, the God of the Jewish prophets and even of Christendom.   Such an interpretation is, as a matter of fact, impossible.   The same texts which make these assertions speak of other deities as coexistent, and show that in using the word "god" the scribe was thinking only of the god most near to him, the god of his nome, the *neter nûti*, " the god belonging to the city," of the texts.   This god was to the writer an all embracing power, yet one which did not exclude the existence of other powers that might, to other minds, hold the first place. Osiris, Horus, Thoth, Râ Tûm Harmakhis, Ptah Tanen, the Nile, Amen Râ, and others are each from time to time severally adored in the texts as one and only god ; but from this it is vain to draw far reaching conclusions as to the fundamental ideas of the Ancient Egyptian religion. Yet although such expressions afford no proof of an original and recurring monotheism held as a creed by the Egyptian people, it cannot be proved from the inscriptions that no such conception existed in Ancient Egypt. In view of the repeated attempts to bring the Egyptian religion forward in evidence, now on the one side and now on the other, in the discussion concerning an early monotheism, the fact must be emphasized again and again that no trustworthy evidence whatever is as yet afforded to either side by our knowledge of that religion. It must never be forgotten that only a small part of the material left to us by Ancient Egypt is as yet at our disposal; much still lies beneath the soil, and much still rests undisturbed in private and public collections. For the religious texts especially, very little has been done. Until more of these have been published and carefully studied it is impossible to obtain any certainty as to the nucleus and origins of the motley confusion now known to us as the Egyptian religion. In the study of Egyptian religion, as in all other branches of Egyptology, our knowledge is as yet very imperfect. We must not therefore conclude that the extra Egyptian tradition of certain facts and systems of thought is untrustworthy because the inscriptions and papyri have hitherto yielded us no testimony on their behalf. Many such conclusions have been emphatically asserted only to be proved erroneous on a closer examination of the texts, and others may at any time be refuted by some crucial discovery. Our knowledge of the subject is advanced by the statements of the inscriptions, not by their accidental silence.

The longest, finest, and at the same time most instructive of the hymns to Amen Râ which have come down to us is now preserved in the Gîzeh Museum, in a copy made on papyrus and dating from the XXth Dynasty.[1] It is written in what may be called verse, the close of each line being marked by a red point. In the following translation each line represents one line of the hymn in the original. The arrangement of ideas and the parallelism of the parts recall the style of the Hebrew psalms, with the wording of which many sentences of the hymn closely correspond; though the comparison does not, of course, extend to the conception of the godhead. The text runs as follows:—

> Praise to Amen Râ!
> To the bull in Heliopolis, to the chief of all the gods,
> To the beautiful and beloved god,
> Who giveth life by all manner of warmth, by
> All manner of fair cattle.
> Hail to thee, Amen Râ, lord of the throne of the two lands,
> Dwelling in Thebes,
> Husband of his Mother,[2] dwelling in his fields,
> Wide-ranging, dwelling in the Land of the South,
> Lord of the Libyans (*Mátaû*), ruler of Arabia (*Pûnt*),
> Prince of heaven, heir of earth,
> The lord who giveth duration to things, duration to all things.

---

[1] Pap. Bûlak, No. 17; MARIETTE, *Pap. de Boulaq*, ii., pls. 11-13; REINISCH, *Chrestomathie*, ii., pls. 45-47. Cf. also GRÉBAUT, *Hymne à Ammon-Râ*, Paris, 1874; the latter, however, imputes to the text a more profound religious perception than seems to me possible.

[2] For the meaning of this title, see above, p. 104.

Alone in his forms (?) in the midst of the gods,
The goodly bull of the Ennead of the gods,
The chief of all the gods,
Lord of truth, father of the gods,
Maker of men, former of the flocks,
Lord of the things which are, former of fruit trees,
Maker of herbage, who maketh the cattle to live,
Fair Power,[1] made by Ptah, youth fair of love.
    The gods give praise unto him;
Maker of things below and things above, he illuminateth
The two lands, he traverseth the upper heaven in peace;
King of Upper and Lower Egypt, Râ the true of voice (*maâ-
    kherû*), chief of the two lands,
Great one of valour, lord of awe,
Chief, making the earth in all its forms,
Making the attributes of every god (?).
The gods rejoice by reason of his beauties;
Acclamations are given to him in the great house (the temple
    of Amen),
Solemn manifestations in the house of flame (*i.e.* when he is led
    forth in solemn procession).
    The gods love his perfume
When he cometh from Arabia (*Pûnt*);
Prince of the dew, he traverseth the land of the Libyans,
Who cometh fair of face [from] the divine land (*ta neter*,
    Arabia);
The gods gather as dogs round his feet,
When they recognize his majesty as their lord.
Lord of fear, great one of terror,
Great of soul, mighty . . . . (?),
Causing offerings to flourish (?), maker of plenty.
    Praises to thee, maker of the gods,
Thou who didst raise the heaven on high, thou who didst put
    down (*lit.* strike down) the earth.

Pause.

    Wake in health (?), Min Amen (*i.e.* Amen as creator),
Lord of the Everlasting, maker of Eternity,

---

[1] For the meaning of the word *sekhem*, "power," or rather, the power incarnate in the figure of a deity, compare WIEDEMANN in *Le Muséon*, xv., pp. 46 *et seq*. Cf. also pp. 242-3.

Lord of adorations dwelling in Thebes,
Established with thy two horns, fair of face,
Lord of the uræus crown, exalted by the two feathers,
Beautiful of diadem, [exalted one] of the white crown of Upper
    Egypt,[1] the kingly land and the two uræi are his (?).
He is adorned (?) in his palace with the *Sekhet* crown,[2] the
    Nemmes cap,[3] and the *Kheperesh* helmet.[4]
Fair of face, he seizeth the *Atef* crown,[5]
Loving its south and its north (*i.e.* the two divisions of
    Egypt which are symbolized by the crown);
Lord of power (?), he seizeth the *Ames* sceptre;[6]
Lord of protection, who holdeth the scourge,[7]
Beautiful ruler, appearing with the white crown,
Lord of rays, making light.
    The gods give praises unto him;
His two hands give gifts to him that loveth him,
He casteth down his enemies by flames of fire,
His eye it is which overthroweth the wicked,
It casteth its lance at the devourer of Nû, it causeth the
    serpent (?) to spit forth what it hath eaten (?).[5]
    Hail to thee, Râ, lord of truth!
Hidden is thine abode, lord of the gods!
Khepera in his bark,
He spake words and the gods were created.
Tûm, maker of intelligent beings,
How many soever they be; making them to live,
Distinguishing their complexions (?) (*i.e.* of the different races)
    one from the other,

[1]

[2] The crown of Upper and Lower Egypt , called in later times
Pschent.

[3]   [4]

[5] A tall cap with a pair of horns and a pair of feathers.

[6] This sceptre has the form of , with a scourge fixed to it.

[7]

[5] This somewhat unintelligible passage refers to the serpent Ápep,
and, as it seems, to a myth according to which Râ pierced this monster and so compelled him to eject the prey that he had swallowed:
cf. above, p. 80.

Hearing the prayer of him who is in affliction,
Kindly of heart towards him who calleth upon him.
He delivereth the timid from him who is of a froward heart;
He judgeth the cause of the poor, between the poor and the
      mighty.
He is the lord of understanding, plenty is on his lips.
He cometh as the Nile to those who love him.
Lord of sweetness, a great one of love.
He [maketh] to live intelligent beings,
He giveth movement to every one (*lit.* to every eye).
He is made out of Nû,
Creating the rays of light.
The gods rejoice in his beauties,
Their hearts live when they behold him.

Pause.

Râ exalted in Thebes, great of splendour in the Benben
      house (at Heliopolis),
Ani (stable one), lord of the festival of the ninth day of the
      month,
To whom is celebrated the feast of the sixth day of the
      month, and the feast of the quarter month,
Sovereign, to whom Life, Prosperity, Health! lord of all the
      gods.
He is seen in the midst of the horizon,
Chief over all beings that are beneath (the sky);
Hidden (*amen*) is his name to his children
In his name of Amen (the hidden one).
   Hail to thee who art in peace!
Lord of joy, mighty one of diadems,
Lord of the uraeus crown, exalted by the two feathers,
Fair by the frontlet, exalted by the white crown.
The gods love the sight of thee,
The Sekhet crown is established upon thy forehead.
Thy graces are moving, traversing the two lands;
Thy rays are shining forth from [thy] two eyes; fair for man-
      kind is thy rising;
Weary are the flocks when thou shinest (in all thy strength).
Thy graces are in the sky of the south, thy sweet pleasant-
      ness in the sky of the north.
Thy beauties conquer hearts,

Thy graces make weary the arms,
The fair things thou hast fashioned make the hands to fall;[1]
Hearts fail at the sight of thee.

Only form, who didst make all that is, one and only one,
   maker of all that have being!
Mankind went forth from his two eyes,
The gods were created on his lips.
He maketh the herbage which maketh the cattle to live,[2]
The fruit trees for men;
He maketh to live the fishes [in] the river,
The fowls beneath the sky (?).
He giveth breath to that which is in the egg;
He maketh the grasshoppers to live,
He maketh the birds to live,
The creeping things and the flying, as well as what belongeth
   to them.
He maketh provision for the mice in [their] holes;
He maketh to live the birds in every tree.
   Hail to thee, maker of all these!
One and only one, he hath many arms (?).
When resting he watcheth over all who repose,
Seeking good for his creatures.
Amen who establishest (*men*) all things,
Tûm Harmakhis!
Praises are to thee when they (the creatures of Amen) all say:
"Praises to thee, for thou restest in us;
Obeisance[3] to thee for that thou didst form us!"
   Hail to thee from all flocks,
Acclamations to thee from every land,
To the height of heaven, to the width of earth,
To the depth of the sea.[4]

---

[1] *I.e.* "It is impossible to praise thee enough," adoration being
offered in Egypt by uplifting the arms.

[2] The word has for determinatives the figures of an ox, an ass,
a pig, and a sheep.

[3] *I.e.* prostration, *lit.* "smelling the earth," the Egyptian
expression of profound reverence.

[4] *Lit.* "great green"; often used for the Mediterranean, but also
for other large sheets of water.

The gods bow before thy majesty;
They exalt the spirits (*ba.ü*) of him who formed them,
They rejoice at the comings of him who begat them;
They say unto thee: " Approach in peace,
Father of the fathers of all the gods,
Thou who upholdest the heaven and puttest down the earth."

Maker of those which are, former of those which have being,
Sovereign, to whom Life, Prosperity, Health! chief of the gods,
We adore thy spirits (*ba.ü*) even as thou madest us;
Thy creatures are we because thou hast borne us (?);
We give praises unto thee, for thou restest in us.

Hail to thee who didst make all that is!
Lord of truth, father of the gods,
Maker of men, former of the flocks,
Lord of corn,
Making to live the herds of the desert.
Amen, bull fair of face,
Beloved in Thebes,
Great one of splendours in the Benben house,
Taking again (?) the diadem in Heliopolis,
Thou who judgedst the dispute between the Twins[1] in the great
    hall,
Chief of the Great Ennead of the gods.

One and only one, without his peer,
Dwelling in Thebes,
Ani in his divine ennead,
He liveth in truth every day.
Harmakhis in the east,
He fashioneth earth, the silver and the gold,
Real lapis lazuli for those who love him;
Balsam (?) and incense together in the land of the Libyans
    (*Mátañ*),
Fresh incense for thy nostril;
Fair of face coming [to] the Libyans,
Amen Râ, lord of the throne of the two lands,
Dwelling in Thebes (*äpt-t-ü*),
Ani dwelling in his sanctuary (*äpt*)!

---

[1] A reference to the occasion on which, according to the legend,
Râ gave final judgment at Heliopolis in the quarrel between the
twin adversaries, Horus and Set.

Pause.

King is he when alone even as in the midst of the gods;
Many are his names, none knoweth their number; he riseth
     in the horizon of the east, he setteth in the horizon of
     the west;
He overthroweth his enemies,
[Giving] provisions (?) the day of each day,
The morning of the birth (?) of each day.
Thoth raiseth his eyes;
He droopeth them before his splendour.
The gods rejoice at his beauties,
Those who are worshipping[1] extol him.
Lord of the Sekti and of the Mâdet bark,
Which traverse for thee Nû in peace,
Thy crew rejoice
When they see the overthrow of the wicked,
Whose limbs are tasted by the knife,
The flame devoureth him,
Punished is (?) his soul for his iniquity,
This wicked one who is saved by his legs (?).[2]
The gods are in exultation,
The crew of Râ are in peace;
Heliopolis is in exultation,
The enemies of Tûm are overthrown. Thebes is in peace,
     Heliopolis is in exultation.
The heart of the mistress of life[3] is glad,
The enemies of her lord are overthrown.
The gods of Babylon[4] are in acclamation,
The dwellers in Letopolis are in obeisance;[5]
They behold him mighty in his power,
As the powerful one of the gods; truth,[6] lord of Thebes,
In thy name, "Maker of Truth, Lord of Plenty, Bull of
     Offerings,"

____

[1] The cynocephali who give praise to Râ.

[2] A reference to the Åpep serpent, which was conquered but not destroyed, and worsted in the fight on one day only to renew his attack upon the Sun on the following.

[3] Name of the uraeus serpent, worn by the king on his forehead.

[4] The fort opposite Memphis, on the east bank of the Nile.

[5] *I.e.* in the act of "smelling the earth."

[6] Apparently this is here one of the titles of Amen.

In thy name, "Amen, Bull (*i.e.* Husband) of his Mother,
Maker of men,
Who createdst the making of all that is,"
In thy name, "Tûm Khepera."
Great hawk, celebrated is [his] body;
Fair of face, celebrated is his eye;[1]
His image is made [many] ells high,
The two uraei fly on wings before him.
The hearts of men fawn (like dogs) before him,
The glorified ones go forth towards him,
The two lands celebrate feasts at his appearing.

Hail to thee, Amen Râ, lord of the throne of the two lands!
Whose city loveth his rising.

[This work] is completed
in peace,
as it was found.[2]

FIG. 19.
AMEN RÂ. (L. D. III. 22.)
Obelisk of Hatshepsû,
at Karnak.

AMEN RÂ is generally figured in human form; he holds the sceptre alone, or the sceptre and symbol of life in his hand, and is crowned with the sun disk and two long feathers, which rise either from a stiff cap, or else from a pair of ram's horns. He was sometimes coloured blue, probably because that was the colour of the heavens in which he ruled as Sun god;[3] and he

[1] Here, as elsewhere, the sun is regarded as the eye of the god.

[2] The orthodox conclusion of Egyptian texts, corresponding to the "explicit feliciter" of the Middle Ages.

[3] It has been brought to my notice that Amen is coloured green in the tomb of Seti I., at any rate. The precise colouring of the deities on the monuments, at present very little studied, would form a profitable subject of inquiry by one on the spot in Egypt, leading to interesting results in regard to the nature of the several divinities.

has the horns of a ram, because in Thebes he was supposed
to be incarnate in a ram.   It must, however, be noted that,
strictly speaking, the horns represented as standing out at
the sides are not those of Amen, but those of Khnûm, and
that in representations of the god with these horns a combination has taken place of the gods Amen and Khnûm,
originally distinct : the horns of Amen curl round the

FIG. 20.—ÀMEN RÂ, HIS SACRED RAMS AND GOOSE. (STELA
IN BERLIN MUSEUM.)

ear.[1] The dromos of the temple of Amen was flanked
along its length on both sides by colossal rams with
coiled horns, which guarded the approach to his sanctuary
as representing the animals sacred to him.   In Thebes
the reverence for the ram in which the god was supposed
to be incarnate was extended in a modified form to all
rams, and they were held exempt from slaughter ; for

[1] Cf. LEPSIUS, *Aeg. Zeit.*, 1877, pp. 8 *et seq.*

since the god had vouchsafed to clothe himself in this form its destruction was a crime; in other Egyptian cities the animal was slaughtered for food without scruple. The Theban cult of the ram headed god Amen penetrated to the Oasis of Jupiter Ammôn, probably about the beginning of the New Kingdom, and there blended with a worship centring round a sacred stone which was probably of Semitic origin. Thence, about a thousand years later, it passed across the sea to Greece, where several temples were erected to Amen. Alexander the Great caused himself to be hailed as the son of Zeus Ammôn, and assumed the characteristic incurvated horns of the god of Thebes on coinage and elsewhere, thus familiarizing the whole Graeco-Oriental world with that deity. The oracles on which the power of the god of the Oasis was founded in the Greek world were delivered also in his native Thebes. Here, from the XXth to the XXIInd Dynasty, his counsel was taken, not only as regards important matters of church and state, but also in connexion with such comparative trifles as the identification of a thief.[1] The Theban kings saw in him whom they invoked as the Lord of Heaven and of the Thrones of the Two Lands and King of the Gods, one who was in an especial sense their constant companion and counsellor. He it was who sent them forth to war; he fought at their side in battle; he it was who got them the victory; and to him therefore was given a great portion of the spoil. In all serious matters, even in connexion with testamentary

---

[1] A British Museum papyrus relating to an inquiry of this nature is discussed by PLEYTE, *Proc. Soc. Bib. Arch.*, x., pp. 41 *et seq.*

arrangements, it was sought to ascertain his views ; judgments were ratified by him, and whoso opposed his sentences, upon him fell the divine curse.[1]

FIG. 21.—ÁMEN RÂ AS A GOOSE. (STELA IN AUTHOR'S POSSESSION.)

According to the inscriptions, intercourse between king

[1] Cf. NAVILLE, *Inscription historique de Pinodjem III.*, Paris, 1883; and MASPERO, *Les Momies royales de Deir-el-Bahari* (*Mém. du Caire*, i. 4).

and god was arranged as follows. The king presented himself before the god and preferred a direct question, so framed as to admit of an answer by simple yes or no ; in reply the god nodded an affirmative, or shook his head in negation. This has suggested the idea that the oracles were worked by manipulating statues of divinities mechanically set in motion by the priests. But as yet no such statues have been found in the Valley of the Nile, and contrivances of this kind could have had no other object than to deceive the people, a supposition apparently excluded in this case by the fact that it was customary for the king to visit the god alone and in secret.   Probably the king presented himself on such occasions before the sacred animal in which the god was incarnate, believing that the divine will would be manifested by its movements.

MÛT was the wife of Amen Râ, " mistress of the gods, lady of heaven, eye of Râ "; and in the city of Samhûd she was held to be the daughter of Râ. The chief centre of her worship was Asher, a spot south of Karnak. Here Amenophis III. built a temple dedicated to the goddess Mût, with a sacred lake attached to it. Votive statues representing the goddess lioness headed, both standing and seated, were dedicated here by the founder and by Sheshonk I. (the Shishak of the Bible) in such numbers that even in ancient times many were transferred to other Egyptian sanctuaries ; almost every great museum of the world now possesses one or more of them.   In wall scenes Mût is more commonly represented in human form. The word *mût* means " mother," and thus itself denotes the maternal function of the goddess in the Theban triad. The ideographic sign used to write her name, the image of a vulture, 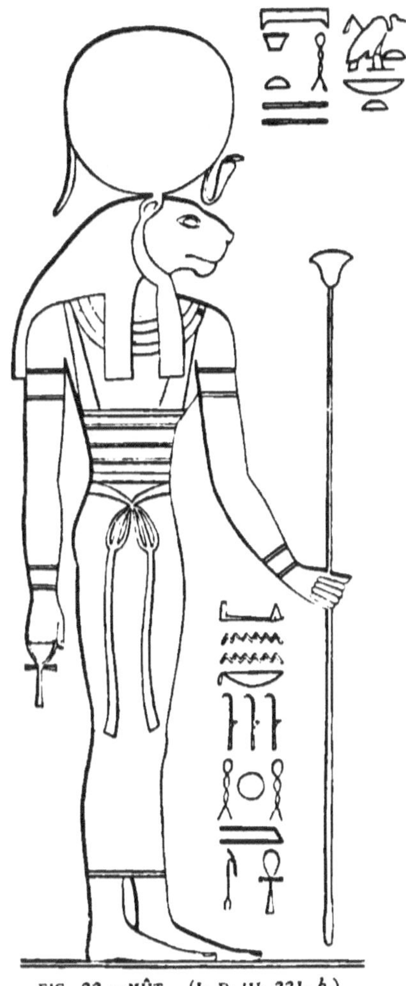, is at the same time in Egyptian the sign for the word "mother." This fact was recognized by Horapollo[1] in his work on hieroglyphics, written as late as the fifth century A.D., of which excerpts have come down to us in Greek.

ÀMENT, another Theban divinity, is sometimes named in the place of Mût; she, however, was not one of the genuine and original deities, but, as the construction of her name implies, merely an artificial creation. Considering her derivation it is not surprising to find that Ament was in even closer affinity to Amen than Mût herself, being represented with the head of a sheep, as corresponding to the ram's head of

FIG. 22.—MÛT. (L. D. III. 221, *b*.)
Karnak, Hypostyle Hall, XXth Dynasty.

___

[1] The best publication of this work is by LEEMANS, Amsterdam, 1835.

her husband.   Notwithstanding the similarity of name this Ament has no connexion whatever with the goddess AMENTI—the Greek Amenthes—the personification of the Underworld.

KHÛNSÛ is in the first place a lunar deity, and as such corresponds almost completely to Thoth ; at Hermopolis and Edfû the two deities were occasionally fused into one under the name of Khûnsû-Thoth.   His name, too, which is derived from the root *khens*—" to traverse "—alludes to his connexion with the heavenly bodies.   He was figured as a hawk headed god crowned with the lunar crescent and the solar disk ; both these symbols being proper to all lunar deities : to Thoth, to Ah, who is purely a moon god, and others.   In its present form, his great temple at Thebes, situate between that of Amen and that of Mût, was begun by Rameses III., and completed and decorated by kings of the XXIst Dynasty.   About that time, as would appear from the Bentresht Stela,[1] Khûnsû was definitely resolved into two distinct forms, the one person being Khûnsû, the Fair-resting One in Thebes, and the second Khûnsû, the Carrier out of Plans.   The first is mentioned in ancient texts ; to the second no early reference is known, but he appears in inscriptions of the XXVIth Dynasty and of the Ptolemaic period.[2]

By the Greeks Khûnsû was sometimes compared to Herakles, not that the latter had ever been apprehended as a lunar divinity, but possibly because Khûnsû may have been regarded as a sun god.   We have at least some testimony in favour of such a view, for at Kom Ombo

[1] Cf. pp. 275-7.   [2] *Proc. Soc. Bib. Arch.*, xiii., p. 274.

Khûnsû took on the composite form of Khûnsû-Hor, and in Thebes that of Khûnsu-Shû and of Khûnsû-Râ. Thus it is clear that he could occasionally assume a solar character, as his hawk head would also indicate.

MENT, Greek Mónth, ranked next in importance to Amen among the chief gods of the Theban nome. Here he was worshipped in a great temple near Karnak, in Medamot, in Taûd, and in Erment on the opposite bank, in fact in so many places as to suggest the idea that he was the true god of the nome and had preceded Amen in that capacity. Since, however, his name seems to be radically connected with *amen*, it is possible that both gods were originally identical and only subsequently differentiated. Ment was emphatically a god of war, fighting with the Egyptian army in their battles, and granting might and victory to the king. In later times he was often combined with the Sun god as Ment Râ, and as such he stands in the prow of the solar bark armed with a lance and

FIG. 23.

MENT.　(L. D. III. 124, *a*.)

Karnak, Hypostyle Hall,
Rameses I.

ready to pierce the enemies who oppose the progress of the Sun. In Erment Râ.t Taûi was recognized as his wife, but in Taûd, ȦNÎT or Hathor. Ment is represented as hawk headed and as wearing the headdress of Amen, ⦗⦘. In

Erment his sacred animal was a bull, Bakh, the Bacis of
the classic writers; and it appears as if the title "strong
bull" borne by the kings of the Theban dynasties was
borrowed from this animal. Bacis is designated by the
texts as the "living soul of Râ," that is to say, an incarnation of the god; thus proving that when this name was

FIG. 24.—BAKH, THE BULL OF MENT. (GRÉBAUT, "MUSÉE," VI. I.)
Stela from Funerary Temple of Prince Unzmes, at Thebes.

first bestowed the fusion of Ment with Râ had already
been accomplished. The animal must have been worshipped also at Taûd, where the god is represented as
wearing his usual headdress, but with the head and horns
of a bull. The cult of Ment is prominent in many of the
later texts; for when Thebes had lost her political and

social supremacy Erment became the capital of the district, and many inscriptions relating to Ment, or rather to Ment Râ, were then placed in temples at Karnak originally dedicated to Amen and his cycle. The mention of Ment in the older texts is chiefly confined to figures of speech in which the king is said to be brave as Ment, to have conquered his foes like Ment, and the like ; but such expressions afford no data for the understanding of the nature and cult of the deity in question. As the Egyptian war god he is occasionally placed in a certain antithesis to the Semitic Baal, and the combined might of Ment and Baal, when granted to a king, was esteemed the very epitome of strength.

MIN [1] was the nome god of Panopolis and an important deity, more or less worshipped throughout the whole of Egypt. He is represented as an ithyphallic figure : the right arm is upraised and waves a scourge above his head. Behind the god there is generally a shrine with trees upon or near it. His sacred animal was the ram. He is the god of the generative power of nature : hence it was to him that the harvest festivals were! dedicated as a sign of gratitude for the abundance which he caused to spring forth from the earth ; and hence also certain gods—particularly Amen Râ—were identified with him when referred to as " husbands of their mothers," *i.e.* as begetters of their divine sons.[2]

---

[1] The name, almost invariably written by an ideogram, has been read by Egyptologists as *Khem* or *Amsi*, as well as *Min*. Variants of Greek times give the correct pronunciation, *Min.*

[2] Cf. p. 104.

KHNÛM or KHNEF, the Khnumis or Kneph of the Greeks, who was specially worshipped in the neighbourhood of the first cataract, was regarded, as his name would indicate, as the "Modeller." In many Egyptian texts he is set forth as being the creator, "he who created all that is, who formed that which is existent, the father of fathers, the mother of mothers"; "he who constructed men, who made the gods, who was father in the beginning"; "the creator of the heaven, the earth, the Underworld, the water, the hills"; "he who formed fowl, fish, wild animals, and all creeping things, in pairs, male and female." Man he had formed and turned upon a potter's wheel; even under the New Kingdom it was sometimes believed that the Pharaoh had been so made, and in the "Tale of the Two Brothers" we read how, at the command of Râ Harmakhis, Khnûm made a beautiful woman, and "the essence of all the gods was in her."[1] According to other texts, he was also a cosmogonical deity; a late inscription at Esneh informs us that "he raised the sky upon its four pillars, he uplifted it from eternity."

His sacred animal was a ram, and he is usually represented as ram headed, with horns horizontally extended, ⫯. As time went on Khnûm was combined with Râ, and at Abaton, near Philae, the sacred ram was called the "living soul of Râ," while in Heliopolis he corresponded to Osiris and his ram was worshipped as an incarnation of that god. The association of these deities with this form of incarnation was in every case

[1] *Pap. d'Orbiney*, p. 9. Cf. PETRIE, *Egyptian Tales*, ii., pp. 50-1.

guided by the idea that the generative power in the
animal was identical with the force by which life is renewed in nature continually, and in man after death.

HEKT, the frog headed goddess, was sometimes considered to be the wife of the
ram god ; she was also supposed to be a form of Hathor
and the mother of Aroëris.
Although frequent reference
is made to her in the texts,
we learn nothing as to her
nature or functions : under
the Old Kingdom great men
prided themselves on being
" prophets " of truth and of
Hekt. The facts that she is
mentioned and figured on sarcophagi, and that lamps dating
from Coptic times bear the
image of a frog with the legend " I am the resurrection,"
show that she played some
part in the doctrine of the
resurrection. The line of
thought which suggested this

FIG. 25.—HEKT. (WILKINSON,
NO. 502.)
Ptolemaic or Roman.

association probably had its rise in the old Egyptian belief,
often mentioned by Greek writers, that frogs were born of
the mud which the Nile fertilized at the annual inundation.
It was even asserted that animals had been observed when
half their bodies still consisted of unformed mud. Hence

the Egyptians came to believe, not only in the spontaneous generation of the frog, but further that this supposed phenomenon was a reason for considering that the first living beings originated in the Valley of the Nile.

SATI is a goddess associated with Khnûm more com-

FIG. 26.—KHNÛM, SATI.T, AND ÂNÛKT. (L. D. III. 63, *d.*)
Temple of Thothmes III. at Ibrim.

monly than Hekt: she, Khnûm, and Ânûkt formed the triad of Elephantine. Her titles "Lady of Heaven, Mistress of the Two Lands, Chief of all the Gods," led the Greeks to identify her with Hera, to whom she had no other resemblance. She plays no part in the myths at present known to us, but is mentioned in several texts as the daughter of Râ. She is represented as wearing the vulture headdress, the horns of a cow, and the crown of Upper Egypt.

ÂNÛKT, Greek Anuki, is compared to Hestia, for which again no intrinsic reason can be discerned. The relation to the king sometimes attributed to her is characterized in a text by these words : " He was a son of Khnûm, born of Sati, nursed by Ânûki." She appears on the monuments as a woman with the sign of life in her hand and a crown of feathers on her head, ⦚. This feather headdress suggests a negro divinity ; and indeed the high honour in which she was held from the cataracts southward and the rare occurrence of her worship in the north alike point to a Nubian origin. Her title "lady of Sati" has misled some writers into regarding her as an Asiatic goddess, but "Sati" as a place name denotes not Asia only, but also the island of Sehel near Philae, which was the chief centre of her worship and from which this title is derived.

PTAH, transliterated Phtha by the Greeks, and by them identified with Hephaestos, bore a name which is probably derived from the root *pth*, " to open," especially as used in the ritual term " opening of the mouth." In the inscriptions there is apparently no trace of any mythological event connected with this name, but Porphyrius,[1] who was well informed in Egyptian matters, tells us that the god came forth from an egg which had issued from the mouth of Kneph. Ptah is represented as a bandaged mummy ; and the pedestal upon which his figure was placed was shaped like a cubit rod, which is the sign for

---

[1] EUSEBIUS, *Praeparatio Evangelica*, iii. 11.

truth and just measurement, 𝕀. Generally he wears a tassel hanging from the back of his neck, in form something like a pendent bell shaped flower, 𝕀. As to the significance of this there has been much idle conjecture, but an examination of the more detailed representations shows it to be here nothing more than the so called *menât*,[1] generally used as a counterpoise to prevent the necklace from falling too low in front. The inscriptions afford no warrant for ascribing to it any mythological significance in reference to the god.

In Memphis, where Ptah with Sekhet and Nefer Tûm or Imûthes formed the divine triad, he was held to have been the first King of Egypt and the creator of the world, and therefore bore the titles: "Father of the mighty fathers (the other gods), father of the beginnings, he who created the sun egg and the moon egg." A bas relief at Philae, with an accompanying and explanatory inscription, displays him in his composite form of Ptah Tatûnen turning the egg of sun or moon upon a potter's wheel. He is also

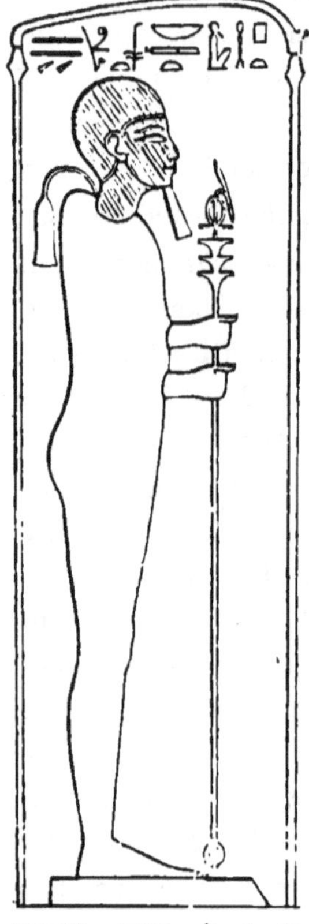

FIG. 27.—PTAH. (L. D. III. 143, *a.*)
Karnak, Hypostyle Hall, XIXth Dynasty.

---

[1] Compare below, p. 295.

called the "creator of his own image, he who created himself, who establishes truth, king of both lands, lord of heaven," etc.   In the Book of the Dead it is stated that he performs the ceremony of "opening the mouth" for the dead, as he had once performed it for the dead gods;

FIG. 28.—PTAḤ TATÛNEN.   (ROSELLINI, "MON. DEL CULTO," PL. 21.)
Philae, Roman.

but in all likelihood this function of his was merely evolved out of his name.

Ptah is often found in combination with other deities. Thus there were *Ptaḥ âten en pet*, " Ptah the sun disk of heaven," a sun god of whom it is said "he enlightens the earth with his rays"; Ptaḥ Nû, "the father of the gods," a form of manifestation of the primeval waters; *Ptaḥ Ḥâpi*,

"Ptah the Nile," who sent the inundation, and by its agency exhibited his creative powers.

PTAḤ TANEN is another of these composite deities, and combines Ptah with the somewhat rare god TANEN or TATÛNEN, who appears to have been an earth god, a counterpart of Seb. Ptah Tanen, however, is not infrequent. We find him, for example, at Abû Simbel, where he is accounted the father of Rameses II., and an inscription says: "So saith Ptah Tanen, wearing the high feathers, equipped with two horns; he who begets the gods every day, ' I am thy (*i.e.* Rameses II.'s) father, who begot thee as a god to make thee King of Upper and Lower Egypt in my place; I gave unto thee the lands which I created.'" The figure of the god here referred to is that of Ptah, except for the addition of a headdress consisting of two horns and two ostrich feathers, 𓋚, symbols of the truth and justice ascribed to him as attributes. In his hand is a sceptre, or occasionally a scourge, 𓌅; but in the latter case we have to do with a further combination, in which the god is connected with the familiar forms—

PTAḤ OSIRIS, PTAḤ SOKARIS, or PTAH SOKAR OSIRIS, which were generally supposed to be incarnate in the Apis bull at Memphis, and are the subjects of innumerable texts. As to the elements of this composite deity, Osiris is the well known god of the dead, while of Sokaris— Egyptian *Seker*—to whom we have already referred on p. 92, in dealing with the Sun's passage through the Underworld, little is known. He seldom appears except in combination, and has then almost entirely lost his original nature. He was primarily a sun god, the incarnation of which was kept in the sacred bark *hennu*. The bark is represented as standing on a pedestal, ; the stern is adorned with the head of a gazelle, and a disk crowned hawk which represents Sokaris himself is perched upon the cabin. At the festival of the god [1] his bark was borne in solemn procession round the walls of the temple of Sokaris. It was, of course, in Memphis that this festival was celebrated with the greatest pomp, but it was also held in other religious centres with certain local modifications, such as adding the Sekti bark to the procession. The festival was connected with the winter solstice, with the "little sun," as the Egyptians called it at that time. In the Ptolemaic period it fell on the morning of the 26th Khoiak (22nd December), while in earlier times it would seem to have been held in the evening. An Egyptian text states, "The Sun is great as Horus, the Sun is little as Sokaris," but this idea was of later growth, and arose at a time when it was sought to safeguard the individualities of the various solar deities by associating each with an appearance of the sun at a particular time of the day or year, whereas originally Râ,

FIG. 29.

SOKAR OSIRIS. (L. D. III. 72.)
From Stela of Amenophis III.
at Thebes.

---

[1] For the festival see BRUGSCH in *Revue Égyptologique*, i., pp. 42 *et seq.*

Horus, and Sokaris had all the same significance and were simply sun gods. The sophistry in these attributions is moreover obvious from the fact that another distinction between Sokaris and Râ was proposed, the former being differentiated as the god of the sun at night. It was this interpretation which led to the combination of Sokaris with Osiris, King of the Under-world. Moreover he gradually became the god κατ' ἐξοχὴν of the Memphite necropolis, where his name still survives in that of the village of Saqqarah. Sokaris is usually represented as hawk headed like Râ, but without the solar disk, and bearing, besides the sceptre, the scourge and crook carried by Osiris as symbols of his rule.

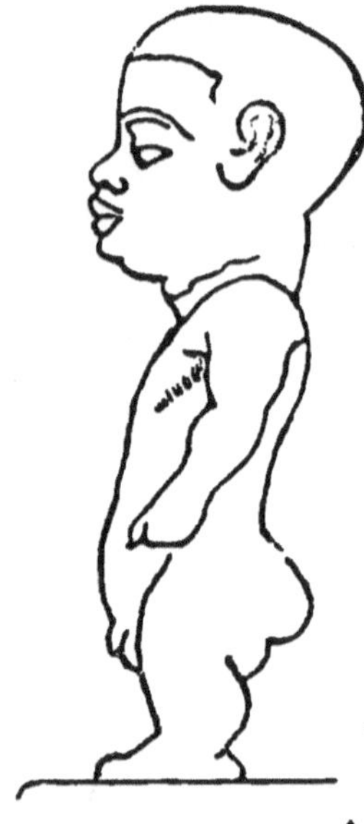

FIG. 30.—ONE OF THE KHNÛ-MÛ. (ARUNDALE AND BO-NOMI, GALL. VII. 10.)

From Statuette in British Museum.

These forms of Ptah compounded with Osiris and Sokaris united the attributes of the three gods'; the resulting deity was at once creator of the world, Sun god, and king of the dead, and became the centre of conceptions of a pantheistic ruling and embracing of all things, and of such thoughts as those expressed in the Hymn to Amen Râ (pp. 111 *et seq.*). This Ptah was, however, more closely associated with life in the world to come than with the characteristics of a solar deity, whereas the reverse was the case with Amen Râ. Ptah has no essential connexion whatever with the Greek Hephaestos ; so far as the evidence of the inscriptions goes, he was never a fire god, as, arguing from this identification, it has been thought. The only grounds for the comparison appear to be that Ptah was described as a modeller, and that his close fitting cap is suggestive of that of a smith.

In the work of creation Ptah had been helped by the KHNÛMÛ, "the modellers," who were generally counted as his children, although later as those of Râ. They were represented as dwarfs, with big heads, crooked legs, very long arms, and long moustaches[1] : grotesque figures which, as Herodotus tells us,[2] excited the derision of Kambyses in the temple of Hephaestos at Memphis. Countless little glazed earthenware figures of these gods are found in Egyptian tombs ; for even as once the Khnûmû had helped in the making of the world, so would they help to reconstruct in all its members the body of the dead man in whose tomb they were laid.

FIG. 31.

SEKHET.   (L. D. III. 201, *d.*)

Speos at Gebel Silsileh, XIXth Dynasty.

SEKHET was recognized in Memphis as the wife of Ptah and the mother of Nefer Tûm or Imûthes. She is represented as a lioness headed woman crowned with the

[1] Query, snakes ? (TRANS.)

[2] HERODOTUS, iii. 37 : cf. WIEDEMANN, *Herodot's Zweites Buch*, p. 236.

solar disk and uraeus serpent. Broadly speaking, she is one in nature with other feline headed goddesses: the lioness headed Tefnût, Mût of Thebes, PAKHT of the Speos Artemidos, and the cat or sometimes lioness headed BAST of Bubastis—all of whom represented the variable power of the sun, from genial warmth to scorching heat. Thus

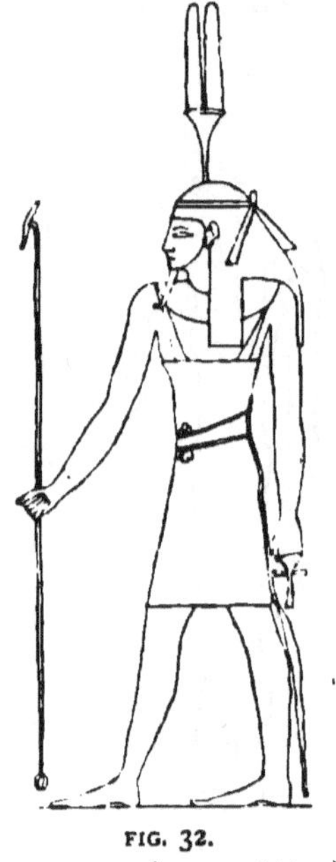

FIG. 32.

NEFER TUM. (L. D. III. 204, c.)

Tomb of Seti II.

a Philae text states in reference to Isis Hathor, who there personified all goddesses in one: " Kindly is she as Bast, terrible is she as Sekhet." As conqueror of the enemies of the gods Sekhet carries a knife in her hand, for she it was who, under the name of the Eye of Râ, entered upon the task of destroying mankind.[1] Other texts represent her as ancestress of part of the human race.[2]

NEFER TÛM, whom the local myths represent as the son of Sekhet, of Pakht, or of Bast, is in the Book of the Dead an unimportant deity mentioned in connexion with the doctrine of immortality. He was figured as a man crowned with an upspringing lotus flower, a symbol of the resurrection and of his power to grant continuance of life in the world to come. At a late epoch, from about the XXVIth dynasty

---

[1] See pp. 59 *et seq.*
[2] Cf. LEFÉBURE, *Tombeau de Seti I.*, ii., pls. 4, 5.

onwards, large numbers of his statuettes were made in bronze and in glazed ware; but beyond this fact we have no precise knowledge of the reasons for his special worship at this period.   At any rate, the importance of Nefer Tûm

was much less than that of Imûthes, who more usually occupies his place in the Memphite triad.

The name of IMḤETEP signifies " he who comes in peace "; the Greeks tran-scribed it Imûthes, and likened him to Asklepios. He is represented as a young man wearing a close fitting cap.   In the Underworld his functions also related to human immortality, while on earth he cured men of their diseases by means of medicine and of magic.   He was generally regarded as a learned deity, and, in the attitude of reading a half opened papyrus roll spread

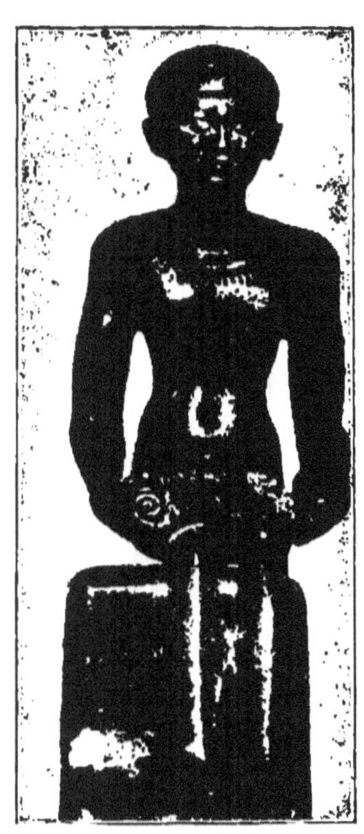

FIG. 33.—IMḤETEP.
(STATUETTE IN BERLIN MUSEUM.)

out upon his knees, in which he is frequently depicted, he seems to be performing the office of chief *kher ḥeb*, *i.e.* chief of those priests whose office it was to recite funerary prayers and formulas.[1]   Small bronze statuettes of the god

[1] Cf. below, pp. 236-7.

are very often found, and are generally remarkable for tasteful execution ; nearly all date from Saite and Greek times, when the worship of Imûthes was much affected in Egypt.

NEITH is a goddess frequently mentioned by the Greeks ; she, Osiris, and Horus formed the triad of Sais.[1] She is named in some of the oldest inscriptions, but did not attain

FIG. 34.
NEITH. (WILKINSON, NO. 510.)

to any prominence until the time of the XXVIth Dynasty, which originated from Sais ; but even then her real influence did not extend beyond the Delta. She is represented as a woman with the green face and hands characteristic of deities of the Underworld. As a warrior she is generally figured with bow and arrows, and it was owing to this circumstance that the Greeks identified her with Athene. She wears the crown of Lower Egypt. The ideogram for her name is the weaver's shuttle, a device which the Libyans wove into their clothing and tattooed upon their arms, so that she would seem to have been originally a Libyan goddess.[2] In Egyptian mythology she ranks as mother of the gods and of Râ in particular, and hence, even in the XVIIIth Dynasty, Sais is called the abode of the mother of the gods. Subsequently she was confused

[1] Cf. MALLET, *Le Culte de Neit à Sais*, Paris, 1889.
[2] On the Libyan origin of Neith cf. PETRIE, *Nagada and Ballas*, p. 64. (TRANS.)

with Isis, and took the place of the latter in the Osirian myth. The monuments describe the festivals of Sais, of which Herodotus also gives an account, and which were dedicated principally to Neith, as the ordinary feasts of Isis.

FIG. 35.—NEKHEBIT. (WILKINSON, PL. XL.)

NEKHEBIT and ÛAZIT are often set over against each other in the inscriptions as tutelary goddesses of Upper and Lower Egypt; little more is known of either goddess.

 The chief seat of the former was at El Kab, and the Greeks identified her with Eileithyia, the goddess of birth. She was usually represented as a vulture hovering over the king. Ûazit was more particularly worshipped in the Delta; she was the Buto of the Greeks, who compared her to Leto and ascribed oracles to her.

FIG. 36.
ÛAZIT. (WILKINSON, PL. XLI.)

She is represented either as a winged serpent or as a woman. Occasionally, when Nekhebit and Ûazit are named together, both take the same form: as winged uraci, vultures, or women. In the Osirian myth Buto was the guardian of Horus, whom Isis gave into her charge while she went forth to seek the body of Osiris.[1]

MAÂT,[2] the daughter of Râ, is the Themis of the Greeks. She was figured as a woman wearing upon her head an ostrich feather, the symbol of truth. She was the goddess of Truth and Justice, and hence was occasionally represented with bandaged eyes, since Justice judges without respect of persons. In the Underworld she was present at the weighing of the heart. She is mentioned in some of the oldest texts; it was esteemed an honour to be one of her priests; and gods and kings of all periods professed that they lived by and from her. Yet she has no place in mythology.

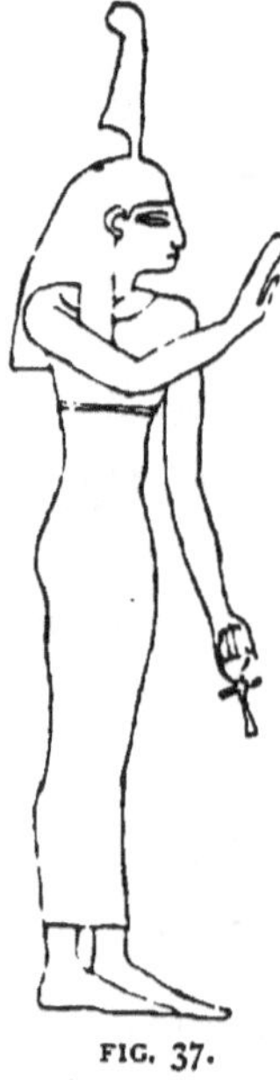

FIG. 37.

MAÂ.T. (L. D. III. 223, c.)

Stela in Hammamat Valley, XXth Dynasty.

HATHOR also was a goddess of whom much mention is made, but no distinct myth ' related. Her name means the "Abode of Horus," and is ideographically written by a sign consisting of the ground plan of a fortress and a standing hawk within it, ▯. She was the goddess of love and joy, to whom many festivals were dedicated, and whose magnificent temple at Denderah is still comparatively uninjured. Here she was esteemed the sum and substance of feminine godhead, and

[1] WIEDEMANN, *Herodot's Zweites Buch*, p. 558.

[2] WIEDEMANN, *Annales du Musée Guimet*, x., pp. 581 *et seq.*

all goddesses were considered as forms or attributes of Hathor worshipped under different names, so that, according to the priests of Denderah, all prayers to them were in reality addressed to Hathor.

(Another goddess bearing the same name and entitled Lady of the Underworld was of independent origin. She sometimes took the place of Nût in giving water to the souls of the dead from the midst of a sycomore. Of independent origin were also the seven Hathors who are said in the inscriptions to help the queen at childbirth and who play the part of fairy godmothers in the tales.)

Hathor is generally represented as a woman, sometimes with the ears, the horns, or even the head of a cow, that being the animal sacred to her.

SEBÀK, the Sukhos of the Greeks,[1] was represented either in the likeness of his sacred animal, the crocodile, or else as crocodile headed. Two distinct deities were comprised under this name. First, there was Sebak a sun god, who was usually combined with Râ and especially worshipped at Ombos, where the sun god Aroëris was the local deity. And, secondly, there was Sebak the counterpart of Osiris. According to certain texts at Denderah, Osiris was wor-

FIG. 38.

HATHOR. (L. D. III. 124, b.)
Karnak, Hypostyle Hall,
XIXth Dynasty.

---

[1] See illustration, p. 192.

shipped under the name of Sebak in the Libyan nome, and especially in the city of Apis ; while a myth of Upper Egypt relates that it was upon the back of a crocodile that the body of Osiris was borne to Philae.   But Sebak was

FIG. 39.--SEBÀK, (STATUETTE IN BERLIN MUSEUM.)

also occasionally reckoned as an evil deity. The crocodiles sacred to him were held to be the associates of Set in the Underworld, and men sought deliverance from them on earth by means of incantations. Although throughout a considerable part of the country fear of the god to whom the creatures belonged prevented their being regularly hunted down, nevertheless in districts where the worship of Sebak did not prevail, this sport was a favourite pastime, especially among the nobles of the Old Kingdom.

ḤÂPI, or the Nile, was the subject of one of the great national cults, and in his honour the largest number, or at any rate the most widely observed, of the Egyptian festivals were celebrated. As Libanius[1] tells us, the god was supposed to be so exacting in regard to these solemnities that, if his feast was not kept rightly, he refused to grant a favourable inundation. Magnificent temples were raised to him at Nilopolis, near Memphis, at Heliopolis, and other places, and were richly endowed by the kings. The god of the river was represented as a fat man with the breasts of a woman, to symbolize fertility, and his worshippers thought to honour him by their own effeminacy. On his head was a crown of flowers. Some-

FIG. 40.

ḤÂPI.   (L. D. III. 175, *d.*)

Stela at Gebel Silsileh,
Rameses II.

times he was resolved into the Nile of Upper and the Nile of Lower Egypt, the lotus being considered emblematic of the

---

[1] *Oratio pro Templis.* References to the Nile by the ancient writers are collected by JABLONSKI, *Pantheon Aegyptiorum*, iv., pp. 140 *et seq.*

former and the papyrus of the latter ; a design consisting of both plants tied together formed a favourite subject for the decoration of the royal throne, as typifying the king's rule over Upper and Lower Egypt, . Sometimes the personality of Hâpi was still further subdivided, and every nome had its Nile god with a more or less complete individuality. A recognized Egyptian method of presenting to the eyes a picture of all Egypt doing homage to Pharaoh was to draw a procession of the Nile gods following each other in single file and presenting their gifts to the king. Hâpi had as his associate deities the god KA, "father of the gods," who bore a frog's head surmounted by a scarabaeus ; the gods ḤÛ, ZEFA, and RESEF, who collectively represented food or plenty ; NEPERÀ, the goddess of grain ; and the snake headed or snake bodied RENNÙT, goddess of the harvest.

There are many hymns in praise of the Nile god and all his benefactions to Egypt ; and more especially of his inundation. The texts are found on papyri, on stelae, and on the walls of cliffs, and their contents are often supposed to be spoken by the king. The following are some of the principal passages of one such hymn, which was engraved upon the rocks at Gebel Silsileh in Upper Egypt by command of Rameses II. ; and in duplicate by command of his son and successor Merenptah ; and again by Rameses III.[1] They will serve to show the general manner and style of these hymns in their most interesting form.

" The living and beautiful Nile who loveth Nû, the father of the gods and of the divine cycle, he who dwelleth in the

---

[1] Cf. STERN, *Aeg. Zeit.*, 1873, pp. 129 *et seq.*

river ; Plenty (*ḥū*), Riches (*ka*), Food (*resef*,—determined
by the signs for fowl and fish—) of Egypt, who maketh all
men to live by his riches (*ka*), who is venerable upon his
path, who hath plenty (*ḥū*) at his fingers. Men rejoice at
his coming. Thou art alone, thou createdst thyself, none
knoweth the place in which thou art (the source or spring
in which the Nile was supposed to dwell). On the day
when thou comest forth from thyself (the beginning of the
inundation), then is every one full of joy. Thou art lord
of many fish and of gifts ; thou givest food (*resef*,—fowl
and fish as determinative—) unto Egypt. The divine cycle
knoweth not where thou art. Thou art its life, for at thy
coming their offerings increase, their altar is filled with
plenty, they shout for joy at thine appearing. Thou dost
provide for us that which is needful that men may live,
even as Râ when he ruled this land."

Then follow a eulogy of the king and his command to
institute two festivals in honour of the Nile, "father of all
the gods, prince of the waters, who feedeth Egypt, from
whose rising come plenty, and riches, and life to all."

CHAPTER VI.

FOREIGN DEITIES.

THE Egyptians did not exclude foreign deities from their pantheon. They never questioned the divinity of the gods of the races with which they came in contact, but accepted it in each case as an established fact. To them an exceptionally powerful nation was in itself a proof of that nation's possession of an exceptionally mighty god, whom the dwellers in the Valley of the Nile were therefore eager to receive into the ranks of Egyptian deities, that they might gain his protection for themselves by means of prayers and offerings, and at the same time alienate his affections from his native land. The acquisition of a god necessarily involved the acquisition of his kingdom ; for to Egyptian thought, as indeed to that of the old Oriental world in general, a war between two nations was primarily a war between their gods, and the people without a powerful god was the sure prey of a neighbour more fortunate in this respect. Among the peoples whose gods the Egyptians had opportunities of appropriating, the Libyans, the Semitic Asiatics, and the Hamitic and negro races of Ethiopia were especially plundered.

It is probable that certain Libyan gods had already been appropriated at the beginning of Egyptian history, in times of which we have no historical tradition ; among them apparently were Bast and Neith. These two goddesses were worshipped in the western parts of the Delta, where the majority of the population were Libyan ; but even under the dynasties which sprang from Bubastis and Sais, the chief centres of their worship, they never attained to importance throughout the rest of the land, especially where the population was more purely Egyptian, as in Upper Egypt.

For the Egyptian appropriation of Asiatic divinities [1] we have better historical evidence. Among such deities Baal, Astarte, Ânta, Reshpû, and Kedesh call for special notice.

BAAL, the Egyptian *Bâl*, first became known to the Egyptians as the chief god of nations with whom, at the beginning of the New Empire, they were at war for centuries : not with invariable success. It was in the course of these wars that the worship of Baal was introduced into Egypt, and the Ramessides had a special predilection for calling themselves as brave and as mighty as Baal in heaven. He had apparently no place in Egyptian mythology ; but since his name in writing is usually followed by the image or by the sacred animal of the god Set, there would appear to have been a recognized affinity between the two gods, and, as a matter of fact, the name of Baal is substituted for that of Set in one of the texts of Edfû relating to the legend of the Winged

[1] The collection, elucidation, and comparison of all the information relating to these deities which is to be found in the texts is a great desideratum in Egyptology. The notices of ED. MEYER, *Zeitschr. d. Deutsch. Morg. Gesch.*, xxi., pp. 716 *et seq.*, are too defective to be considered as forming an authoritative work on the subject. (W. MAX MÜLLER, *Asien und Europa nach Altaegyptischen Denkmälern*, pp. 311 *et seq.*, has specially dealt with this subject.—TRANS.)

Sun Disk.[1] In Egypt Baal was regarded as a god of the sky,—a conception which fairly corresponds to his original nature,—and as a great but essentially a destructive deity. Broadly speaking, his worship was confined to the eastern part of the Delta, where the Semitic population was proportionately large : his chief temple was in the fortified frontier city of Tanis.

ASTARTE was worshipped in several Egyptian temples.[2] An inscription dating from the XXIst Dynasty mentions a priest of Memphis who served both her and the moon-god Ah ; and in Ptolemaic times a small chapel dedicated to her stood near the Serapeum. It must have been either this chapel or an earlier one on the same site to which, by a curious misconception, Herodotus refers as the temple of the " strange Aphrodite," whom he further confounds with the Helen of Homer. The western quarter of Tanis was dedicated to Amen, the southern to Sûtekh, the northern to Bûto, and the eastern to Astarte, to whom also a temple seems to have been established not far from Tanis, on the shores of the Serbonian lake. In magical texts she is mentioned along with Ânta as a goddess who " conceives but never brings forth." In the treaty made between the Kheta (Hittites) and the Egyptians, she appears as a national goddess of the Syrian Kheta, and this at a time when her worship had become so far familiar to the dwellers by the Nile that Rameses II. called his son Mer-Â(s)trot.t after her ; and several proper names compounded with her name were current. She found but a late entrance

---

[1] NAVILLE, *Textes rel. au Mythe d'Horus*, pl. 4.
[2] Cf. WIEDEMANN, *Herodot's Zweites Buch*, p. 433.

into Egyptian mythology : in the scenes illustrative of the legend of the Winged Sun Disk [1] she is lioness headed, and, mounted on a quadriga, drives her horses over the bodies of the foe. She is entitled " lady of horses and of chariots," and this designation betrays the late origin of the mythological episode in which she figures, since the horse apparently was only introduced into Egypt in the time of the Hyksôs, and never appears in any of the older myths. Reference to Astarte is made in the Osirian myth as related by Plutarch, but there she is euhemeristically explained to have been a queen of Byblos.

ÂNTÂ is named along with Astarte in the Kheta treaty,

FIG. 41.—ÂNTÂ. (PRISSE, " MON.," PL. 37. Stela in British Museum. XXth Dynasty.

whence it would seem that she also was a goddess of this Syrian people. She figures on Egyptian monuments as " lady of heaven and mistress of the gods," with helmet, shield, and lance, and swinging a battle axe in her left hand ; sometimes she is represented on horseback. She is often mentioned in the inscriptions of Rameses II. and

[1] NAVILLE, *Textes rel. au Mythe d'Horus*, pl. 13.

Rameses III., both of them warlike princes, and the latter even gave to his favourite daughter the Semitic name of *Bent ânta*, " daughter of Ânta."

RESHPÛ is represented with helmet and lance. His Semitic origin is obvious from the outline of his profile, and he corresponds to the Phoenician Resef, who was worshipped both in Cyprus and in Carthage. His titles "great god, lord of heaven, ruler of eternity, lord of might in the midst of the divine cycle," are simply borrowed from Egyptian divinities, and are useless for determining his nature.

FIG. 42.—RESHPÛ. (PRISSE, " MON.," PL. 37.)
Stela in British Museum.
XXth Dynasty.

KEDESH is the goddess represented as accompanying Reshpû. She holds flowers in her right hand and a serpent in her left ; usually she wears as her headdress the sun disk embraced by two horns, and she stands upon the back of a lion. She and Râ, together with the Egyptian god Min, were grouped into a triad ; but as a matter of fact she was merely goddess of the city of Kadesh, the capital of the Syrian confederation of the Kheta, upon whose dominions Rameses II. in particular found himself obliged to make war. In all likelihood Kedesh was originally a local modification of Astarte. On Egyptian stelae of the XVIIIth and XIXth Dynasties she is entitled "lady of heaven, mistress of all the gods, eye of Râ, who has none like unto her, daughter of Râ, *âsa.t* eye of Tûm, beloved of the Sun god." On the same monuments prayers are also addressed to her for gifts of life and health, and after extreme old age a good burial in the west of Thebes, the latter request proving that the god was recognized in the capital of the country.

The above named deities changed neither name nor identity by their transference to Egypt; but the influence of Semitic thought which occasionally prevailed there had a far wider and more profound importance, and effected organic transformations in the ideas of the Egyptians as to the natures of their own national gods. A conspicuous example of this influence is discernible in the belief in

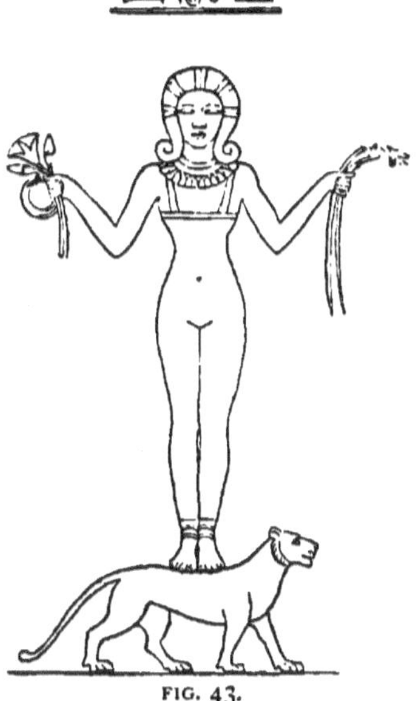

FIG. 43.
KEDESH. (PRISSE, "MON.," PL. 37.)
Stela in British Museum. XXth Dynasty.

sacred inanimate objects as incorporations of deity, particularly stones, the Bethels or Betyls which are known to have been such important objects of adoration among the Semites that the worship of them was carried wherever Semitic colonists penetrated. They were set up in connexion with Astarte in Paphos, Apollo in Ambracia, Zeus Teleios in Tegea in Arcadia, and in many other

places besides.   The oracular image of the Oasis of
Jupiter Ammon was a stone which in shape is said to have
resembled a navel, and which at festivals was borne in
procession, richly decorated with jewels.   An Egyptian
origin for this stone as the representative of Amen
is impossible ; only the animal incarnation, in a ram,
was derived from Egypt and characteristic of it.   The
second symbol of the deity worshipped in the Oasis was
introduced in all likelihood from one of the Phoenician
settlements on the north African coast, between which
and the Oasis an active connexion always subsisted.   The
population of the Oasis was, it is true, but half Egyptian.
A similar form of worship, however, was established in
Egypt, in Heliopolis, the most renowned of all her
temples : one incorporation of the Sun god of Heliopolis
was a stone (pp. 16-17, 24).   The form of the stone seems
to have varied with the course of time ; now it is spoken
of as a pyramid or an obelisk, and again as a conven-
tionalized column, ⬤ or ⬤, the hieroglyphic sign which
was used from earliest times as the ideogram for *An*, the
name of the city of Heliopolis.   As reference is also
occasionally made to the presence of a similar column
in other sanctuaries, this form of worship had evidently
commended itself to the colleges of priests, owing to
the influence of the temple at Heliopolis.

Another Egyptian god who was occasionally regarded
as incorporate in a stone was Set.   This is proved by
the fact that the sign of an oblong stone, ▭, is the
usual determinative of his name, although no specific
statements on the point have been found in the in-

scriptions. In this as in other matters relating to this god Semitic influences had undoubtedly prevailed.

Trees were also worshipped in Egypt as well as stones, but there is no evidence that hill worship ever obtained there.[1] The worship of springs could hardly come into consideration, since they were almost entirely lacking in the land, and the worship of water was necessarily confined to that of the Nile. One spring, however, there was: that near Heliopolis, and this was dedicated to the Sun god (p. 18). Special instances of tree worship are comparatively rare. In Ptolemaic times a systematic attempt was made to introduce this form of cult into the temple of every nome : according to the contemporary lists relating to the subject, twenty-four nomes worshipped the Nile acacia, seventeen the *Corda myxa* (?), sixteen the *Zizyphus spina Christi*, while other trees, such as the sycomore, the *Juniperus phoenicea*, and the *Tamarix nilotica*, are named but once or twice. Ten kinds of sacred trees are here mentioned in all, of which as many as three were sometimes worshipped in the same nome.[2] But the connexion of

---

[1] The Ethiopian kings of 800—700 B.C. speak of the hill of Gebel Barkal as the " sacred hill," but it is not clear whether the hill was considered sacred in itself or only on account of the rock cut temple at its base.

LEFÉBURE, *Muséon*, xiv., pp. 316 *et seq.*, has endeavoured to prove that the Egyptians were also fire worshippers, but the illustrations which he adduces only show that fire was sometimes regarded as an attribute of various deities whose functions were compared to the action of fire, especially in the case of the solar deities, and so on ; but that the Egyptians were genuine fire worshippers, in the same sense as the Iranians, is a conclusion which cannot be drawn from Egyptian texts.

[2] Cf. MOLDENKE, *Ueber die in altaeg Texten erwaehnten Baeume*, pp. 8 *et seq.*

this cult with the main worship of the temple was very
loose. The texts do occasionally mention the sacred tree
of Heliopolis growing near the spot where the Âpep
serpent was slain by the solar cat ; out of which also the

FIG. 44.—TÛM, SAFEKHT, AND THOTH INSCRIBING NAME OF RAMESES II. ON
SACRED TREE OF HELIOPOLIS. (L. D. III. 169.)
Temple of Rameses II. at Gûrnah.

phoenix arose, and on its foliage Thoth, or else SAFEKHT,[1]
the goddess of learning, inscribed the name of the king,

[1] For the reading of the name of this goddess cf. CHASSINAT,
Rec. de Travaux, xvii., p. 55.

who by this act was endowed with eternal life. We also read of the sacred tree which grew over the chest containing the body of Osiris,[1] of the tree in the west in which dwelt the goddess Nût or the goddess Hathor (pp. 143, 233), and of others. It is, however, a curious fact that the palm, a tree otherwise so intimately associated with Egyptian thought and feeling, may be said to have no place in this cult.[2] The belief of Porphyrius[3] that the Egyptians deemed it wrong to injure vegetation was the outcome of a late idea founded on pantheistic views.

Although the worship of vegetable life[4] did not, to any appreciable extent, affect the Egyptian religion as displayed in the temple inscriptions, nevertheless I should hesitate to say that it was not indigenous. In the same way little account is taken of animal worship by the Egyptian texts, and yet we know from the testimony of Greek writers that it played a considerable, if not the principal, part in the popular religion. Now these writers were more familiar with the people than with the priesthood and the upper classes, and in Egypt, as elsewhere, the beliefs of the great mass of the nation were not in precise accordance with the doctrine of the priests. Due reverence and tribute were paid to the gods of the great

[1] Cf. DEVÉRIA, *Mémoires*, i., pp. 123 *et seq.*

[2] It is only very occasionally that the palm tree is substituted for the sycomore of Nût, as in the bas relief from the tomb of Naai, now in the Egyptian Museum at Berlin, No. 7322.

[3] PORPHYRIUS, *De Abst.*, i. 21.

[4] For a comprehensive treatise on tree worship, or the cult of vegetable life, based primarily upon the well known investigations of Mannhardt, see J. G. FRAZER : *The Golden Bough*, London, 1890.

temples, but it was to the minor divinities[1] that the people turned in their personal joys and sorrows, and to whom they addressed their prayers and their complaints. Recent investigations have shown how this condition of things developed among the Indo-Germanians, more particularly among the Greeks and Romans;[2] and in Egypt it was not otherwise. Here too it was the first impulse of the peasant to present his humble petitions to his own rustic deity rather than to the god who dwelt within the city in his magnificent abode. Among such deities were many of the sacred animals,[3] and the sacred trees must also be placed in the same category. The shade giving sycomore was the special object of such homage, and it is peasants who are represented on the monuments as paying their devotions to that tree, even as it was the lower orders of the people who zealously offered their prayers and dedicated stelae to the sacred beasts. The upper classes among the Egyptians would look down upon these rustic and plebeian deities with the same contempt as was felt by the cultured Greeks, and Romans for the uncouth gods of the countryfolk. Few of them were admitted within the great temples, and to such as gained admission very insignificant places were usually assigned : often they were deprived of their essential natures and merged in the god

[1] "Sondergötter" (isolated gods) is the present designation in Germany.

[2] On this question cf. more especially the excellent work by H. USENER, *Götternamen*, Bonn, 1896.

[3] On this subject see WIEDEMANN, *Zum Thierkult der alten Aegypter*, in *Mélanges, Charles de Harlez*, Leyden, 1896, pp. 372 *et seq.*

of the temple, either as his incorporations, his attributes, or his symbols; or they were relegated to inferior positions in his court or household. So far as we can judge, the reception of tree worship into temple service and mythology was always the result of a compromise : the priests were compelled to make concessions to the faith of the masses and admit into the temples the worship of the people's divinities; but they did so grudgingly, and this explains the apparent insignificance of the official cult of vegetation in Egypt as compared with the worship of the great gods and their cycles.

The representations of Libyan and Asiatic deities were almost entirely conformed to those of Egyptian gods, in physical appearance, attitude, and symbolism. It was otherwise with gods of African origin, which outwardly resembled the negro human fetish of to-day, and were figured as deformed, monstrously fat, hideous, and frightful; whereas, so far as the rules of Egyptian sacred art admitted, the true Egyptian gods were represented in conformity to the ideal.

BES[1] was the most important of the African gods. He was represented as a bearded dwarf with large ears and with crooked legs, on which he is sometimes resting his long arms, ⚘. He is dressed in the hide of a beast with the tail hanging down behind him, and wears a crown of feathers recalling the headdress of Ânûki, a goddess worshipped in Nubia (p. 131). A further distinction between Bes and the Egyptian gods is that he is generally

---

[1] See an excellent treatise by KRALL in the *Jahrb. d. Wiener kunsth. Samml.*, ix., pp. 72 *et seq.*

drawn in full face while they are ordinarily presented in profile. Many names were given him, such as ḤAIT, ÀḤTI, SEPD, KHERAÛ, in later times especially, but these implied

FIG. 45.—BES. (L. D. IV. 83, c.)
Birth House of Temple of Denderah. Roman Period.

no change in the apprehension of his nature. His usual name was at all periods Bes, a name derived from the word *besa*, which designates one of the great *felidae*, the

Cynaelurus guttatus. It was the skin of this beast which formed his clothing, and most probably he was named after the animal in which, according to Egyptian ideas, he

FIG. 46.—BES. (WOODEN SPOON IN BERLIN MUSEUM.) XVIIIth Dynasty.

sometimes became incarnate. The worship of Bes was an ancient cult; there are indications that it was known in the Old Kingdom, and certainly it was in force at the beginning of the New Kingdom ; while from the time of the XXVIth Dynasty downward it became so popular that many proper names were compounded with his name ; and this fashion was transmitted both to the Greeks in Egypt and to the Copts. The Copts had lost all sense of the meaning of the word, and one of the Christian martyrs of Alexandria is still known to us as Besas. Bes was known in Roman times chiefly by means of his oracle at Abydos, which was often consulted even down to a late period. The figure of Bes supplied a subject to Alexandrian decorative art, and found besides somewhat extended application in the Hellenistic and Phoenician. This explains sufficiently its later appearance on Arabian coins, which, however, affords no proof of any close connexion between the Arabians who used this money and the great centres of Bes worship.[1]

One of the oldest representations of the god Bes is found in a bas relief at Deir el Bahri, in a temple built by Queen Râmâka, better known as Queen Hatshepsût, about 1600 B.C. It occurs in a scene relating to the birth of the founder. In the middle of the top register is the royal mother, sitting in a chair, and holding the new born child in her arms. Left of her are five goddesses who have apparently assisted as midwives, each holding the sign of life in token that life has come to the child by their means ; among them are Isis and Nephthys. In front of the queen kneel four female forms waiting to attend to the infant, and to its *ka*, born at the same time ; they are stretching out

---

[1] Cf. ERMAN, *Zeitschrift für Numismatik*, ix., pp. 296 *et seq.*

IARI," II., PL. LI.)
ri.

their hands in readiness to receive the former. In the middle
row squat three human headed, four crocodile headed, and
one ram headed demon, each of them presenting the sign of
life to the child ; in their midst are symbols signifying that
life, stability, eternal duration, shall be its portion. Immediately below these symbols, and in the lowest register, are
others denoting divine protection, and the sovereignty to
which the babe is destined ; on either side of them are
divinities, mostly in attitude of invocation. Two are hawk
headed ; and the figure of a third, together with that of a
third jackal headed god, doubtless occupied the blank space
to the right of the symbols. The hawk headed gods—
Horus, Àmset, and Ḥapi, according to the Book of the
Dead—are the souls of Pe, the temple of Bûto, and were
held to be the spirits of the North ; the jackal headed
figures—Horus, Dûamûtef, and Kebehsenûf—are the
souls of Nekheb, that is the spirits of the South. Thus
the homage of these divinities symbolically expresses the
homage of Northern and Southern Egypt to the new born
Pharaoh. Near them stand the god Bes and the goddess
Taûrt. All is transacted in the presence of Meskhent, the
goddess of birth, who is shown seated on her throne. The
accompanying texts promise the new born princess life,
stability, might, health, joy, and the rule over Upper and
Lower Egypt on the throne of the god Horus. The subject
of this scene is found, similarly treated, in a bas relief in
the temple of Luxor which represents the birth of King
Amenophis III.[1] There is a similar scene in a temple
of Denderah,[2] dating from about the time of Trajan and

---

[1] Lepsius, *Denkmäler*, iii. 74.   [2] *Ibid.*, iv. 82 *b*.

representing the birth of the Sun god. Here Bes is a seated divinity with the name Ahti. In like connexion the figure of Bes appears in all the " Birth Houses" of Egyptian temples. The "Birth House" of a temple was supposed to have been the birthplace of the god of the temple, and was long known as the Typhonium, because

FIG. 48.—BES AND HAR-
POKRATES. (ARUNDALE
AND BONOMI, PL. 23,
FIG. 82.)
Bronze in British Museum.
Roman Period.

of the grotesque figure of Bes always to be found upon its walls, and which was held to represent Typhon, the god of evil. But this view was altogether unwarranted, and was necessarily relinquished after the decipherment of the hieroglyphics.

In all these scenes Bes is one of the divinities attending the birth of the king, or of the Sun god. He is also shown holding Harpokrates, the young Sun god, upon his left arm while giving him food with his right hand, or bearing the child on his shoulder. But his services to the child were not confined to supplying it with food ; he had also to provide for its amusement, and so he is represented as laughing at it, dancing grotesque dances, and playing on the harp before it. Thus, gradually he came to be considered as the god of the dance, of music, and of jollity, a part to which he seemed predestined even by his absurd appearance. Another office also fell to him as guardian of the young Sun god : serpents being the

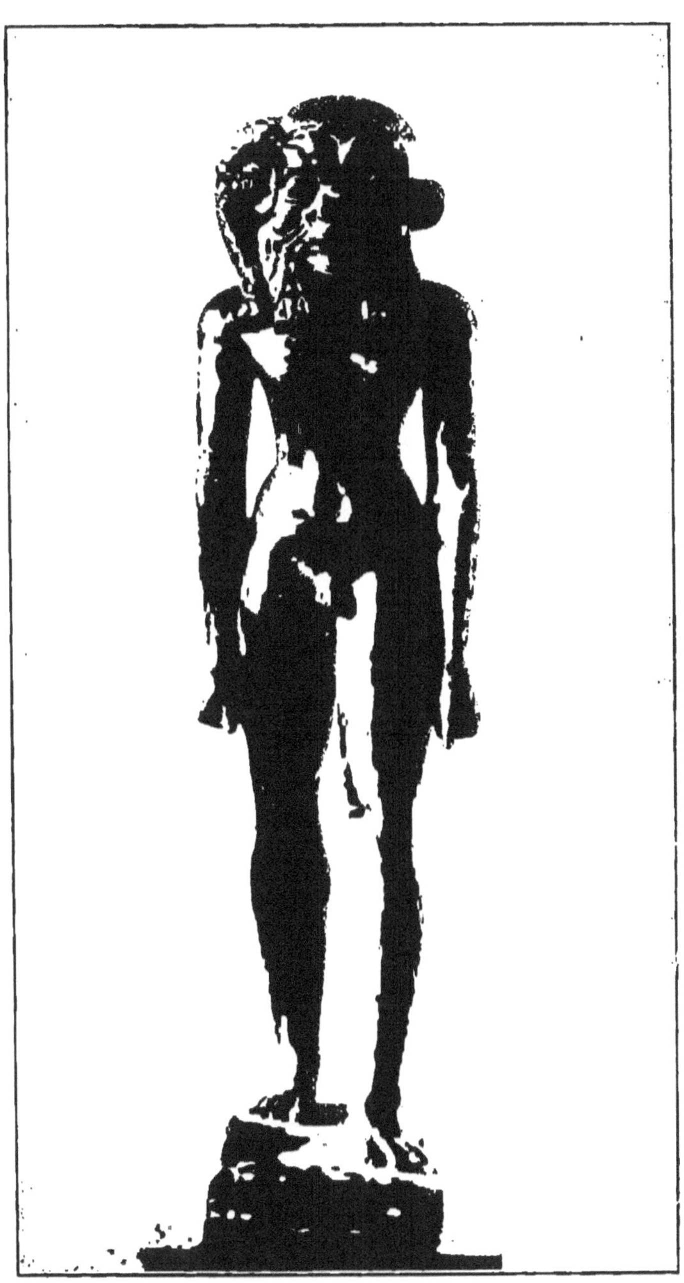

FIG. 49.—SEPD. (BRONZE STATUETTE IN BERLIN MUSEUM.)

chief enemies of the Sun god, Bes was therefore the foe of serpents. He is frequently represented as gripping and strangling them in his hands, or biting them to bits, as does the goddess Taûrt. At the end of the New Kingdom he was fused with his ward, endowed with all the attributes of the young Sun god, and represented like him as sitting upon a lotus flower and wearing the side lock of youth. The solar lions also became connected with him, and he was regarded as one with the god Sepd, lord of the east, conqueror of the hill tribes of the Sinaitic peninsula. Ultimately he was entirely confused with the hawk headed Horus. This, as well as his identification with Amen and even with Osiris Amen, was due to the prevailing syncretism of the Ptolemaic period.

As a solar deity Bes was god of the east. He was therefore lord of Pûnt, *i.e.* of the southern countries on both shores of the Red Sea, and in later times of Arabia in particular, the supposed home of the Sun god and of his sacred bird the phoenix. This comparatively late connexion of Bes with the land of Pûnt is no argument for his Arabian origin. His whole appearance and attire point rather to an African and indeed a negro country to the south of Egypt as the place from which he sprang. In the early days of Egyptian history negroes appear to have dwelt on the southern frontiers of the kingdom, but afterwards a series of Hamitic peoples occupied large territories south of the Egyptian, the negroes having been enslaved or driven farther to the south. The civilization of these Hamitic peoples was dependent on that of the Egyptians ; they therefore venerated, not the original

African conception of Bes, but the form which was then adored in Egypt, only they often represented him as a full grown man instead of as a dwarf.

In the Underworld Bes appears in a somewhat different character. Here, though on purely Egyptian territory, his dwarf form was changed into that of a full grown man, or even of a giant. The Bes of the Underworld was an avenging deity: his distorted face inspired terror; he menaced the wicked with his knife, threatening to tear out their hearts, and hence he was called the Warrior. Subsequently the attempt was made to ascribe this character to him on earth also, except that he was there to be regarded rather as the friend of the good than the enemy of the wicked, and as such he was represented bearing a shield and wielding a sword ready to smite down all who should dare to withstand those who were under his protection and wore his image as an amulet.

TAÛRT, "the great one," is generally figured as a female hippopotamus standing on her hind legs, with a disproportionately large belly and pendent breasts, her fore feet resting on the amulet which represented the blood of Isis. Her headdress is composed of the solar disk and two tall feathers, . Occasionally the figure is human headed, or altogether that of a woman, the head being surmounted with the cow horns which all Egyptian goddesses appear to have been at times entitled to wear. Taûrt was regarded as the mother and nurse of the gods, and assisted at the births of gods and kings alike. She had a counterpart in ÂPET, the hippopotamus goddess of Thebes, to whom a small temple was erected there in Ptolemaic times. Here Apet was supposed by some to have given birth to Osiris, while elsewhere the honour was claimed for the temple of Ombos. Later still Taûrt was known simply as RERT, the female hippopotamus, and represented as dwelling in

FIG. 50.—TAÛRT AND HATHOR COW EMERGING FROM MOUNTAIN OF THE WEST. (L. D. III. 231, *b*.)
Rock tomb at Anibeh, Rameses VI.

the "House of Suckling." Earlier than this, however, the prevailing syncretism had identified her with Isis Hathor, and again with Bast of Bubastis, Bûto of Pelusium, the lioness headed MENḤIT of Heliopolis, RENPT, *i.e.* the

year personified, of Memphis, and other goddesses. Her
image in glazed earthenware formed a favourite amulet,
which, like that of Bes, was held to be a great prophylactic
at childbirth, and was one of the commonest of the many
Egyptian amulets which passed into foreign lands. It
also passed to a certain extent into foreign art, and there
are reminiscences of the figure of Taûrt in Mykenaean
wall scenes.[1] In the cult of the dead the functions of
Taûrt coincided with those of the Hathor Cow, and she
was supposed to be the guardian of the Mountain of the
West through which the road to the realm of the dead lay.
At the end of the New Kingdom she, as well as Bes, found
her way back to Ethiopia, where it would seem that she
had originated when that country was inhabited by negroes
who knew nothing of Egyptian culture. In Egypt proper
her popularity, like that of Bes, dates from the New
Empire, and it greatly increased during the later period in
the history of Egyptian religion, when there was a decided
preference for all that was most extraordinary in the older
texts, special significance being attached to it both in
worship and in belief.

It is a striking fact that at this time, when the tendency
of the Egyptian religion to combine and utilize every
religious phenomenon was so strong, there was apparently
no inclination whatever to be influenced by the religion of
the Greeks. The language, too, which had shown itself to be
very receptive as regards Semitic words, was closed against
both Greek and Latin, and rarely indeed made use of a
term borrowed from either in place of any Egyptian word.

[1] Cf. *Ephemeris archaeologike*, 1887, pl. 10.

In the same way the Egyptian religion remained apparently altogether uninfluenced by the faith of the Macedonian rulers of the land. Only very isolated indications of Greek ideas can be found, such, *e.g.*, as the substitution of the name " Hades " for Dûat (the Underworld) in the texts.[1] At the very time when the Hellenes were displaying the greatest zeal in appropriating the strange gods, simply accepting some of them and proclaiming others as counterparts of their own deities, the Egyptian religion had renounced its former liberality and ceased to adopt foreign deities.

The hatred and contempt of strangers which characterized the Egyptian of the decadence, and which he took pleasure in exhibiting even to his foreign rulers, were feelings which he also ascribed to his gods. They too had a like contempt for this young barbarian people from the north together with all its gods, gods which, as Plato would express it, were without history, and therefore without that trustworthy proof of their reality which ancient traditions afford.

[1] BRUGSCH and DÜMICHEN, *Recueil*, iv., pl. 50, no. 14.

CHAPTER VII.

THE WORSHIP OF ANIMALS.[1]

THE worship of animals has always been regarded as a striking phenomenon of the Egyptian religion : Fathers of the Church considered it one of the most frightful aberrations of the heathen spirit ; Christian apologists employed it as an illustration of the senseless follies of heathen worship ; while Greek philosophers, on the other hand, thought to see in it profound symbolic teaching. Among modern critics of Ancient Egypt also, a similar divergence of opinion prevails on this point. By some the Egyptian worship of animals has been adduced in proof of the existence of a carefully excogitated pantheism, and an appreciative sympathy with animal life ; by others it is likened to the fetishism of the negro, and advanced as evidence of the low plane upon which thought and feeling anciently moved in the Valley of the Nile ; others again take it for a survival of the prehistoric religion of the people, and yet others as the outcome of steady degradation in religious thought.

[1] WIEDEMANN, *Le Culte des Animaux*, in *Le Muséon*, viii., 211, 309 *et seq.; Herodot's Zweites Buch*, pp. 271 *et seq.; Zu dem Thierkult der alten Aegypter*, in *Mélanges Charles de Harlez*, pp. 372 *et seq.*

Something may be said in support of each of these views, yet none is free from error. There is little likelihood now of any attempt being made to exalt animal worship and view it as a particularly noble phase of spiritual life in Egypt, but in this chapter we shall endeavour to show how the Egyptians came to adopt this form of worship by a logical development of belief in accordance with their whole habit of religious thought. In dealing with the subject a clear distinction must be made between two different points of view, subsequently associated and blended : the worship of individual animals, and the setting apart of certain species as sacred.

The idea of an animal incarnation of deity is thoroughly Egyptian. The Egyptian imagined the next world to be even as this, the life of the blessed dead to be as that of the living upon earth, and that the dead also ate and drank, hungered and thirsted, rejoiced and suffered, having in one thing only the advantage over the living : they were no longer tied to a single form, but could change their shapes into those of animals, or plants, or even of gods. Nor was there any essential distinction between gods and men. The life of a god was indeed longer than that of a man, but death put an end to the one as to the other ; and the power of a god, though greater than that of a man, was none the less limited. In every sphere of thought man, and man only, was to the Egyptians the measure of all things.

Since a body is necessary to the exercise of the functions of life, the soul of the dead could not be imagined as an intangible immaterial being, but only as something which lived by means of a body. A god also was in like case ; and in order to associate with mankind he must of necessity become incarnate, otherwise he could not express himself in human speech, nor act with visible effect. We learn from the texts how, in the long conversations between god and king, the god would nod or extend his arms, and how the goddess would act as midwife at the birth of a prince and feed from her own breast the child who was born to rule on earth as representative of the god that had begotten him. To us such ideas are almost necessarily allegorical ; not so to the Egyptian. He was altogether lacking in any faculty for comprehending abstract thought, and could only apprehend what was presented as a concrete reality. The use made of ideograms in the Egyptian script testifies to this realistic state of mind : the Egyptian wished not only to gather the meaning from the characters, but to see it, and hence drew the picture of a crocodile after its written name, of a man drinking after the word "drink," of a figure in the act of striking after the word "strike," and so on. Even for ideas which admitted of no exact representation he devised ideograms, often by means of somewhat complex processes of thought ; for instance, the word meaning " to hunger " is followed by the sign of a man with his finger to his lips, a method of suggestion prompted by the same train of ideas as that which leads the modern Italian beggar to point to his mouth as he says, " Morio di fame ! " Again, the word " bad " is followed by the image of a small bird, birds being the commonest agricultural pest in the country, and the word " pure " by the sign for water, or by that of a man over whom water is being poured ; while words expressing purely abstract ideas, such as "good," "beautiful," etc., were determined by the sign of a papyrus roll, because as written words they had a visible reality. The same impulse moulded the language as well as the script, and Egyptian sentences are so constructed and arranged as to read like the text descriptive of a series of pictures.

This incapacity for abstract thought had its effect upon the Egyptian religion also. The Egyptian was not content to pray trusting that his prayer might be heard by an unseen power, but sought rather to confide it to the very ears of his god. Led by instinctive impulse to picture the deity to himself in human form, he thought to have found this incarnation in the king, who was entitled "the beautiful god," "the great god," "the Horus," and to whom in this capacity petitions were addressed which he himself fulfilled or else transmitted to his parental deities, the celestial gods whose descendant upon earth he was, and with whom he held constant communication. "Thou, O King Merenptah! art as the image of thy father the Sun who riseth in heaven. Thy rays reach even unto the caverns. There is no place where thy goodnesses are not. Thou appointest the law in every land. As thou restest in thy palace thou hearest the words of all lands. Thou art provided with millions of ears. Thine eye is brighter than the star of heaven ; it knoweth to see better than the sun disk. If the mouth utter aught in a cavern, nevertheless it cometh to thine ears. Thine eye seeth that which was done in secret, merciful lord, creator of breath!"[1] This belief in the divinity of the king was maintained throughout Egyptian history : a special cult was instituted in his honour, specially appointed priests officiated in connexion with it, and offerings were made to him. At times the reverence for the divine person of Pharaoh was so excessive that even the kings themselves worshipped themselves, some attempt being made to mitigate the inherent absurdity of the proceeding by the supposition that the king's prayers were not addressed positively to himself, but to his ka[2]—the ka of a man being one of the immortal constituents of his being— and no incongruity was felt in the idea of lengthy conversations between the king and his own ka, in which the ka graciously granted him Joy, Prosperity, Health, and Power at his heart's desire.

But though looked upon as a god the king was by no means regarded as the only one : other members of the Pantheon ranked with him and above him. Nor was he omnipresent. If the king resided in Tanis, then Memphis would be without visible deity, and so on : a state of matters intolerable to the Egyptian, who always desired the possibility of daily and even hourly communion with his gods. The natural resource was to imagine other gods as dwelling on earth in human form besides the god incarnate in the king ; and indeed the historic titles of the nomarchs would seem to indicate that these princes also had been regarded as gods in prehistoric times. But in later times we find

---

[1] *Anastasi Papyrus*, iv., p. 5, ll. 6 *et seq.* = *Anastasi Papyrus*, ii., p. 5, ll. 6 *et seq.*

[2] For a definition of the ka see below, pp. 240-2.

only isolated instances of such a practice. We see, for
instance, from a funerary stela that a high official early in
the XIXth Dynasty was entitled " the god," and worshipped
as such by one of his subordinates ; and at a later date,
according to some of the earliest Christian writers, it was
the practice in Anabe—a place of which we know no
other mention—to choose out a man for worship and
to make offerings to him.[1] But for the rest, and apart
from the recognized divinity of the king, living human
incarnations of deity were in historic times everywhere
supplied by other, and particularly animal, incorporations.

The cause of this change may doubtless be ascribed, in
the first place, to considerations of practical expediency.
If other men than the kings were regarded as gods
incarnate, it might very well happen that the differences of
opinion which would inevitably arise among them would
set the gods at variance one with another, and thus bring
about a condition of affairs highly dangerous to the
stability of the state.   The worship of animals involved no
such dangers.   On the one hand, through their sensibility
and power of action they were able to express their desires
by movements, and also to eat and drink ; and thus they
exposed themselves to that material apprehension of which
a deity must have been capable in order to suit the Ancient
Egyptian mind.   And, on the other hand, it was easy so to
manage them that movements apparently made at their
own impulse were in reality the response to given signals
by means of which the priests, or even the king himself,
brought about the supposed expression of the creatures'

WIEDEMANN, *Proc. Soc. Bib. Arch.*, xiv., p. 335.

will. For in the strength of his belief in his own divinity the king would be blind to the absurdity of wilfully imposing upon himself by extorting from the god consent to his own wishes and the answer which he had himself determined upon. The Egyptian was certainly not so consciously reverent as to subordinate his wishes to the will of his gods—nay rather, he sought to force his own views upon them. If the sacred beasts could not or would not help in emergency, they were beaten ; and if this measure failed to prove efficacious, then the creatures were punished by death. Similar superstitious practices are to be found among the lower classes of widely alien races. When Heaven does not fulfil the desires of the people, the offence is visited by them upon idols, or statues of the saints, according to nationality. But in the Valley of the Nile such ideas were not cherished by the people alone ; it was particularly among the upper classes that these low conceptions of deity prevailed, and it was the priests themselves who condemned and executed the sacred animal. Afterwards, indeed, they sought to secure its immortality by the embalmment of the body, thereby hoping to appease the wrath of the god, lest he should avenge the killing of the creature in which he had been incarnate.

In fixing upon certain animals as being respectively the incarnations of certain deities, the Egyptian was guided by what he considered the salient characteristics of the different divinities and of the different species of animal in question. To the gods of nature in its annual rejuvenescence were assigned animals supposed to be possessed of exceptional procreative vigour, such as the bull and ram; while animals such as the cow were dedicated to the fertile and food producing deities; and serpents owed their deification to their stealthy movements, to their deadly power, and also to an occasional trustful familiarity by which all nations have been impressed. The association of the hawk with sun gods was obviously suggested by the bird's soaring and hovering in high heaven; and the crocodile, lying inert upon the bank, but terrible and devouring when roused, was the embodiment of the dignity and self conscious power which have always appealed to the reverence of Orientals. A list of the sacred animals of Egypt would contain not only all the more important representations of the Egyptian fauna—mammals, fish, reptiles, and insects,—but many imaginary creatures, such as the sphinx, the animal of the god Set, and the griffin. To the Egyptian these were no creatures of fancy, but real inhabitants of the desert, no matter how rarely they might be seen of men. A XIIth Dynasty representation of a hunting scene exhibits, side by side with gazelles and other animals, quadrupeds with heads of monsters, with heads growing out of their backs, etc.—creatures which the high official in whose tomb they are figured believed himself to have seen during his lifetime, although it might be only in the distance.[1] They are, indeed, scarcely to be classed as mere creatures of imagination. To primitive man all things which his fancy paints or

---

[1] LEPSIUS, *Denkmäler*, ii. 131; GRIFFITH and NEWBERRY, *Beni Hasan*, i., pl. xxx.

a dream presents to him are realities, and a firm faith
in the existence of fabulous monsters has always been
characteristic of races dwelling in the desert ; they are
convinced that these things have been seen either by
themselves or by their forefathers.   Alone and helpless in
the darkness of night, and thus left a prey to impressions,
they took the simplest occurrences for the most terrible
phenomena, and afterwards felt no hesitation in announcing
as facts the illusions of their fear.

A sacred animal was "the renewed life" of the god
incorporate in it : that is, it was a renewal of the life which
had perished with the animal's immediate predecessor in
the temple.   It was distinguished from others of its
species by certain marks known to the priests.   The Apis
is said to have had twenty-nine such marks, but they are
differently specified by different writers.   According to
Herodotus the bull was "black, with a square spot of
white upon his forehead, and on his back the figure of
an eagle; the hairs on his tail are double, and there is
a beetle on his tongue."   But there is some uncertainty
as to the accuracy of these data : we find, for example, in
images of the Apis that the spot upon its forehead is
triangular.   When the right animal had been found and
had passed through a certain training it was then solemnly
introduced into the temple.   It was long assumed, and still
the assumption is current, that the Egyptian temple centred
round a statue.   This was not the case.   The numerous
statues set up in a temple were votive images dedicated
either by kings or private individuals for the adornment
of the building and the future welfare of the bestower ;

the processions did indeed pass before them, but generally speaking it was not to them that the temple prayers and offerings were made, but to something alive—in short, to the sacred animal of the place.[1]

In a passage quoted by Origen[2] from the work of Celsus against Christianity we read : " If a stranger reaches Egypt he is struck by the splendid temples and sacred groves that he sees, great and magnificent courts, marvellous temples with pleasant walks about them, imposing and occult ceremonies ; but when he has entered into the innermost sanctuary he finds the god worshipped in these buildings to be a cat, or an ape, or a crocodile, or a he goat, or a dog." With this statement Clemens of Alexandria and Lucian alike agree. Their testimony on this point is often rejected as a malicious invention, but such a man as Celsus would have been far more disposed to pass over in silence whatever might detract from the dignity of the Egyptians than to invent anything to their ridicule. His mention of such a thing is the best proof that it was a reference to a known fact, to an institution regarded by the Egyptians as a matter of course.

And in fact how could an Egyptian, believing that he

---

[1] This statement of course applies only to temples in which, according to Egyptian views, the godhead was supposed to dwell, and not to temples elsewhere dedicated to the same form of the same deity but only occasionally visited by him, and which must have contained an image of the god which should represent him in the intervals of his visits. Thus, for example, in Thebes Amen Râ of the great temple of Karnak as incarnate in a ram, could reside in his own temple only ; all other temples there dedicated to him could possess but his symbol, and this would generally be his statue.

[2] iii. 17.

possessed his god himself in animal form, be ashamed to
admit the possession so long as he retained any conviction
of the existence and power of his gods ; and of these he
never seriously doubted.   However divergent the views
which the Egyptians cherished concerning their gods, and
however variously they pictured the life beyond death and
the relationship to deity which man would assume in it, a
genuinely atheistic attitude of mind was utterly foreign to
the Egyptian race.   It was not until they had come to
know something of higher forms of religious belief that the
people began to perceive the anomalous nature of the
worship of animals, and to explain it as the mystic cult of
mere symbols of deity, this change being due to the combined influences of Greek philosophy and of Christian
teaching, influences which even Egyptian heathendom
could not altogether evade.   But in so far as the Egyptian
religion remained intact the divine nature of certain
animals never ceased to be one of the fundamental dogmas
of its doctrine.

The death of the. sacred animal did not involve the
death of the god whom it represented, nor the loss of its
own personal identity.   Though the dislodged deity at
once sought fresh incarnation in another animal of the
same species and appearance as that which had died, the
soul of the latter was immortal.   According to the doctrine
which taught that the dead man became an Osiris, so did
the dead Apis become an Osiris Apis, the dead ram of the
temple an Osiris ram, etc.   In all these cases the same
rites were performed for the animal as for the human
mummy : it was embalmed and provided with amulets for

that world beyond death in which its soul would henceforth
live for ever.   The increasing number of the Apis bulls, of
the divine rams and crocodiles which he was thus re-
legating to the next world, suggested no embarrassments to
the Egyptian, although he believed the soul of each sacred
animal to be of unconditioned divinity ; for thus too the
deceased Pharaoh was supposed to remain King of Upper
and Lower Egypt in the next world, notwithstanding the
presence there of his predecessors on the throne, who
continued to hold the same rank and were rivals therefore
for the same position.   The Egyptians did not attempt
to systematize their eschatological beliefs, and on such
matters the illogical and absurd presented to them no
occasions of stumbling in their processes of thought.

Considering how great a part was assigned to the sacred
animals in worship, we cannot fail to be struck by the
comparative rareness with which they are represented in
the wall scenes : among other representations of deity the
images of animals occur scarcely in the proportion of one
in a thousand, the gods being shown either in human form
or as having human bodies and animal heads.   A deity
figured in human form generally bore the features of the
reigning king or of his consort.   The Egyptians, who laid
special emphasis on the divine power of voluntary trans-
formation, naturally supposed that the higher being would
occasionally assume human form for the purpose of holding
converse with the king on equal terms, and they further
represented the god as exactly resembling the king because
the latter was always accounted his son.   But the composite figures, part animal and part human, were not

intended to present any real forms of the divinity : they
were simply used as ideographic substitutes for the divine
image, and this for artistic reasons.   It was a strict canon
of Egyptian art that in the composition of a scene all the
figures should be drawn as of the same height ; excepting
only that a deity among common men, a Pharaoh among
his subjects, a master among his servants, is represented
as greatly excelling his subordinates in stature, this being
the pictorial expression of his superiority in rank.   Since
king and god were regarded as of equal rank, both
must therefore be represented as of the same stature, and
the effect would have been absurd had the god been
figured altogether in the likeness of his sacred animal.
Imagine the composition of a scene in which a crocodile
stood as tall as the king, with its body drawn in full
proportion !   Occasionally the expedient was adopted of
placing the sacred animal on a pedestal and thus raising
him to the required height ; but the style usually preferred
was that in which the god was figured in human form and
the animal signified by the head which he bore.   This
method of representation had the further advantage that
the composite figure could be shown as in the act of
moving hands and feet, of embracing the king, of presenting him with the sign of life ; or if a goddess were in
question she might even be represented as suckling the
sovereign, a situation which would at once strike the
spectator as strange were she figured simply as her sacred
animal.[1]

   In considering some of the ideas connected with the

   [1] Such representations are, however, occasionally met with : for

worship of sacred animals which were counted as gods, and the slaughter of which by a layman was regarded as deicide and punished by death, it is to be noted that an animal thus honoured was always a single individual of its kind and differentiated from the rest of its species by certain outward marks. But the respect in which whole species of animals were held in the different nomes is quite another thing. In these cases the animals were not honoured as gods, but rather as specially favoured by the gods ; because it was believed that the animal form in question was that assumed by preference during his sojourn upon earth by the deity to whom it was sacred, and protection was extended to the whole species lest any one representative might happen to be killed at a moment in which it was serving as the incarnation of the god. In some places also uncertainty as to the marks distinguishing the animal which was the incarnate god from the rest of its kind induced the inhabitants to spare the whole species in order to obviate any risk of injury to the one sacred animal. This respect for whole species of animals was but loosely connected with the prevalent religion of the land, and even down to the present day we may find similar instances of it among very various races : in many parts of Germany, for example, the peasant thinks it a serious crime to hurt a stork. Animals, as species, were not worshipped in Egypt, but they were in

instance, a bas relief at Florence, No. 1225 (PETRIE, *Photographs*, No. 232), represents the king Horemheb sucking a cow, the embodiment of the goddess Hathor, and there is a similar scene in the Hathor Shrine at Deir el Bahri.

certain instances tended and held exempt from slaughter, and sometimes were also embalmed. The latter attention was bestowed apparently in order to assure to the creatures the full and perfect immortality to which mummification was essential; and it was assumed that the god who favoured the particular species would show his gratitude to any who ensured complete immortality to one of his favourites. Deceased animals so treated also became Osiris animals, but they were not divinities of the next world like the Osiris Apis; they took no higher rank there than here, even as the Osiris of a slave remained a slave, and the Osiris of a peasant a peasant.

Different species were protected in different nomes, and down to the times of the Roman emperors these differences led to positive wars between nome and nome, the populace of one nome refusing to tolerate that animals which to them were sacred should be killed and eaten in an adjacent district. To the present time popular respect for certain kinds of animals has lingered on in Egypt. So long as there were crocodiles in the Valley of the Nile, so long were they objects of reverence to the Egyptian; and cats, which his forefathers believed to be favourites of several of the goddesses whom they worshipped, are regarded by him to this day with peculiar affection. In the case of the cats, the attempt to explain away this heathen survival of sentiment and practice as Muhammedan, by alleging Muhammed's fondness for cats as its origin, is obviously futile, since the creatures are if anything more respected by Copts than by Muhammedans.

Among the sacred animals which were accorded divine

honours as individuals, and not merely respected as belonging to certain kinds, four are of exceptional importance
and are often mentioned both by Greek writers and
in the inscriptions. These are the Apis bull, the Sukhos
crocodile, the Phoenix, and the Sphinx. The first and

FIG. 51.—APIS BULL. (BRONZE IN FRANKFORT MUSEUM.)

second of these were real animals actually dwelling in
the temples, but Phoenix and Sphinx had their being only
in the imaginations of their worshippers.

APIS, Egyptian *Hapi*, was the name of the sacred bull
of Memphis. The worship of the Apis is as old as
Egyptian history, and was still practised in Roman times:

monuments dating from the time of the IVth Dynasty make mention of its priests, and we read of the disturbances which attended the discovery of a new Apis in the reign of Hadrian, and that a solemn induction of a sacred bull took place in Memphis even under Julian. The Apis was supposed to have been begotten by a deity descending as a ray of moonlight on the cow which was to become the mother of the sacred beast ; hence he was regarded as the son of the god. The bull elect was known by his marks, and when the old Apis died the priests sought among the Egyptain herds for its successor, traversing the whole land in their quest, but sometimes without much result for a year. When at length they succeeded a rich guerdon was bestowed upon the owner of the divine bull, great reverence was paid to the cow which had borne him, and a temple was raised in her honour. The discoverer of the new Apis also received large sums of money, sometimes amounting to as much as one hundred talents of gold. The animal itself was led to Nilopolis in Lower Egypt, and here its training was so far accomplished as to admit of its being duly brought into Memphis, whither it journeyed at moonrise in the gilded cabin of a sacred bark, henceforth to dwell in the temple of Ptah. Here, in Strabo's time, visitors who were not satisfied with gazing at the animal through a window in its stall might behold it bounding in the magnificent courtyard which had been built for it by King Psammetichus.

Great honours were paid to the Apis : the Pharaohs expended their riches lavishly on its cult, and Alexander the Great and even Titus deemed it necessary to present it with offerings. But chiefly it was renowned for its oracles, which were imparted in very various ways. When the bull licked the garments of the celebrated Eudoxus of Cnidus this signified the astronomer's approaching death; a like fate was predicted to Germanicus when it refused to eat at his hand; and the conquest of Egypt by Augustus was announced beforehand by its bellowing. Some inquiries were answered by the animal's passing into one or other of the two rooms placed at its disposition, and others by dreams which were vouchsafed to inquirers who slept in the temple and which were explained by the sacred interpreters. Other inquiries, again, though presented to the creature itself, found their reply through the voices of children playing before the temple, whose words assumed to the believing inquirer the form of a rhythmic answer to his question. Prophecies of a general kind took place during the procession of the Apis. " Then the youths who accompanied him sang hymns in his honour, while the Apis appeared to understand all and to desire that he should be worshipped. Suddenly the spirit took possession of the youths and they prophesied."[1]

Thus honoured, the Apis lived on in the temple until it died a natural death. This event was the occasion for a national mourning, and the body of the bull was solemnly embalmed and carried to its last resting place. The tombs of the sacred bulls of Memphis, at least from the middle of the XVIIIth Dynasty, that is from about 1500 B.C. onward, were discovered by Mariette in 1851. The

---

[1] PLINY, *Hist. Nat.*, viii. 185.

gigantic and generally monolithic sarcophagi, weighing on an average fifty-eight tons each, stand singly in separate

FIG. 52.—APIS STELA.　(IN BERLIN MUSEUM.)

rooms, which in some cases lie apart beneath small chapels, but in others are connected by an extended system of passages. / Mariette found that some of the sarcophagi still contained the mummies of the bulls, and one of the tombs which he opened had been left absolutely undisturbed from the time that it had been closed after the interment of the Apis : the footprints of the last Egyptian who had left the chamber some three thousand years ago were still visible. Within and without the chapels were many votive stelae and statues, dedicated by pilgrims who had journeyed to the spot once more to do reverence to the Apis who had recently departed, in hopes of thereby gaining his favour and the fulfilment of their various wishes. The soul of the Apis was supposed to have been received into heaven as the Osiris Apis, and was regarded henceforth almost as a Double of Osiris. It was indeed in this form that Osiris was generally recognized by the Greeks, who, having endowed him with attributes derived from Pluto and Asklepios, named this half Greek, half Egyptian deity SARAPIS or SERAPIS. Under the Romans the worship of Serapis extended throughout the empire, having its devotees in every province ; wherever Roman legions penetrated inscriptions making mention of his name have almost invariably been found, and he rather than Osiris himself was regarded as the consort of Isis. And since Egyptian symbols and amulets were considered necessary to a proper observance of this cult, both in temple and in home, genuine Egyptian antiquities of all sorts and sizes, from tallest obelisk to tiniest amulet, are found in abundance in all countries which once formed part of the Roman Empire.

SUKHOS, the crocodile, was the incarnation of the god *Sebâk*,[1] and dwelt in a lake near Krokodilopolis, in the

---

[1] See above, pp. 143-5.

Fayûm. To its priests the creature was tame, and Strabo,[1] who was in Egypt during the reign of the Emperor Augustus, gives the following account of his own visit to the crocodile god: "Our host, a highly respected man who showed us the sacred things at Krokodilopolis, went with us to the lake, taking with him from the table a small cake of bread, roasted meat, and a flask of honey wine. We found the animal lying on the bank. The priests approached it, and while some opened its jaws another put into its mouth first the cake, and then the meat, and

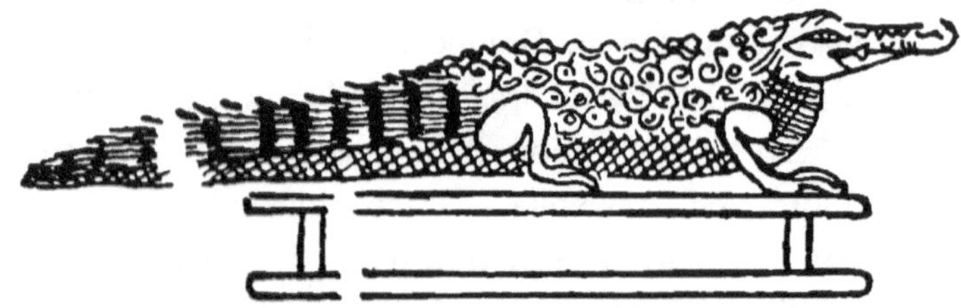

FIG. 53.—SEBÀK (SUKHOS), THE CROCODILE GOD OF THE FAYÛM.
(PLEYTE, "PAPYRUS OF LAKE MOERIS," PL. II.)
Late Ptolemaic.

afterwards poured in the honey wine. Then the animal plunged into the lake and swam to the opposite bank. Meanwhile there came another visitor bringing a like offering; this the priests received and went round to the other side of the lake. When they had found the animal they gave it the fresh offering after the same manner as before." As with the worship of Apis, so also with that of Sukhos: it lasted far into Roman times, the god being then known by the name of *Petesûkhos*, "the gift of its Sukhos"; he is even mentioned in Fayûm papyri of the

[1] xvii. 812.

third century A.D. Sukhos also had his oracle : when on one occasion he would neither listen to King Ptolemaeus nor give heed to his own priests, this signified the approaching demise of the sovereign. After death the body of the sacred reptile was carefully embalmed and laid away in one of the subterranean chambers of the Labyrinth, and so sacred was the place of interment that Herodotus was not allowed to visit it.

The PHOENIX,[1] Egyptian *bennû*, which classic and Christian artists often represented as an eagle, was imagined by the Egyptians rather as a heron, and was depicted with two long feathers growing out at the back of its head, and sometimes also with a tuft hanging from its breast,  . The name *bennû* signifies "that which revolves" or "turns back." Myths told how the bird was born from the midst of flames which arose from out of the summit of a tree in

FIG. 54.
THE BENNÛ (PHOENIX).
(LEPS., "TODT." CH. 83.)
Ptolemaic Papyrus.

Heliopolis, and that it was known to men by the beauty of its song, to which even the Sun himself loved to listen. The Phoenix symbolized the morning sun arising out of that fiery glow of dawn which dies away as the new born luminary ascends the sky, and hence was regarded as the bird of Râ. But since the dead Sun was held to become an Osiris and the new Sun to arise from the embalmed body of the old which had been duly brought to

[1] WIEDEMANN, *Aeg. Zeit.*, 1878, pp. 89 *et seq.*

Heliopolis, in like manner also the Phoenix was supposed to be a form of Osiris in which the god returned to his own country. Further, as on the death of the Sun it was from the Osiris Sun that the Phoenix Sun arose, so it was taught in the case of humanity also that it was from his own Osiris that there sprang the new man of the resurrection, and of this resurrection the Phoenix became a symbol from a very early date. Hence, even in funerary texts of the Old Kingdom the deceased was likened to the Phoenix : later it continued to serve as a symbol of the resurrection, and as such it is mentioned in patristic literature and figures in earliest Christian art.

The SPHINX of the Egyptian had little in common with the Sphinx of the Greeks, beyond the name given to it by the latter people. When the Greeks first came into the Valley of the Nile and there saw figures of human headed quadrupeds, they remembered that at home also there was the tradition of such a creature, and that it was named "sphinx." This name they bestowed, therefore, not unnaturally, upon the creature of Egyptian myth, undisturbed by the fact that there was no real similarity between the two conceptions. The Egyptian sphinx plays the part of guardian of a temple or deity, and hence the god ÀKER, the watchman of the Underworld and the guardian of the god Râ during the hours of the night, is generally shown as a Sphinx with the body of a lion when represented as going forth to destroy the enemies of the Sun god. As the image of the Winged Solar Disk over the door of a temple by its mere presence prevented any evil thing from entering within the sacred halls, so the couchant sphinxes guarding

FIG. 55.—GREAT SPHINX OF GÎZEH.
As excavated by Brugsch Bey in 1886-7.

the approach served to keep back any enemy of the god of the place from the gates of the divine abode. In tombs also, especially those of later date, sphinxes were placed in the capacity of guardians. In one such instance the sphinx is made to address the deceased as follows : " I protect the chapel of thy tomb, I guard thy sepulchral chamber, I ward off the intruding stranger, I cast down the foes to the ground and their arms with them, I drive away the wicked one from the chapel of thy tomb, I destroy thine adversaries in their lurking place, blocking it that they no more come forth."[1]

Primarily the sphinx represented an imaginary quadruped living in the desert, human headed, and supposed to be the favourite incarnation assumed by Râ the Sun god when he desired to protect his friends and adherents. This is the conception embodied in the gigantic Sphinx near the pyramids of Gîzeh, hewn out of the living rock and standing seventy-five feet above the plain of the desert. Sculptured in remote antiquity, here it couched even in the time of Khephren, builder of the second pyramid, guarding the necropolis against the approach of evil genii. It faced the east and the rising sun, being itself one of the manifestations of the Sun god, and more especially dedicated to the Sun of the morning, banisher of the mists of the night. Hence it bears the name of Khepera as well as Râ Harmakhis. Between the fore feet was a small temple approached by a flight of steps and containing stelae and inscriptions relating to the worship of the Sphinx ; but the temple was by no means always accessible, for in ancient

[1] BERGMANN, *Aeg. Zeit.*, 1880, p. 50.

times as now it was repeatedly buried by the whirling sands of the surrounding desert. An extant stela [1] tells us how one day when Thothmosis IV. was out hunting and took his siesta in the shadow of the great Sphinx, the god Râ Harmakhis himself appeared to him in a dream, ordering him to clear away the sand from the divine image. But the work of the king was of no lasting avail; the sands soon drifted back again, covering the stela erected to commemorate the royal excavation. Later the Sphinx would seem to have been cleared by Rameses II., for his name frequently recurs in the inscriptions of its temple; but again the sands swept back. No mention of the great image is to be found in Herodotus, although reference is made to it by later Greek writers. More than once in the present century the sand has been cleared away, only to return as of old. Nothing is now to be seen but the face, gazing out over the desert, still majestic, though sorely mutilated by the Arabs. To them the Sphinx is known as the " Father of Terror," as if in recollection of its ancient significance. And so obviously does the figure produce the impression which it was intended to convey that, long before its exact office was made known to us by the decipherment of the hieroglyphics, the great Sphinx of Gizeh was described by travellers as the guardian of the necropolis near the pyramids.

Few indications of the existence of sphinxes in the Old Kingdom remain; the predilection for them prevailed

---

[1] LEPSIUS, *Denk.*, iii. 68, translated by BRUGSCH, *Aeg. Zeit.*, 1876, pp. 89 *et seq.*

chiefly from the time of the XIIth Dynasty to that of
the Ptolemies. The face of this manifestation of the
deity was generally modelled after that of the reigning
sovereign, for similar reasons to those which led the
Egyptians to represent their gods in the likeness of their
Pharaohs (p. 183); and since the sovereign was usually a
king, as a rule the sphinxes were male sphinxes, as in
the case of the Amasis sphinxes at Sais mentioned by
Herodotus. But the sphinxes of a temple founded by
a queen might well be female sphinxes, more especially
if they were also intended to serve as representations of a
goddess. For a sphinx was not regarded as belonging
exclusively to Râ: its form was not only adopted by
the god Aker in his capacity of guardian to the Sun god,
but also by various other tutelary deities, as, for example,
occasionally by Isis when she appears as the guardian
of her spouse Osiris.

This fact further explains how it came to pass that a
sphinx was sometimes sculptured with other than a
human head—for example, the head of a hawk or of
a jackal—the animal head substituted being that ascribed
to the sacred animal of the deity who was supposed
to have chosen the sphinx for his incorporation. But
the stone rams, lions, etc., which we find as amulets,
or which in many instances occupy the same position
before Egyptian temples as the sphinxes, must by no
means be confounded with the sphinxes: each was
simply an image of the sacred animal of the god of the
place, of the creature in which he took incarnate form,
and each was therefore the equivalent of the statue of the

god. There is no authority whatever for calling these objects by the name of sphinxes, and the mistaken nomenclature has arisen only from the fact that their office was the same, architecturally speaking.

The Egyptian temple was built with a double end in view. It was, in the first place, the abode of the god, or rather of his sacred animal, and provided accommodation for the assembling together of his worshippers with prayer or offerings. In the second place, from prehistoric times it was the fortress from which god and worshippers might defend themselves against the common foe in the days when nome strove against nome for the supremacy, and no Pharaoh had as yet appeared to compose their differences and prevent the opposition of individual interests and party passions from issuing in violent outbreaks. Then, as now, where savage races are concerned, the conquest of a country or district involved the destruction of the local deity and the slaughter of his sacred animal, and Kambyses and Okhus did no more than follow the example of the early Egyptians themselves when the one attempted to kill the Apis and the other commanded the slaughter of the sacred bull and of the ram of Mendes. It was to guard against such contingencies that the abode of the god was made the fortress of his domain, the citadel into which his followers flocked together for their final stand against the foe. But the defensive character of such buildings was maintained in the Valley of the Nile even after the consolidation of the empire and the gradual formation of a national pantheon which included all local divinities had abolished or

minimized this threatened danger to the temples of the
gods. From earliest to latest times the ground plan of
the Egyptian temple remained practically unchanged in
its essential parts.

The chief room of the temple
was the sanctuary, and within
this was the naos, a rectangular
box opening in front, often with
a door of lattice work, and
serving in some cases as the
cage of the sacred animal, and
in others for whatever object
was supposed to be the incorporation of the god. But in
those exceptional temples where
several deities were alike
honoured there might be several
sanctuaries side by side instead
of one only. The sanctuary was
more or less surrounded by
chambers, generally dark, and
which served as storerooms for
the temple furniture, sacred
garments, processional barks,
standards, and the like. In
front of the sanctuary and its
surroundings lay the hypostyle
court, lighted dimly by windows
near the roof and opening to the sanctuary by a narrow
and somewhat low doorway. Opposite to this, on

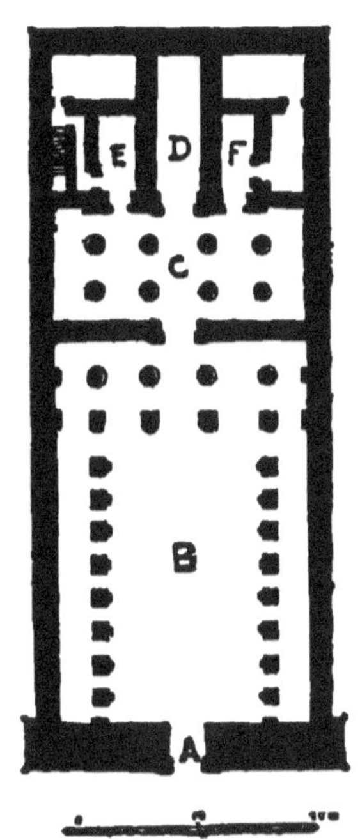

FIG. 56.—PLAN OF SMALL TEMPLE
OF RAMESES II. TO AMEN, AT
KARNAK. (WIEDEMANN, "GESCH.
ALT. AEG.," P. 287.)

A. Entrance Pylon.
B. Hypaethral Court.
C. Hypostyle Hall.
D. Sanctuary.
E & F. Store Chambers.

the other side of the hypostyle hall, another and hardly larger doorway led into a second court, open to the sky. This court was as a rule colonnaded only on either side, but occasionally also a series of columns traversed the centre, as is the case in the temple of Karnak. It was entered from without through a colossal gateway mainly consisting of two great and wide towers, each tower having its four sides sloping regularly and slightly inward. The passage between the towers was but narrow and could easily be defended from their parapets. Such gateways are now known to us as pylons, and the entrance from the hypaethral to the hypostyle court was also, generally speaking, through a pylon. The passage of the great pylon was often fitted with wooden doors plated with precious metal and glittering in the sun. In addition to the chief entrance there were only small side posterns by which admission to the temple could be gained ; and these could easily be barred against a foe, and from them, if need were, sorties could be made.

Generally an obelisk was erected before each tower of the pylon ; between either tower and its obelisk was placed a seated statue of the royal founder, and in front of the pylon were four or eight tall masts from which gaily coloured streamers waved,[1] and which were intended to serve in some mystic way to ward off evil from the temple, as was also an image of the Winged Sun Disk over the doorway. The inner walls of the temple from pylon to sanctuary were adorned with scenes arranged, as it would

---

[1] LEPSIUS, *Denkm.*, iii. 243 (temple of Khûnsû at Karnak); MARIETTE, *Mon. Div.*, pl. 30*a* (temple of Ptah at Memphis).

seem, in a certain prescribed order. The whole series
formed a kind of guide book for the use of the king
on his visits to the temple, representing as they did the
course of the various ceremonies which it was incumbent
on him to perform on such occasions. The series
commences at the outer pylon and extends to the innermost chamber, the right and left walls always corresponding
in subject. Almost invariably the god of the place is
represented as facing towards the entrance and the
king as advancing into the building to meet him. The
ceremonial order of the scenes was but rarely interrupted
by historical texts, scenes of battle, or the like, these being
more usually sculptured upon the outer walls of the temple.
Yet they also were considered as being essentially temple
texts and scenes, for to the Egyptian every war in which
his country engaged was a holy war, counselled and planned
by the great god himself, even in such details as a command
that the king should not go out to fight in person—a command, by the bye, which, when inculcated on Merenptah,
was very favourably received by that king, who does not
seem to have been remarkable for his personal valour.
But if the king himself went forth to battle with his
host, then the god hovered over him as a bird, protecting
him, granting victory to his arms, and even assuming
human form to fight at Pharaoh's side in his hour of peril.
Since the god had conducted the war, it was to him that
the victorious king made offering of all the best of the
spoil—gold, slaves, and the revenues of cities—while inscriptions celebrating the main incidents of the war, and more
especially the victory, were duly placed within his house.

For were not these in truth the deeds of the god, and the king the divine son who had acted throughout the war only as the instrument and in the interests of the god? The front walls of the pylon were almost invariably sculptured with a scene of victory. We see the king as he slays before his god a group of imploring prisoners, and this not only represented an actual occurrence—the human sacrifice celebrated by the Pharaoh before his god after a victorious return from war[1]—but also served as a terrible example to the enemies of that god, who might see depicted here the fate of all those who attempted to oppose the divine power.

A wall, or more commonly an earthwork, surrounded the temple temenos, and occasionally included other temples, groves of trees in which birds made their nests, lakes upon which the temple barks floated, dwellings also for the priests, and sometimes even palaces, as it would seem. The only access to the temenos was through gates in the enclosure wall directly opposite to the pylons. Sacred ways led up to them, and along these funerals passed, images of the gods were borne in procession, and the king came to make offerings in the temple. These ways were connected with the Nile by flights of steps, at the foot of which the barks for the service of the temple and of the dead were anchored; they were often flanked on either side by a row of sphinxes placed at regular intervals and confronting each other across the road, or more generally by images of the sacred animal of the temple inscribed in honour of the royal founder and occasionally holding

---

[1] Cf. WIEDEMANN, *Le Muséon*, xiii., p. 455.

his statue between the outstretched paws. These stone figures of the sacred animals were numbered by thousands; at Thebes, for example, there were whole avenues of rams. They guarded the Via Sacra and marked the boundaries of the sacred domain. Even in processions the god had no need to leave his own property, for sacred ways passed from temple to temple, through cities and fields, and also to the place of embalmment and to the tombs; for the dead who were carried thither had themselves become as gods and were protected as far as possible from passing along unconsecrated ground.

The barriers presented by the rows of sphinxes or sacred animals and by the enclosure wall of the temple were the only ones which separated god from man in the Valley of the Nile. He who had a pure heart and was a faithful follower of the gods might walk the sacred way at festivals and enter the temple in the train of the procession; he might listen to the chant of the priests and reverently gaze into the mysterious and lamp lit darkness of the Holy of Holies, wherein the god himself moved in his animal form. No division of the people into Esoterics, with a knowledge of the hidden mysteries of the religion, and Exoterics, who assisted at the sacred rites only from without but might not enter into the temple, or at any rate into the sanctuary, is mentioned in Egyptian texts, whatever theories may have been advanced on the subject by modern scholars. Of course the Egyptians would no more have allowed than we ourselves should that any manner of man might enter a temple at his pleasure and pass without restrictions into the Holy of Holies. To this end a certain preparation was exacted, chiefly consisting in prayers, fasting, and ablutions; but no one was of necessity excluded from the mysteries of the Egyptian religion: these were as accessible to the people as to the nobility, however true it may be that the former troubled themselves but little on the subject, and left it to the priests to take thought for the offerings. The people would naturally have more faith in the power of amulets and magic than had the cultured classes, yet fundamentally the religious belief of all classes was the same. The rites of their religion presented mysteries only to the ignorant, or to such as were careless of inquiring into their meaning; but necessarily the subject must always have been both difficult and tedious because of the involved complexity and abounding paradox of the doctrines.

CHAPTER VIII.

OSIRIS AND HIS CYCLE.

OUR fullest account of the myth of Osiris and Isis is that given by Plutarch in a work composed about 100 A.D.[1] Omitting unessential details and the author's remarks by the way, Plutarch's story may be rendered as follows : Rhea (Nût), the wife of Helios (Râ), had had secret commerce with Kronos (Seb). When this became known to Helios he cursed her with the curse that in no month and in no year should she give birth to her unborn children. But Hermes (Thoth) also had been the lover of Rhea, and playing at draughts with Selene he won from that goddess one seventieth of each day in the year, and out of these pieces of time made five whole days, which he intercalated at the end of the three hundred and sixty days of the Egyptian year. These new made days were outside the range of the curse of Helios, and upon the first of them Osiris was born, a voice from heaven proclaiming that the lord of all things had appeared. It was also revealed to a certain Pamyles in Thebes that he should loudly announce the birth of the great king, the beneficent Osiris, whom Kronos forthwith entrusted to his care. On the second of the five new days Aroëris (*Her-ûr*, " Horus the Elder ")

---

[1] *De Iside et Osiride*, cap. 12-19

was born, on the third day Typhon (Set), who tore his way through his mother's side, on the fourth Isis, and on the fifth Nephthys. Osiris and Aroëris were considered as the children of Helios, Isis as the child of Hermes, Typhon and Nephthys as the children of Kronos; but some accounts state that Osiris and Isis had been lovers before birth, and that Aroëris was their son. All accounts, however, agree in stating that Osiris and Isis were eventually married, as were Typhon and Nephthys.

When Osiris came to his kingdom the Egyptians were living a life little better than that of animals; but he changed their miserable existence, taught them the art of agriculture, gave them laws, and instructed them in the worship of the gods. Subsequently he traversed the whole world on a mission of civilization, and scarcely needed to employ force in furtherance of his ends, but won his way by persuasion and teaching, by song and music; and it was for this that the Greeks identified him with Dionysos. During the absence of Osiris, Typhon was powerless to effect any changes, for Isis was continually on the watch and made a stout resistance; but after the return of the king the evil one caught him by guile. Having secured the confederacy of seventy-two men and of Queen Aso of Ethiopia, Typhon privily took the measure of the body of Osiris, made ready a richly decorated chest of like dimensions, and brought it with him to a royal feast, at which it was greatly admired. Typhon, as if by way of a jest, promised it to any one present whose body should exactly fit it. One guest after another tried it in vain; but at length Osiris stepped in and lay down. Then the confederates sprang forward, shut fast the lid, nailed it down, soldered it with melted lead, and carrying it to the river sent it forth to sea by the Tanitic mouth of the Nile. This befell on the 17th day of the month Athyr, in the twenty-eighth year of the life, or, according to other accounts, of the reign, of Osiris.

When Isis learned what had happened her mourning was great; she wandered far and wide seeking for the body of her husband, until at length she heard from some children through which mouth of the Nile the chest had passed out to sea. She also learned that Osiris had once lain with her sister Nephthys, taking her for Isis, and seeking for their child she found it and cared for it. The child was known as Anubis, and became her guardian and companion in her wanderings. In the meantime the chest containing the body of Osiris had floated ashore at Byblos, where it was soon surrounded and overgrown by the stem of a magnificent *Erica*. The king of the land seeing the tree had it cut down, and set it up as a pillar of his house, not suspecting that within it was the chest. So Isis came to Byblos, and by reason of the sweet smell which emanated from her she found favour with the women servants of the palace, obtained entry there, and was appointed nurse to the king's child. The goddess nursed the child, placing her finger instead of her breast to his mouth, and by nights burned away all that was mortal from his body, while she herself flew mourning round the column, in the form of a swallow. But at length she was surprised by the queen, Astarte, who cried out when she saw the child in the midst of the flames and thus deprived him of immortality. Then the goddess revealed herself and asked for the column, drew it out easily from under the roof, and cut away the *Erica* from about the coffin. The column she wrapped up in a linen cloth, poured myrrh over it, and gave it to the king : thus it was that she made " the wood of Isis," worshipped by the people of Byblos down to a late date. Then she flung herself upon the coffin, sobbing aloud, and finally carried it away by ship. When at length she was alone she opened the chest, laid her face to that of the dead, and kissed him, and wept.

Afterwards she concealed the coffin and journeyed to her son Horus, who had been brought up at Bûto in Lower Egypt. Typhon, hunting by moonlight, found the coffin, recognized the body, tore it into fourteen pieces, and scattered them far and wide. As soon as Isis learned this she took a canoe and traversed the Delta in search of the scattered members of her husband's body. All but one she found, and at each place of discovery a tomb of Osiris was raised. In the meantime Horus had grown up ; he armed himself to fight against Typhon ; the combat lasted many days, and ended in his victory. Typhon was put in chains and delivered up to Isis, who, however, did not slay him, but let him go. At this Horus was enraged and tore the crown from off the head of Isis, or, rather, he cut off her head, which Hermes replaced by that of a cow. After the death of her husband Isis again became with child by him, and bore prematurely the boy *Her-pe-khred*, " Horus the Child," whose lower limbs were dwarfed and stunted.

This is Plutarch's account, but no such continuous story can be substantiated from the monuments. Nevertheless it is thoroughly Ancient Egyptian in character, and nearly all the incidents are mentioned incidentally in the texts and continual allusions are made to them : apparently the myth was so well known that it was considered unnecessary to give any complete account of it. The falsity of the conclusion based on certain statements of Herodotus that the Osirian myth was a religious Mystery is best disproved by a popular story current in the XIXth Dynasty and known as the Tale of the Two Brothers. In this a number of incidents and particulars are derived from the myth, and in part at least the tale must have been unintelligible to any hearer ignorant of the story of Osiris. In treating of the latter in detail, however, we will confine ourselves to the incidents that are of most importance and vouched for by the inscriptions.

The Old Egyptian year consisted of twelve months of thirty days each, and in order to bring this into closer conformity with the true year there were added to it the so called Epagomenal days, which even at an early period were celebrated in certain temples as those on which the five gods of the Osirian cycle were born. The third of these days, which was held to be the anniversary of the birth of Typhon, was reckoned unlucky, whereas the beneficent character ascribed to Osiris is marked even by his name of *Unnefer*, "the Good Being "—which was at once his commonest title and one of his names as king. The statement that the 17th Athyr was kept as the anniversary of his murder is confirmed by a reference in a XIXth Dynasty papyrus,[1] giving that date for the

[1] IV. *Sallier* : see below, p. 264.

mourning for Osiris in Sais, a coincidence all the more noticeable since most Egyptian texts place both anniversary and mourning at the end of the month Khoiak. This striking divergence [1] is explained by the fact that two divinities had been merged in Osiris : the dying and dead Râ, and the god man and king Osiris. The former died at the end of Khoiak, on the shortest day of the year. Other races also have regarded this as the day of the Sun's death, and of its new birth, which in the case of Râ too, followed immediately on his death. Different considerations should have determined the day upon which the death of Osiris was to be celebrated ; but none the less the Athyr date was discountenanced, especially in later times, when all the gods were more and more regarded as solar. It still, however, continued to be generally recognized, and is regularly quoted by the classical writers. The earliest allusion to the death of Osiris as occurring in the month Khoiak is found in an inscription of the XVIIIth Dynasty. [2]

In other ways also the fusion of Râ with Osiris affected the conception formed of the latter, and tended to obliterate its original character. The original Osiris was the ideal man, or rather king, whose life was the pattern life, whose death showed how all, even the best, must die, and whose life beyond death showed too, how by the exercise of

[1] Occasionally the birth of the Osirian gods was fixed as having taken place on other than the Epagomenal days, and indeed, generally speaking, the Ancient Egyptian dating of mythological events was very uncertain. Cf. WIEDEMANN, *Rec. de Trav.*, xviii., p. 126.

[2] WIEDEMANN, *Proc. Soc. Bib. Arch.*, xi. 417.

virtue all might attain to a like continuance of personal identity. Although of divine descent, Osiris was not supposed to have been a god while he lived, yet an inscription of the XVIIIth Dynasty asserts[1] that he is "the creator of the world, which he formed with his hand, of its water, its air, its plants, all its cattle, all birds, its reptiles, its quadrupeds," thus assigning to him the same work which, according to the usual acceptation, had been carried out by Râ, and placing him in a position which is not in logical harmony with that which he occupies in the myth. But even this very text alludes to the myth at length, and says : "Isis the Shining One, the avenger of her brother (Osiris), sought him and rested not while full of mourning she roamed through the whole land ; she rested not until she had found him. She made light with her feathers, wind she made with her wings ; she gave unto him funeral panegyrics. She took his seed from the god and formed for him an heir, she suckled the child," etc.,[2] the child in question being he whom the Greeks called Harpokrates and supposed to have been conceived after the death of his father.

In later times the wanderings of Isis were a favourite subject of Egyptian legend. It is related, for instance,[3] how after the death of Osiris Set shut up Isis and Horus in a house, but she, counselled by Thoth, fled forth together with her child. The episodes of the flight are

---

[1] LEDRAIN, *Mon. de la Bibl. Nat.*, pls. 21-7. Cf. CHABAS, *Hymne à Osiris*, in *Rev. Arch.*, xive-année (1857), pp. 65 *et seq.*, 193 *et seq.*

[2] *Hymne à Osiris*, ll. 15, 16.

[3] *Metternichstele*, ed. GOLENISCHEFF, Leipzig, 1877. Cf. *Aeg. Zeitschr.*, 1879, pp. 1 ff.

related in detail, and it is interesting to note that on one occasion Isis was changed into a cow and Horus into an Apis bull, that they might go together to the place of Apis in the Libyan nome "to see the god Osiris." Neither the change into this animal form nor the visit to the city, which lay outside the route of the goddess, has any meaning in the Osirian myth : both incidents are borrowed from the legend of Râ. It was at this spot, known as " The Abode of the Cow," that Râ had retired on the back of a cow at his abdication.

Incidents connected with the nurture and youth of Horus were also interwoven in these legends. While in quest of her husband's body Isis had committed Horus to the charge of the goddess Ûazit (Leto), in the city of Buto, in the midst of the marshes of the Delta. Here, though safe from Set, the child was exposed to other perils, and one day suddenly fell lifeless to earth, stung by a scorpion.[1] Then Isis called the god Râ to her help, and the sun bark stayed in its course. The god Thoth disembarked in all the power of his magic, and restored to life the child, destined as a man to ascend the throne of his father Osiris and to avenge his death upon Set. The texts make frequent reference to the episodes of this long struggle between Horus and Set, which was carried on from one end of Egypt to the other, generally bringing it into connexion with the war of Horbehûdti against the enemies of Râ, among whom Set also appears. All the battles end in favour of Horus, but his victory is never final ; Set ever raises his head

---

[1] *Metternichstele*, l.c.

anew. The theory that Seb settled the strife by making
Horus king of the north and Set king of the south of
Egypt, placing their frontiers somewhat south of Memphis,[1]
seems to have been a comparatively late invention. The
strife was by nature interminable, for Horus, or rather
Osiris whom he represented, was the good, and Set the
evil principle always coexistent in the world however
often Evil may be overcome by Good. Set is likewise
Death, which temporarily conquers Osiris; but Good
triumphs over death, and not only lives again in the world
to come, but also remains upon earth, inasmuch as it leaves
there as its representative, Horus, a being similar in all
respects to itself.

The burial of Osiris is the subject of long texts, and
the laments which Isis and her sister Nephthys are supposed to have chanted at his coffin, and which represent
him sometimes as a Sun god pure and simple, are preserved in several examples varying in detail only.[2] The
annual festivals in commemoration of his death, which
were held in the month Khoiak and which set forth his
burial and resurrection, are described minutely in a long
text in the temple of Denderah,[3] and at the same time
there is given an enumeration of the different places
containing "graves of Osiris." Other texts amplify this

---

[1] Stela of the time of King Sabako : cf. PLEYTE, *Aeg. Zeit.*, 1876,
pp. 51-2.

[2] HORRACK, *Lamentations d'Isis et de Nephthys*, Paris, 1866;
PIERRET, *Études Égypt.*, pp. 20 *et seq.*; BUDGE, *On the Hieratic
Papyrus of Nesi-Amsu, Archæologia*, lii., pp. 11 *et seq.*, 65 *et
seq.*: cf. *Proc. Soc. Bib. Arch.*, ix., pp. 13 *et seq.*

[3] LORET, *Rec. de Trav. rel. à l'Égypte*, iii., pp. 43 *et seq.*; iv.,
pp. 21 *et seq.*; v., pp. 85 *et seq.*

list and state also what portion of the god's body was
preserved as a sacred relic in each of the sanctuaries
named : thus, in Memphis it was the head, in Letopolis

FIG. 57.—OSIRIS *ASAR* ENSHRINED ON FRONT OF A SQUATTING FIGURE.
(STATUE IN BERLIN MUSEUM.)

the neck, in Athribis the heart.　The inventories not
being made on any uniform plan many relics appear twice
over ; the head, for instance, is at Abydos as well as at

Memphis, and legs enough to supply several men are duly accounted for. In Greek times there were forty-two of these Osirian temples, and the Greeks called them Serapeums, borrowing the name from the Serapeum at Memphis, without regard to the distinction between the tomb of a dead bull which had become an Osiris and the sepulchre of the god man Osiris himself. But to the Egyptians they were the sanctuaries of Osiris, of "him who dwells in the Underworld."

After his death Osiris became king of the world beyond the grave. This was the capacity in which he was worshipped by the Egyptians: he ruled over the dead, and it was in his presence that the judgment was given which decided on admission to his kingdom ; all must therefore seek to secure his favour. Hence it is that by far the greater number of prayers for the dead and the formulas of funerary offerings relate to him, and in thousands upon thousands of funerary inscriptions we may read : "May a royal offering be given to Osiris, that he may grant all manner of good things, food and drink to the *ka* of the deceased, M. or N." Other gods are named again and again in these texts, but Osiris is always invoked with them, or rather before them. The figure of the god was drawn as that of a man, generally swathed in mummy wrappings to show that he was a god dead and buried ; only the hands, grasping a sceptre, were left free, and the green face adorned with the long stiff beard which denoted the dead who had become as gods. His headdress consists of the crown of Upper Egypt and the two feathers of Truth : it was originally peculiar to himself, and is worn

by any other god only if he had been merged in Osiris ;
thus, for example, Râ has become Osiris when he is
represented as a hawk with the Osirian crown.[1]

FIG. 58.—ISIS, *AS.T,* STANDING BEHIND OSIRIS. (L. D. III. 242, *d.*)
Stela from tomb at Saqqarah, XIXth—XXth Dynasty.

ISIS Egyptian *Hes.t* or *As.t*, the wife and sister of
Osiris, is represented as a woman holding the sign of

[1] Cf. for Osiris, LEFÉBURE, *Le Mythe Osirien*, I. *Les Yeux
d'Horus*, II. *Osiris*, Paris, 1874-5.

life in her hand, or a papyrus stem, ⎍, the usual sceptre
of a goddess ;[1] on her head is a throne. This throne or
chair denotes nothing peculiar to the nature of the goddess,
but is merely the ideogram used in writing her Egyptian
name, the meaning of which is unknown. The Greeks
imagined it to have some connexion with the word *ás*,
"old," the Egyptians with the ejaculation *ás*, "behold,"[2]
neither of these etymologies being a happy one. Isis was
considered to be the true type of wife and mother, and
also a most learned magician ; it is in the latter capacity
that she appears in the legend of Râ.[3] The cow was
sacred to her as to all maternal deities, and hence she is
occasionally represented as cow headed, but more generally
as wearing the horns only, ⎍. Isis, like Osiris, had many
centres of worship, but honour was more especially paid
to her at Abydos and Mendes, or rather Busiris. The
triad of Osiris, Isis, and Horus is a common one. In late
times Philae was the centre of her cult ; here magnificent
temples were raised to her, and we know from an inscription that she was here still regarded as a goddess
even in 453 A.D., that is, seventy years after the edict of
Theodosius prohibiting the worship of Egyptian deities.
Offerings were more particularly made to her then by
the Blemmyes, savage nomad tribes who continually
menaced Egypt, and were hardly held at bay and kept
from pushing on to Lower Egypt by all the power of the
Roman and Byzantine governors.

[1] The Decree of Canopus, l. 31, σκῆπτρον παπυροειδές, ὁ δ'εἰώθασιν
αἱ θεαὶ ἔχειν ἐν ταῖς χερσίν. It has often been thought to be a con-
ventionalized lotus.

[2] DŨMICHEN, *Kal. Insch.*, L. b. 2.   [3] See above, pp. 54 *et seq.*

NEPHTHYS, Egyptian *Neb-ḥat*, the "Lady of the House," often appears in the texts, and is occasionally named as the mother of Anubis, the wife of Set, and the like. She was worshipped in several cities, but was really nothing more than the associate of Isis in her funeral lamentation for Osiris. Even as once she had protected the body of Osiris, so would she do for the pious dead among men ; and when engaged in this office she, like Isis, is represented standing with wings outspread in pro-

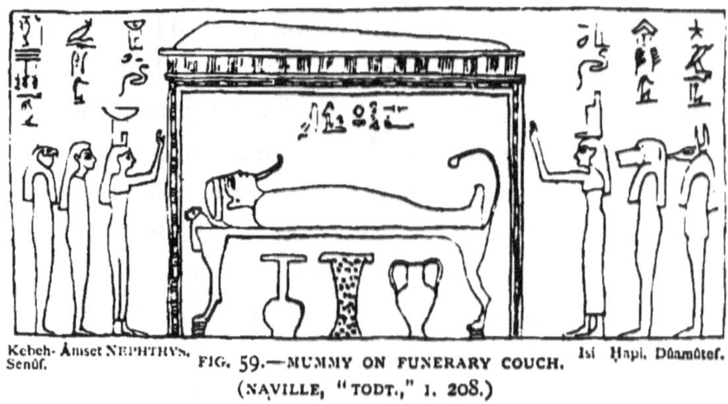

FIG. 59.—MUMMY ON FUNERARY COUCH.
(NAVILLE, "TODT.," I. 208.)

tection of the mummy. For the rest she is in human form and wears her ideogram as a headdress, this being absolutely necessary, it alone distinguishing her from Isis, or indeed from any other goddess. Sometimes she wears the cow horns and sometimes a solar disk, but this affords no grounds for regarding her as a solar deity.

SET, the brother and murderer of Osiris,[1] was in every

---

[1] PLEYTE, *La religion des Pré-Israelites*, Utrecht, 1862 ; *Lettre à Deveria*, Leiden, 1863 ; *Set dans la barque du Soleil*, Leiden, 1866 ; MEYER, *Set-Typhon*, Leipzig, 1875.

respect his opposite ; he was the personification of Evil as opposed to Good, of the desert as against the fertile land, of drought as against the Nile, of darkness as against light, of foreign lands as against Egypt, of illness as against health. The evil of his nature favoured rather than hindered the prevalence of his worship. It was in love that offerings were made to Osiris, but Set was worshipped out of fear; for he was strong and mighty, a terror to gods and men. The kings were therefore anxious to secure his favour : in the Old Kingdom they describe themselves as being at once both Horus and Set, that is, the embodiment of the powers of Good and of Evil ; and Seti I. and other Pharaohs of the New Kingdom by their names marked themselves as adherents of Set. It was only in late times that the fear of him was overcome by aversion to his wickedness, execration taking the place of worship, and that he was persecuted in the persons of his adherents, viz. red haired men, who were devoted to him, and the animals sacred to him, such as crocodiles, asses, and hippopotami. He was also regarded as the god of foreign lands, and foreign deities, as for example Baal, were often represented in his figure, which was human and held a sceptre, 𓌅, but with the head taken from some animal. This head bears some resemblance to a camel's head, and is the same as that of the long tailed fabulous beast, the supposed incarnation of Set, 𓃩.

In Tanis, and in several cities under Tanitic influence, the position of Set was peculiar. Here he was held to be a solar deity who pierced the Âpep serpent with his lance, and was called "the beloved of Râ," "the son of Nût" (who was almost invariably regarded as his mother), "mighty in the sun bark," etc. But according to the original conception of Set he was not so much the foe of the Àpep serpent as that serpent itself: the new character in which he appeared at Tanis was undoubtedly the result of his equation with Baal.

FIG. 60.—ḤEREMḤEB BETWEEN HORUS AND SET. (L. D. III. 122, *a*.)
Speos of Gebel Addeh, Nubia.

In the New Kingdom Set is very commonly known as SÛTEKH, and the legend as to the outbreak of the war of expulsion against the Hyksos states that Apepi, the Hyksos king, endeavoured to make this deity his sole god, not serving the other gods of the country. Under the XVIIIth and XIXth Dynasties we find Sûtekh spoken of as the god of the Kheta, and in this character he stood in a certain antagonism to Râ the god of the Egyptians. Radically the names Set and Sûtekh are one, differentiated only by the addition of kh—a method of word formation of which there are other instances, and which is in harmony with the Egyptian, and indeed with the Semitic, tendency to develope stems containing three radicals out of roots consisting originally of two.

From early times Ombos in Upper Egypt was an important centre of the cult of Set. Here he was worshipped as lord of the South Land, and occasionally regarded as one with Sebak, the crocodile god. He had a temple at Thebes, and several temples in the Western Delta—especially in Tanis

FIG. 61.—HORUS THE SON OF ISIS, HER-PE-KHRED. (L. D. IV. 63, c.)
Erment, Late Ptolemaic.

—where he was generally worshipped under the name of Sûtekh.

HORUS the son of Isis appears in the Osirian legend, first as the child HER-PE-KHRED, " Horus the child," Harpokrates, with his finger in his mouth ; secondly as the avenger of his father ; and finally as his father's successor on the throne of Egypt. His original nature can no longer be determined ; even in prehistoric times he had already been blended with Horus the Sun god, from whom there is no distinguishing him in the texts. Harpokrates is sometimes the young Sun, just risen, and his double, Aroëris, is almost purely a Sun god. Apart from the Osirian legend, little remains to show that Horus had not entirely lost his original nature : some few of its characteristics were still, however, left to him ; thus, when the kings claim to have ascended the throne of Horus, the reference is to Horus the son of Isis, for Horus the Sun god was never reckoned as having been king of Egypt. In the lists of the divine dynasties this

FIG. 62.—HORUS AND AMENOPHIS II.
(L. D. III. 63, d.)
Speos of Amenophis II. at Ibrim.

position is reserved for Râ, Shû, etc., and it was as their successors also that the Pharaohs ruled over the land. It is because of his equation with the Sun god that Horus the son of Isis is represented as hawk headed and wearing the disk, instead of being shown in human form, as might have been expected for the son of an essentially anthropomorphic deity.

THOTH,[1] in Egyptian *Dḥût.i,* "belonging to the ibis," plays a comparatively small part in the Osirian myth, appearing only as a counsellor, or as one who can by

FIG. 63.—IBIS OF THOTH. (FIGURE IN BERLIN MUSEUM.)

magic make good wrong which has been done. Thus it was he who placed a cow's head upon Isis after Horus had cut off her own. Originally a lunar deity, he was often connected with Khûnsû, and with the moon god Àḥ, and

[1] Data concerning Thoth have to some extent been collected by PIETSCHMANN, *Hermes Trismegistos,* Leipzig, 1875.

had for his sacred animal the cynocephalus, whose sexual life was supposed to be regulated by the phases of the moon. More usually, however, he was represented by the ibis. Ptah and Mût were considered as his parents, but not universally : in Thebes, for instance, where he

FIG. 64.

THOTH, DḤÛT.I. (L. D. III. 223, *a*.)
Stela in Hammamat Valley, XXth
Dynasty.

was occasionally substituted for Set as the husband of Nephthys, he appears as the third member of a triad consisting of Khûnsû, Mût, and himself. Generally he was depicted in the form of an ibis headed man, , usually crowned with the solar disk and with the lunar crescent, inasmuch as he was a god of time.[1] It was owing to the importance of the moon in the measurement of time that Thoth gradually came to be considered as god of time, even in cases where the moon had nothing to do with his functions or with the divisions of time in question. Thus he, alone or together with

SAFEKII.T, the goddess of writing, inscribes the king's name

[1] Star worship in any strict sense of the term was extremely rare in Egypt; two references only are made to it on the monuments, and both date from the XIXth Dynasty. Cf. WIEDEMANN, *Rec. de Trav.*, xvii., pp. 11 *et seq*.

for its everlasting duration upon the sacred sycomore ;[1] it is he who promises the sovereign "the years of Tûm, the dominion of Horus, and millions of years"; and to him the first month of the Egyptian year and the sixth hour of the day were dedicated.

Since the moon is a divider of time the lunar Thoth became also the god of just measurement. The cubit, which was dedicated to him, was the measure used in the planning of temples. Once, too, he had measured out the world and given it laws ; hence he is the guardian of all law, acting in this capacity both for himself and at the command of Râ. Moreover he was the god of writing, the scribe of the gods, and the god of letters—especially of religious literature. Scribes regarded him as their tutelary deity and invoked his aid at their work. He was supposed to have written the most sacred books and formulas with his own hand, and therein to have set down his knowledge of magic, in which art Isis only was his rival. His pre-eminence in magic naturally led to his becoming the god of medicine, for magic was fully as important to the medical practitioners of the Nile Valley as knowledge of remedies.

But it was after death that man most needed the help of Thoth. When Osiris died Thoth had undertaken to provide him with the correct magic formulas to use in fighting against his foes, the powers of darkness, and thus to make him king of the world beyond death. Each Egyptian hoped to receive like help in his own extremity : it was Thoth who would restore to him his speech, teach him to recite the true formulas, with Anubis conduct him

---

[1] See illustration on p. 156.

to the Judgment Hall, note down the final judgment, and perhaps even speak for him as his advocate.

FIG. 65.

ANUBIS, *Anepu.* (FIGURE IN BERLIN MUSEUM.)

The Greeks identified him with Hermes with whose nature as conceived by the Alexandrians and Neoplatonists his was not without affinity; and the Greek method of marking the distinction of their god by calling him Hermes Trismegistos, "Hermes the thrice great," is not unlike the Egyptian: in later times especially we find Thoth qualified in the inscriptions as "twice great."

In the Râ legends also Thoth is prominent as the adviser and scribe of the gods. The popularity of his worship culminated at the beginning of the New Kingdom, when the Pharaohs were called after him, *Dhutmes* (Thothmosis), "Son of Thoth," or *Ahmes* (Amasis), "Son of the Moon," after the planet which was his.[1] Temples, however, were rarely raised in his honour.

ANUBIS, Egyptian *Anepû*, was depicted in human form, but with the head of his sacred animal, the jackal, 𓃣. This animal was mistaken by the Greeks for a dog, and hence it was as a dog that Anubis was introduced into Roman Isis worship. From time to time the Egyptians themselves had fallen into this mistake, and isolated mummies of

FIG. 66.—ANUBIS AND MUMMY. (NAVILLE, "TODT.," I. 174.)

dogs have occasionally been found in the jackal cemetery at Lycopolis. Yet, generally speaking, the dog was not held sacred, although it was domesticated and kept both for hunting and in the house. Anubis was usually considered the son of Osiris and Nephthys, but in a magical text[2] Râ is named as his father, probably only because

---

[1] The correct translation of these names is probably " Thoth," or " the Moon—has born (a child)," giving a sense analogous to the name Rameses = Râ-mes-sû, " the Sun god has borne him."

[2] CHABAS, *Pap. magique Harris*, 101.

Râ and Osiris were regarded by the writer as one. In the legend he is the assistant of Isis. According to Egyptian belief he was a special patron of the dead, guarding them and superintending their embalmment, he or Thoth being their guide into the next world and leading them by the hand into the Hall of Judgment. Temples were raised to him in many places, but the chief centre of his cult was Lycopolis in Upper Egypt, the Siût of to-day. Here he was worshipped under the name or rather title of *Apûat*, "The Opener of the Way," *i.e.* of the Underworld. Lycopolis in the Delta was also dedicated to him, and probably these were the two places which the Egyptian had in mind when speaking of the Anubis of the South and the Anubis of the North, and placing upon funerary stelae two jackals as guardians of the deceased. This procedure illustrates the fact that though the Egyptians recognized that divinities of the same name in different centres of worship were distinct, yet this did not imply any belief in more than one Anubis. It was the Greek mythographers who from similar premisses first drew this inevitable conclusion : they assumed that there must be more than one Herakles, Hermes, etc., because it seemed impossible to unite into one biography all the myths relating to each.

SEB, or, as his name was also written, KEB,[1] was god of the earth, for which his name was used as an equivalent in expressions such as " on the back of Seb." The Greeks

---

[1] Cf. BRUGSCH, *Aeg. Zeit.*, 1886, pp. 1 *et seq.*; RENOUF, *Proc. Soc. Bib. Arch.*, ix., pp. 83 *et seq.* ; also *Aeg. Zeit.*, 1893, pp. 125 *et seq.* ; *Rec. de Trav.*, xvii., pp. 94 *et seq.*

identified him with Kronos, probably only because as father of Osiris he might be considered as senior among the gods. Shû was supposed to be his father, and Nût his wife. According to the lists of the divine dynasties in Memphis and Thebes, he was the fourth king of Egypt, and therefore to be reckoned as one of the younger gods. But the mention of him in the texts does not seem to favour this view, for there he is called, not king, but nomarch (*erpâ*) of the gods, as if at the time when his worship arose there had as yet been no king in Egypt. His sacred animal was the goose, and sometimes he is supposed to be connected or even identical with the goose which laid the egg whence issued the world.

FIG. 67.—SEB (KEB) SEPARATED FROM NÛ.T BY SHÛ. (BRUGSCH, "MYTHOLOGIE," P. 210.)

In the Legend of the Destruction of Mankind he is installed as king in immediate succession to Râ. His connexion with the cult of the dead is very slight; nevertheless he is often named incidentally in the texts.

NÛ.T, usually represented as a woman, is the female personification of the sky, of which she forms the vault by arching her body over the earth and resting her weight upon her hands and feet; Shû is sometimes seen standing below to support her in this uneasy posture. On her

travel the heavenly bodies, over which she also was supposed
to exercise some control.   She was "lady of heaven,"
"mistress and mother of the gods," "lady of earth." [1]

This goddess must be distinguished carefully from the
god named NÛ or NÛN, who represents the celestial
ocean, the water traversed by the solar bark, who was

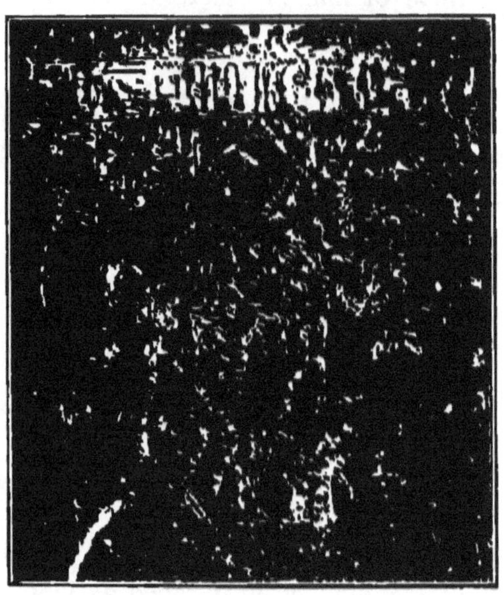

FIG. 68.—NÛ.T POURING WATER FROM A PALM TO DECEASED AND
HIS SOUL. (STELA IN BERLIN MUSEUM.)

the father of the gods, the source of creation, and from
whom all came forth.   In late times he was sometimes
considered the first of the falsely so called gods of the
elements, and to represent, together with his feminine
manifestation NÛ.T or NÛN.T, the waters of the Nile.

[1] For Nût as a cow, see illustration p. 65, and pp. 62-4.

This second Nût is sometimes figured as a woman seated within a palm or sycomore and pouring waters of refreshment from a libation vase on the hands of a soul (*ba*) crouched at the foot of the tree.[1] The remaining deities of the group to which Nûn and this Nût belong, and which bear the names HEH and HEH.T, KEK and KEK.T, NENÛ and NENÛ.T, would seem to be male and female forms of Eternity, Darkness, and the Inundation. This interpretation is, however, uncertain, although better substantiated than the older explanation that they were personifications of the four elements : Water, Fire, Earth, and Air.[2]

[1] Cf. pp. 143, 157.
[2] Cf. LEPSIUS, *Ueber die Götter der vier Elemente bei den Aegyptern, Abhandlung* of the Berlin Academy, Berlin, 1856, an article collecting all the data given in the inscriptions.

CHAPTER IX.

THE OSIRIAN DOCTRINE OF IMMORTALITY.

WE have already seen one series of Ancient Egyptian
ideas of a future state to be closely connected with
the myth of the Sun god Râ, and his journey through
the Underworld. These, however, formed the belief of a
very restricted number : for the vast majority of Egyptians
of all periods conviction of a life beyond death was bound
up with the worship of Osiris, and on this groundwork
they pictured for themselves in detail the fate of soul and
body, and developed a doctrine of immortality which in
precision and extent surpasses almost any other that has
been devised. The scientific importance of the Osirian
doctrine arises first from its extreme antiquity—for even
in Pyramid times it was complete in all its essential parts—
and also from its many points of affinity to Jewish and
Christian dogma.

A follower of the Osirian religion held that when a man
had died, when his heart had ceased to beat and his body
had become cold, nothing remained of him upon earth but
a lifeless hulk : the corpse. This was named the KHA, and
its ideogram was a dead fish, , the sign for any noisome,
putrid thing. The preservation of the Kha was the first
duty of the survivors, and shortly after death it was

handed over to the embalmers that they might so mani-
pulate it as to render it proof against corruption. But in
the hot climate of Egypt it was impossible to preserve the
body intact : the intestines, heart, lungs, and liver, and
also the brain were removed, either to be buried or cast
away, or else to be placed in vessels apart ; although in
some exceptional cases they were thickly smeared with
asphalt, and in this unnatural condition restored to the
body. The body now consisted of bones, flesh, and skin
only, and after being thoroughly dried and shrunk by
means of natron, it was coated with asphalt and became
what we call a mummy, a black corpse which might
remain unchanged for thousands of years in the dry
climate of the Nile Valley, but which gradually falls into
decay when brought into the damp atmosphere of Europe.
In the cavities of the body were laid all manner of
amulets ; others were placed on different parts of the
body, especially about the neck, and all was then swathed
in linen bandages. Each rite which had to be performed,
each prayer which had to be repeated, was exactly prescribed, and directions for them are contained in several
papyri which have come down to us.[1] It is true that the
same ceremonial was not observed in all cases ; the rites
were more or less complicated in proportion to the sums
which the survivors were able or willing to devote to the
service of their dead.

The swathed mummy was laid in a coffin inscribed with

[1] *Rhind Papyri*, edited by BIRCH, London, 1863, and BRUGSCH,
Leipzig, 1865 ; Hieratic Papyrus at Vienna in BERGMANN,
Hieratische Texte, Vienna, 1887 ; others at Bûlak and Paris in
MASPERO, *Mém. sur quelques pap. du Louvre*, Paris, 1875.

prayers for the deceased together with his names and titles, and invocations of the different deities charged with his future welfare, all illustrated by vignettes. In the matter of coffins also, the difference between rich and poor was great, the latter having to make shift with few texts and often without coffin at all, while the wealthy found their last resting places within three and even four sarcophagi, placed one within another and adorned with innumerable inscriptions and vignettes.

The body was returned to the family in its coffin ; sometimes, if the deceased had died in a foreign land, he was thus brought back to his native city to be laid in the tomb which it was the care of an Egyptian to prepare for himself during life. The mummy was borne in solemn funeral procession, accompanied by the family, the wailing women, and the priests, from the eastern shores of the Nile, where most of the cities were built, to the necropolis among the western hills. If city and necropolis both lay on the same side of the river, still the crossing was performed, at least symbolically, by traversing the sacred lake invariably attached to a city of the dead. When the tomb, the "eternal house," had been reached, the coffin was set up on end, with face turned towards the south, on a small sandhill intended to represent the Mountain of the West—the realm of the dead. There the deceased was approached by various persons who prayed before him and performed many sacred rites, the chief functionary being the *Kher heb*, who may best be described as master of the ceremonies. He conducted the whole ritual ; papyrus roll in hand, he assigned to

FIG. 69.—THE MUMMY AT THE TOMB. (PAPYRUS OF ANI, PL. VI.)
XVIIIth Dynasty.

each his place, and prompted each with the words he had to speak, or else recited them in his name. With the *Kher ḥeb* stood a servant, a friend, and a son of the deceased, two mourning women, one representing Isis and the other Nephthys, the sacrificial priest, and other persons who seem to have been merely present at the proceedings without taking part in them. The whole ceremony was intended as a reproduction of what was supposed to have taken place round the coffin of Osiris.

There is no occasion for entering into the details of these complicated proceedings : from full and precise descriptions of them which have come down to us[1] it is evident that their main object was the restoration of all bodily functions to the mummy preparatory to the long journey which lay before it in the next world. The mouth was symbolically opened that it might speak and the eyes that it might see ; a bull was slaughtered that the dead might have food to hand ; rites were performed to enable it to make use of garments, unguents, and many other things, in fact to make it in all things like a living human body. The mummy itself remained undisturbed ; the coffin only was manipulated. For the most part, the end in view was to be accomplished by reciting the right prayer and touching the mummy case with a wand shaped like the hieroglyph ⌒ ; sometimes the symbolical passes were made, with the same effect, upon a statue of the deceased instead of upon his coffin. After

---

[1] SCHIAPARELLI, *Il Libro dei Funerali*, Turin, 1881-90; MASPERO, *Rev. de l'Hist. des Rels.*, xv., pp. 162 *et seq.* ; *Études de Mythologie*, i., pp. 283 *et seq.*

this ceremony was completed the body was lowered into the grave and the shaft closed, and when all was over a funeral feast was held in the antechamber of the tomb.[1]   Henceforth there was nothing more that the friends and relatives of the deceased could do for him except to present him with offerings either directly or through the gods, and to constrain the gods with magic formulas to deal kindly by the dead.

In addition to his body, thus made into a perfect mummy, or, as the Egyptians would have called it, an OSIRIS, man had also an immortal soul. This was not considered, as among most races, a simple entity, but a composite one : in life the component parts had been united ; at death they parted, each to find its own way to the gods.[2]

First among these parts was the so called KA, imagined as similar to a man and yet not a man, and which stood to him somewhat in the same relation as the verbal expression of some tangible reality to that reality itself, or as the name of any one to the person whom it designates. The notion of a Ka was probably suggested by the fact that the image of the dead or of one who is far away may be seen in thought or dreams. Hence it was believed that man was not simply a material being who could be in only one place at once, but that he included a second self, able to pass through walls or barriers, bound neither

[1] An exceptional practice sometimes, however, prevailed of keeping the mummies in accessible chambers above ground. See *Proc. Soc. Bib. Arch.*, xvii., p. 156.

[2] WIEDEMANN, *The Ancient Egyptian Doctrine of Immortality*, London, 1895.

by time nor space, and which might exist for thousands
of years. The Ka has thus several points of affinity with
the REN, or name of a man,[1]—the sound of which evokes
an image of him in the mind of the hearer—and with a
portrait statue. Similar conceptions of personality as
apart from a person are found among the most divergent
races, but an extreme development of the idea in one
direction was peculiar to the Egyptians: they turned this
abstraction back into the concrete, and endowed it with
a tangible form dependent upon food for its continued
existence.

At death a man, as such, ceased to be. His body was
made into a mummy and placed within a coffin, and
this experience had shown that no mummy could ever
leave. The Ka, which had been the companion of the
body in life, at death attained to independent existence.
It was to the Ka that funerary prayers and offerings were
made; to the mummy alone they were useless. But
when the Ka returned to the mummy, entered into it,
animated it, and became " the Ka living in its coffin," then
the two united were able to lead something of the same
life that they had led together on earth, eating, drinking,
and going to and fro to visit the survivors and remind
them of their duty in the matter of funerary offerings.
This procedure was more incumbent upon the poor man's
Ka than upon that of the rich, who could in his lifetime
ensure for himself the needful supplies by entering into
a contract with the priests of the dead in his own
neighbourhood, making over to them land and property

---

[1] See below, pp. 293-5.

in exchange for their bond to present his Ka with carefully specified offerings on certain feast days. The poor man could make no such provision for himself: he was dependent after death upon the piety of his family.

A great proof of the firm root which this idea of the Ka had taken in the Egyptian mind is afforded by the fact that it was believed to be an indispensable constituent of every being which had life, Kas being ascribed to the gods themselves even in Pyramid times.

The ÀB, or heart, the second of these immortal parts, will be dealt with in the chapter on amulets.

The third part was the BA, which best corresponds to our idea of the soul. It was imagined as being in the form of a bird, usually with human head and hands. At death it flew to the gods; but it was no more immaterial than the Ka, and equally dependent upon renewed supplies of food and drink. In Egyptian art the Ba is sometimes shown perched on the coffin, tenderly caressing it, and taking farewell of the mummy within.

In the fourth place we have the SÂHÛ, figured as the swathed mummy of the deceased, the empty form of himself which, having come to him from the godhead, could therefore at death return to it. And there was the KHAIB, or shadow of a man, which also passed for a separate entity that might be parted from its owner, and was indeed invariably parted from him when he died. The Khaib was usually symbolized as a sunshade. Again, there was the KHÛ, the Shining One, a conception apparently suggested by the idea of a glorified and luminous mummy, and the SEKHEM, the personified power .or strength of the deceased,[1] not to mention other constituents of a man's being less frequently insisted upon. But far more important than any of these, and the chief immortal representative of man as a whole, was his Osiris.

The OSIRIS was the immortal counterpart of the mummy. The equipment of the mummy was the equipment of the Osiris; the amulets bestowed upon the mummy, the furniture placed in its tomb, all became possessions of the Osiris. But even as the other immortal parts of a man left him at death, so also did his Osiris.

These supposed entities are obviously very similar in function; several, such as Ka, Osiris, and Sâhû, personify almost the same idea, and it would seem that in these cases we have to do with the different conceptions of an immortal soul which had arisen in separate places and prehistoric times, and were ultimately combined into one doctrine, the Egyptians not daring to set any aside for fear it should prove to be the true one. All, therefore, were retained, regardless of the logical embarrassments inevitably brought about by such a course. The fusion of these beliefs took place at a very early period and its history cannot now be traced : even in the times of the Pyramid builders it had already been accomplished, and there can be little profit in speculating as to how it came about until better evidence for the settlement of the question is forthcoming. One thing, however, is clear : the Osirian doctrine was that which obtained the largest following, for it put all other theories into the background. While little or nothing is stated

---

[1] Cf. WIEDEMANN, *Le Muséon*, xv., pp. 46 *et seq.*

in detail as to the fate of the other immortal parts of a man's being, and we are only told that at death they left the body and were dispersed, but were reunited in the Osiris after the Last Judgment, with the fate of the Osiris himself the texts deal at wearisome length. And this is because the Egyptian hope of eternal life was bound up in the god Osiris, and therefore preference was given to that conception of the soul which had such affinity to Osiris as to be called by his name.

The most important and widely diffused of all Egyptian religious writings is the so called BOOK OF THE DEAD, which is specially devoted to the Osiris. It is a collection of prayers and formulas to be spoken by him in traversing the regions of the Underworld, and secured to him victory over evil demons and protection from good ones. The oldest copies of the work date from the Middle Kingdom ; these, however, are rare. Commoner use was made of it in the New Kingdom, and in later times a copy of at least some portion of the book was placed with every mummy of the ·better class.[1] The contents of the

---

[1] The oldest of these texts are given by LEPSIUS, *Aelteste Texte des Todtenbuches*, Berlin, 1867 ; MASPERO, *Mém. de la Miss. au Caire*, i. 155 ff.; LEPSIUS, *Denkm.*, ii. 98, 99, 145-8. Later texts may be found in NAVILLE, *Das ägypt. Todtenbuch der* 18—20 *Dyn.*, Berlin, 1886 (cf. MASPERO, *Le Livre des Morts*, in *Rev. de l'Hist. des Rel.*, 1887); DE ROUGÉ, *Rituel funéraire*, Paris, 1867. Very late texts are given in LEPSIUS, *Das Todtenbuch der Aegypter nach dem hieroglyphischen Papyrus in Turin*, Berlin, 1842 ; *Pap. Cadet*, in *Descr. d'Ég. Ant.*, ii.; etc. A translation of the whole work on the basis of the Turin text has been made by BIRCH in BUNSEN, *Egypt's Place in Universal History*, v., pp. 123 *et seq.* ; by PIERRET, *Le Livre des Morts*, Paris, 1881 ; and lastly, working from Naville's text, by LEPAGE RENOUF, *The Egyptian*

different transcripts vary. The whole work consisted of
separate chapters or books, each intended for some
particular emergency; the rich and pious Egyptian had
as many of them as possible transcribed on the papyrus
placed in his grave, or upon the walls of his tomb and on
the inside and outside of his mummy cases : for the poor
a few of the more important extracts had to suffice. The
chapters altogether amount to over two hundred, but there
is no one manuscript containing them all ; a selection was
always made, partly at the choice of the purchaser, partly
in accordance with the taste and tendencies of the time,
sometimes one and sometimes another set of extracts being
in favour. In the course of centuries the material for
selection increased : the oldest of the transcripts are somewhat short, but as time went on they grew longer and
longer. It is not known at what period the work originated.
The pyramids contain comparatively few passages that
were utilized later in the composition of the Book of the
Dead : their texts do indeed provide magic formulas for use
in the next world ; generally, however, these are worded
differently. But as they presuppose a knowledge of all
the main incidents in the Osirian legend, and also allude
in detail to the doctrine of immortality based upon it,
presumably these texts represent more especially the forms
of belief prevailing at Memphis, and not the Osirian
doctrine as taught even then at Heliopolis and Abydos.

There is no systematic arrangement in the Book of

Book of the Dead, in *Proc. Soc. Bibl. Arch.*, xv., etc. ERMAN
in *Aeg. Zeit.*, 1894, pp. 2 *et seq.*, has given an example of how
individual chapters arose.

the Dead any more than in other religious texts of the Egyptians. It is a rare thing to find two copies in which the chapters follow the same sequence ; the order of the chapters or groups of chapters seems to have been entirely optional. Nor was any attention paid to the logical and natural sequence of events ; for example, the prayers by means of which the beatified soul was enabled to take on various forms generally precede the chapter whereby it was to attain to beatification. And, though not quite so embarrassing, still it is inconvenient that the deceased should receive from the beginning the epithet to which he only becomes entitled later, and is invariably spoken of as *maå kherū*, " true of voice " (or rather, according to the usage of the word in the Book of the Dead, " pronounced justified "[1]), although it is only the sequel that can show whether he possessed or even in the end attained the presupposed attribute. The practice was probably based on feelings akin to those with which the Germans habitually speak of their dead as *selig*, " blessed," hoping that blessedness may indeed be their lot.

The teachings of the Book of the Dead are supplemented by many other texts, usually of a later date. In Ptolemaic times and even earlier there was a demand for compilations of passages from the Book of the Dead and other works which should contain only the most essential formulas, and which were intended for the private use of small circles of believers, or even for individuals, and not for the great majority, who still held fast by the Book of the Dead itself. Some of these collections had

[1] For the meaning of this word, see below, pp. 279-80, and note.

a comparatively wide circulation, as, for instance, "The Book of the Breath," "The Second Book of the Breath," "The Book of Journeying in Eternity," "The Book of 'May my Name flourish,'" etc., while others are found in single examples only and probably never existed in duplicate.[1]

The texts dealing with the Sun's journey through the Underworld yield a tolerably clear picture of a world to come, but this is not the case with the Book of the Dead, and it would be impossible to set down as in a map the regions which it describes. Mention is made of rivers, of several territories, of gates which must be passed, of chapels wherein dwell gods, of demons lying in wait for souls at various points, of lakes of fire, and of islands; but how all these details fitted together was obviously outside the apprehension even of the Egyptian priests, otherwise there would be at least some thread of consistency running through the description of the journeyings of the Osirian soul. In view of this confusion and because the isolated incidents are of comparatively slight importance in any attempt to deal with the Egyptian religion as a whole, we may here dismiss these journeyings from our further consideration. Suffice it to note that by help of the formulas of the Book of the Dead the soul succeeded in overcoming all the evil spirits,

---

[1] BRUGSCH, *Saï en Sinsin*, Berlin, 1851; DE HORRACK, *Le Livre des Respirations*, Paris, 1877; VON BERGMANN, *Das Buch vom Durchwandeln der Ewigkeit, Sitzungsber.* of Vienna Akad., 1886, pp. 369 *et seq.*; LIEBLEIN, *Le Livre Égyptien : Que mon nom fleurisse*, Leipzig, 1895; *Pap. Louvre* No. 3283, edited by WIEDEMANN, *Hierat. Texte*, Leipzig, 1879.

constraining all the good ones to show it favour, in opening all doors, and eventually in coming to judgment in the Hall of the Two Truths, *i.e.* Truth and Justice.

Here, upon a chair beneath a canopy, sat "Osiris the Good Being, the Lord of Life, the Great God, the Lord of Abydos, the King of Eternity." In his hand he held a royal sceptre and a flail, and his crown was upon his head. Some representations of this scene place the symbol of Anubis in front of Osiris; in others Anubis is engaged on the other side of the hall in introducing the soul, which must otherwise make its entry alone. Before Osiris sat the forty-two judges of the dead, each summoned from a different city in Egypt, each to pronounce sentence upon the dead with regard to some particular sin. There also stood before the god the four funerary genii : the human headed ÁMSET, the ape headed ḤAPI, the jackal headed DÛAMÛTEF, and the hawk headed KEBEḤSENÛF.[1] These had charge of the viscera of the dead and were bound to appear at the judgment, because, according to Egyptian belief, it was not the divine Ego of a man which sinned, but only his internal organs. The deceased was received by the goddess or goddesses of truth. He proceeded to speak in his own justification, declaring that he had not committed any one of the forty-two sins, and then the truth of his words was tested by weighing his heart in the scales against the symbol of truth. Horus superintended the weighing, occasionally assisted by Anubis or Thoth, the latter being usually present as Scribe of the Gods to set down the result of the proceedings.

[1] See illustration on p. 220.

If the dead was found to be righteous he received back
his heart, the rest of the immortal parts of his soul were
reunited in him, and he was again built up into the man
who had walked the earth, but who now entered upon
new and eternal life. What befell, according to the
Osirian doctrine, if judgment went against him is uncertain. Presumably for such an one there was no re-
edification, and the Osiris died a second death, followed
by his complete annihilation. In many representations
the figure of a female hippopotamus may be seen in the
judgment hall. She is indicated as the Devourer of the
Underworld, and has often been supposed to be a monster
to whom the unjustified dead were handed over : how far
this interpretation is correct we cannot determine. Generally the animal seems to have been placed there simply
as guardian of the entrance to the Fields of the Blessed,
but sometimes it is likened to Set. Elsewhere it is said
that the judges of the dead slay the wicked and drink
their blood. In brief, here also we have conflicting statements, and can only gather that there seems to have been
no general agreement among the dwellers in the Valley
of the Nile as to the ultimate lot of the wicked.

The judgment before Osiris forms the subject of Chapter
CXXV. in the Book of the Dead, and here we have
specified the words which the deceased was to speak in
the judgment hall. In the Turin text the first part of
this chapter is as follows :—

" Hail to you, ye lords of the Two Truths ! Hail to
thee, Great God (Osiris), Lord of the Two Truths ! I come
unto thee, thou my lord ; I draw nigh unto thee to behold

thy beauties. I have learned and know thy name; I know the names of the forty-two gods who are with thee in the Hall of the Two Truths, who live and keep watch on the wicked, who eat of their blood on that day of trying words before the Good Being, the Justified (*maâ kherû*) One (Osiris). Hail! Twofold Spirit! Lord of the Two Truths is thy name. Hail! I know you, ye lords of the Two Truths; I bring unto you Truth, I destroy Evil for you!

"I have not committed fraud and evil against men.

I have not oppressed my fellow men (?)—otherwise said, my comrades.

I have not diverted justice in the judgment hall.

I have not known meanness.

I have not committed wickedness.

I have not (as overseer) caused a man to do more than his day's work.

I approach the bark of the offering (?), I approach the place of him who offers the prescribed offerings.

I have not given way to anxious care.

I have not been empty (of good).

I have not been weak.

I have not been wretched (?).

I have not done that which is an abomination to the gods.

I have not caused a slave to be ill treated by his overseer.

I have not brought any to hunger.

I have not caused any to weep.

I have not committed murder.

I have not caused any to be guilefully murdered.

I have not wrought deceitfully against any man.

I have not spoiled the bread of offering in the temples.

I have not taken away from the bread of offering of the gods.

I have not stolen the garments or wrappings of the glorified ones (the dead).

I have not committed fornication.

I have not defiled myself as priest of the god of my city.

I have not added to, (and)

I have not diminished the offerings.

I have not added to the weight of the balance.

I have not taken milk from the mouths of children.

I have not taken cattle in their pasture.

I have not taken in nets the birds of the gods.

I have not taken the fish in their (the gods') fishponds.

I have not turned aside the water (from a neighbour's field) at the time of inundation.

I have not cut off an arm of the river in its course.

I have not extinguished the fire in its season (*i.e.* the time during which it was to be kept alight).

I have not defrauded the Ennead of the Gods of that which was theirs (?).

I have not driven back (from my fields ?) the herds of the temple lands.

I have not turned back a god at his coming forth (in procession from his temple)."

After some intervening formulas in which the deceased declares himself to be one of the blessed ones who have risen from the dead, there follows a second " Negative Confession." This is distinguished from the first in that it is divided into forty-two lines, each opening with the invocation of a certain demon, genius, or spirit whose dwelling place is duly named, and concluding with the mention of a sin which the deceased asserts that he has not committed. The formula runs : " O thou Strider forth, who proceedest from Heliopolis, I have not done evil "; " O thou Opener of the Mouth, who proceedest from Babylon (now Old Cairo), I have done no injury," etc. The sins repudiated are on the whole the same as those enumerated in the first confession ; many of them are, however, specified in greater detail in order to bring up the number to forty-two. But let it be observed that here also the deceased claims that he has not robbed, nor been covetous, has slain no temple cattle, has not been an eavesdropper, has not been furious, has not been deaf to words of truth, has cursed none, and especially not the king, his own father, or a god.

The significance of this Negative Confession lies in the fact that it gives us the standard of Egyptian morality, showing the nature and multiplicity of the misdeeds to be avoided by him who would enter into the realm of Osiris. This testimony to the emphasis which the Egyptians laid on morality is confirmed from the most various sources. We have several examples of papyri containing exhortations to good conduct, and strict injunctions as to the right course to pursue under varying circumstances. The oldest of them dates from the XIIth Dynasty and is known as the Prisse Papyrus, being called after the name of its discoverer ; the latest is written in demotic ; and there are texts of similar import which are of intermediate date. In much of their matter, and sometimes even in verbal expression, these papyri recall the collection of proverbs in the Bible, the Wisdom of Solomon, the Proverbs of Jesus Sirach, and many of the other Biblical exhortations. For instance, in the Prisse Papyrus the Fourth Commandment is found in almost identical terms : " The son who hearkens to the word of his father, he shall grow old thereby." Other texts exhort to the study of wisdom, to regard and respect for parents and superiors, to mercifulness, generosity, discretion, integrity, sobriety, chastity, and the like. In the funerary inscriptions the dead often plead their good deeds. " I did that which was right," says one Egyptian; " I hated evil ; I gave bread to the hungry and water to the thirsty, clothing to the naked, succour to him who was in need." " I harmed not a child, I injured not a widow; there was neither beggar nor needy in my time ; none were anhungered, widows were cared for as though their husbands were still alive." " I did that which was pleasing to my parents; I was the joy of my brethren, the friend of my companions, honourably minded towards all my fellow citizens. I gave bread to the hungry and shelter to the traveller ; my door stood open to him who entered from without, and I refreshed him."[1]

The Confession was heard in silence by Osiris and his

---

[1] PRISSE, *Facsimile d'un Papyrus Égyptien*, Paris, 1847 (cf. VIREY, *Étude sur le Papyrus Prisse*, Paris, 1887); MARIETTE, *Pap. de Boulak*, i., pls. 15-23 (cf. CHABAS, *L'Égyptologie*, 1876-8); PIERRET in *Rec. de Trav.*, i., pp. 40 *et seq.* (cf. LEPAGE RENOUF, *Origin and Growth of Religion illustrated by the Religion of Ancient Egypt*, London, 1880, pp. 71 *et seq.*).

assessors : they testified neither approval nor disapproval : the truth of the affirmations would be settled by the weighing of the heart.   This being concluded in his favour, the new man was conducted into the FIELDS OF ÀALÛ (or ÀARÛ), into the kingdom of the blessed followers of Osiris, which was a country modelled altogether on earthly lines, but especially resembling the Delta: a Nile ran through it divided into many branches and forming many islands.   Here the dead ate and drank, went hunting, fought with their foes, enjoyed themselves with their friends at games of draughts, made offerings to the gods, and went out in their boats upon the canals. But the chief occupation was agriculture, which differed from that of earth only in that the harvest never failed, and the corn grew far more luxuriantly, its stems surpassing the height of a man.

The Fields of Aalû were tilled to provide the dead with food, in so far as their wants were not met by offerings, and by magic formulas made and spoken for them on earth. The possibility of being obliged to till the ground in the world to come could hardly have been a pleasant prospect to Egyptians of rank or wealth who had never laboured upon earth, and so they tried to find means of averting this necessity.   The earliest expedient seems to have been the sacrifice of human beings at the tomb, in order to send them after the deceased as servants of his to all eternity. Afterwards the idea was to secure the immortality of those who had been a man's servants upon earth ; their bodies were embalmed, their statues were placed in his tomb, prayers were transcribed for them, and in gratitude for

all this the servants were expected to work for their lord
in the next world. But in time more humane influences
prevailed ; it was felt that death knew no distinction of
persons, and that hence the poorest and humblest might
claim to lead a future life free from care and independent
of the caprices of a master. So the rich man could no
longer hope to keep his servants after death, and would
have lived haunted with the fear that he might have to
guide the plough himself, if a new expedient had not been
devised for his relief. From the XIIth Dynasty onward
the practice prevailed of making little mummiform statuettes, the so called ÛSHEBTIÛ, inscribed with a magic
formula by means of which it was hoped that they would
attain to life in the world to come, and there by diligence
in labour testify their gratitude to him who had evoked
them into being. Their labours began immediately after
his death, when they were expected to recite a lament for
him ; but this they did only at the command of the godhead. In order to relieve the latter from the trouble of
giving the order, it was set down in writing and the
document laid in the tomb.[1] Afterwards the main task
of the little figures was ploughing and reaping, and hence
they are represented as carrying hoe and basket.

It is to the working of the same idea which led to the
use of these statuettes that we must ascribe the presence
of the numerous articles of furniture, toys, weapons, etc.,
found in tombs. With these the dead could set up house,
and thus escape the labour of procuring such things for

---

[1] MASPERO, *Rec. de Trav.*, ii., pp. 13 *et seq.; Mém. de la
Miss. au Caire*, i., pp. 594 *et seq.*

himself in his new abode. Provision was also made for his intellectual interests : papyri were buried with him for the entertainment of his Osiris, containing tales, love songs, and even rules for the game of draughts.[1] But comfortable and pleasant as his life in the Fields of Aalû might thus be made to the wealthy Egyptian, nevertheless he devoutly trusted not to be restricted to remaining there in his form of an Osiris. By help of magic formulas he expected to be able to visit at pleasure all his familiar earthly haunts ; to come forth as a crocodile, a hawk, a phoenix, a heron, a dove, a lotus flower, even as the god Ptah himself ; or to enter and animate his mummy, and in this guise return to look upon the places dear to him in life. Thus he might still remain in touch with the life of this world, to which mankind has always clung ; and since to the Egyptian the life which he had led upon the banks of the Nile seemed an ideal existence, it was on this model that he pictured for himself the life of the world to come.

On the whole, each chapter of the Book of the Dead appears to be complete in itself. These chapters were indeed modified in the course of time, but the alterations almost exclusively affected the wording rather than the contents. The changes are rarely marked in the texts embodying them, and at most only by the phrase " other-

[1] For instance, the papyri containing stories : MASPERO, *Contes populaires*, 2nd edition, Paris, 1889, and PETRIE, *Egyptian Tales*, London, 1895 ; the love songs of Papyrus Harris 500, treated by MASPERO, *Études Égyptiennes*, i., p. 217, and about to be published in Germany by W. MAX MÜLLER ; and the Games Papyri of Turin and Bûlak discussed by WIEDEMANN, *Actes du Congrès des Orientalistes de Genève*,—all of which were found in tombs.

wise said," which is followed by a variant taken from another manuscript than that from which the rest of the text is copied. One chapter only forms an exception : Chapter XVII. in the Turin copy gives numerous variants apart from its own text, and provides commentaries to a whole series of passages, introducing each commentary by the words, "What does this mean?" The chapter is found in the Middle Kingdom substantially in the same form as in late texts, except that the earlier versions are more briefly expressed. It used to be regarded as one of the oldest expositions of the Osirian doctrine, but this view is refuted by closer investigation. The chapter really represents a comparatively late stage of development in the Egyptian religion, and was manufactured with the definite purpose of advancing a syncretic treatment of the Egyptian gods and creeds. This will best be shown by giving a translation of the first section of it as found in the oldest known version, that on the coffin of Mentûhetep at Berlin, together with the more important additions from the Turin copy as published by Lepsius. These additions are here printed in italics and preceded by the letter T. The deceased says :—

I AM TÛM, I AM THE ONLY ONE, T. *in the primeval water Nû.*

I AM RÂ AT HIS FIRST APPEARING, T. *at his appearing at the beginning of his dominion which he exercised. What is that? Râ in his appearing at the beginning of his dominion which he exercised is the beginning of Râ who appears in Heracleopolis magna, when the god Nû was uplifted; he was on the staircase in*

17

Heracleopolis magna, he destroyed the children of the rebels on the staircase at Heracleopolis magna.

I AM THE GREAT GOD WHO CREATED HIMSELF, T. *namely the water, that is the god Nû, the father of the gods,* THE CREATOR OF HIS NAME, THE LORD OF THE DIVINE ENNEAD. T. *What does that mean? Râ, namely the creator of his limbs, these gods arose who are in the train of Râ.* NONE AMONG THE GODS MAY WARD HIM OFF. T. *What does this mean? Tûm is in his sun disk. Otherwise said: Râ is in his sun disk, which rises on the eastern horizon of heaven.*

I AM YESTERDAY, I KNOW TO-MORROW, NAMELY OSIRIS. T. (*after the word "To-morrow"*) *What is that? Yesterday is Osiris, To-morrow is Râ. That day on which were destroyed the enemies of the Lord of All (Osiris) and on which he established his son Horus* (as King). *Otherwise said: That day on which is established the feast of his installation* (*i.e.* as Lord of the Underworld), *namely the burial of Osiris by his father Râ.*

THERE AROSE ·STRIFE AMONG THE GODS WHEN I SPOKE. (Instead of these words T. has :) *He* (Râ ?) *made strife among the gods when he commanded that Osiris should be Lord of the Mountain of the West.* IT IS THE WEST WHICH WAS THE SCENE OF STRIFE. T. *What does that mean? The West belonged to the spirits of the gods when he decreed that Osiris should be Lord of the Mountain of the West. Otherwise said: The West marks the boundary to which Râ causes each god to attain. Behold! he* (*i.e.* that god) *fighteth because of them* (*i.e.* the various dead gods would not permit that Osiris should be King of the West, of which they considered themselves to be the lords, and therefore they fought against him).

I KNOW THE NAMES OF THIS GREAT GOD WHICH IS IN IT (the Underworld). T. *What does that mean?* *Osiris.* Variant : PRAISES OF RÂ IS HIS NAME. T. *Soul of Râ is his name; he begat himself.*

I AM THAT GREAT PHOENIX WHICH IS IN HELIOPOLIS, WHICH IS THERE, T. *I am* THE ORDERING (?) OF ALL THAT IS AND EXISTS. WHAT DOES THAT MEAN ? T. *It is the Phoenix.* OSIRIS, T. *which is in Heliopolis.* IT IS T. *the Ordering* (?) *of that* WHAT IS AND EXISTS, T. *his body.* Variant : ETERNITY AND UNENDING TIME. T. *Eternity is the day, Unending Time is the night.*

I AM MIN AT HIS APPEARING ; THERE ARE GIVEN UNTO ME HIS TWO FEATHERS ON MY HEAD. WHAT DOES THAT MEAN ? HIS TWO FEATHERS ARE THOSE OF HORUS, THE AVENGER OF HIS FATHER. (T. after " What does that mean ? " has :) *Min is Horus, the avenger of his father, Osiris ; they are his manifestations, his birth.* THEY ARE HIS TWO FEATHERS. T. *On his head the Coming of Isis and Nephthys who are placed behind him, that they may be the two Mourning Sisters. Behold, they stand on his head.* Variant : THE TWO URAEI, T. *the Very Great,* WHO ARE AT THE FOREHEAD OF HIS FATHER TÛM. T. Variant : *His two eyes (i.e.* Sun and Moon) *are the two feathers on his head.*

I AM IN MY LAND, I HAVE COME FROM MY CITY. WHAT DOES THAT MEAN ? [From] THE SUN MOUNTAIN OF MY FATHER TÛM.

So the text goes on. The deceased declares himself

to be one with each and all of the gods, thus postulating a general equation of deities of which pantheism would have been the logical outcome. This, however, never did result, for the Egyptian could not bring himself to sacrifice the distinct individualities of his deities, notwithstanding that he regarded them all as identical. Chapter XVII. held its place in spite of all its doctrinal deviations from the belief in anthropomorphic and individual deities which otherwise characterizes the Book of the Dead, and in spite of the contradiction between its fundamental theory, that the dead are merged in the gods and in the Universal Whole, with the leading doctrine of the rest of the work, which taught that the immortal life of man after death in all things but duration resembled his life on earth.

CHAPTER X.

MAGIC AND SORCERY.

IN Egypt all was ruled by the godhead : not that there was any one supreme deity ; to each god of the Pantheon his own sphere was assigned, and nomes, cities, temples, all were dedicated to specific deities, though not altogether to the exclusion of other divinities. Some of the gods were also limited as to the times during which their functions were exercised. Each month was presided over by a certain deity, Thoth, for instance, being the god of the month Thoth, Hathor the goddess of Athyr, and Khûnsû the god of Pakhons, in certain cases at any rate the months being named after the gods. Late texts represent every day of the month as dedicated to a certain deity—the first to Thoth, the second to Horus the Avenger of his Father, the third to Osiris, the fourth to seventh to the four funerary genii, etc., the five epagomenal days being generally regarded as belonging to the five chief gods of the Osirian cycle, who were supposed to have been born on these days. In Ptolemaic times a day would sometimes be named after the reigning sovereign instead of after its god ; thus the 30th Mesori, which was the birthday of Ptolemy Epiphanes, and the

17th Mekhir, which was the date of his accession, were both called after him. This division of time among divine beings was also carried out into still greater detail, and the hours of day and night were severally ruled by separate goddesses—not indeed those of the great cycles, but beings created to this end only.

Besides the gods of time in its divisions there were also gods of the heavenly bodies which regulated these divisions—of the sun, the moon, the planets, certain of the fixed stars, and the constellations. All alike were supposed to have power over events which took place in the periods subject to their control, and to determine the fates of those born under their rule. Their powers, however, were not arbitrary, but exercised rather in accordance with laws of their own beings, and fates could be predicted by one to whom these laws were known. Hence arose the idea of horoscopes, calculations of which we find mention in Egyptian writings ; and in late papyri we have " spheres," that is, tables by means of which the fate of a man could be calculated from certain data, such as the hour of his birth, and the like. From the Egyptians and the Chaldeans, who also held similar ideas, these practices were passed on to the Greeks, and from them to the learned men of the Middle Ages ; and in their last outcome—far removed indeed from their original religious nature—they still play a great part in modern books of prophecy. It was not always necessary to make use of " spheres " and calculations to look into the future ; this could be done more readily by consulting calendars in which it was stated under each day whether it was auspicious or inauspicious, or both, what should be done or left undone on it, what would be the fate of those born on that day, and other information of a similar nature. These statements were founded on the belief that on a given day some mythological event had taken place imparting a certain significance to the recurrence of the date for all time to come. In a XIXth Dynasty papyrus known as Sallier Papyrus IV.[1] we have a specimen of one of these calendars for several months of the year, and from this the following extracts are given :—

4TH PAOPHI :. Inauspicious, auspicious, auspicious (*i.e.* varying in influence). In no wise go forth from thine house on this day. He who is born on this day will die by the plague.

5TH PAOPHI : Inauspicious, inauspicious, inauspicious. In no wise go out of thine house on this day ; approach not a woman. On this day men shall make offerings to the gods. The majesty of the god Ment was content on this day. He who is born on this day shall die by love-making.

6TH PAOPHI: Auspicious, auspicious, auspicious. Day of rejoicing for Râ in heaven. The gods are in peace before the god Râ ; the Ennead of the gods completes the ceremonies before [Râ]. He who is born on this day will die drunken.

9TH PAOPHI : Auspicious, auspicious, auspicious. The gods rejoice, men are in exultation, the enemy of Râ is

<hr>

[1] Published in *Select Papyri of the British Museum*, i., pls. 144-168 ; discussed by CHABAS, *Le Calendrier des Jours Fastes et Néfastes de l'Année Égyptienne*, Chalon, 1870.

overthrown. He who is born on this day dies of the feebleness of old age.

22ND PAOPHI : Inauspicious, inauspicious, inauspicious. Bathe in no water on this day. He who goes in a boat on the river on this day will be torn in pieces by the tongue of the crocodile.

29TH PAOPHI : Auspicious, auspicious, auspicious. He who is born on this day will die honoured of his fellow-citizens.

17TH ATHYR : Inauspicious, inauspicious, inauspicious. Arrival of the superior and inferior Great Ones in Abydos, of Those who shed many tears. Great lamentations of Isis and Nephthys for their brother Ûnnefer (Osiris, who, according to Plutarch, was murdered on the 17th Athyr) in Sais, a lament which may be heard even to Abydos.

10TH KHOIAK : Auspicious, auspicious, auspicious. He who is born on this day dies bread in hand, beer in mouth, his eyes looking upon food.

13TH MEKHIR : Inauspicious, inauspicious, inauspicious. In no wise go forth on this day. It is the day on which the eye of Sekhet was terrible and the fields were filled with devastation.[1] Go not forth at sunset on this day.

Similar prognostications were common down to the end of Egyptian history, and testify to the wide diffusion of the ideas on which they were based. Thus Cicero asserts that he was born when the Dogstar was in the ascendant, and that he was therefore certain to be drowned

---

[1] Evidently an allusion to the Legend of the Destruction of Mankind ; see pp. 58 *et seq.*

at sea; and Pliny states that whoever rubs himself with the juice of the plant called mouse-ear will not suffer from bloodshot eyes all the year.

Many other races have held similar ideas, and believed that whatever natural phenomenon had followed on a supernatural event the recurrence of the one would always bring about the recurrence of the other, and in order to facilitate prophecies based on this assumption, lists of marvellous occurrences were made. Such lists have never yet been found in the Nile Valley, but Manetho, whose views were fundamentally Egyptian, repeatedly makes mention of marvels such as the Nile flowing with honey, the birth of an eight-legged lamb, and the like, and hence we may feel certain that the Egyptians also believed in the peculiar significance of supernatural or unusual phenomena.

But if all lots were thus decreed they were not always and altogether inevitable. In the first place the gods might interfere to spare those whom they delighted to honour the melancholy fate before them, or to bring about the overthrow of their enemies. And by the help of magic man also could control fate; by the same means too he not only obtained power over his fellow men, but also over the dead, and even over the gods themselves, no matter how high their rank. One chief use of magic was to send or procure dreams.

Among all peoples dreams have played a great part, their kaleidoscopic pictures seeming to be real things and the words apprehended in them to have been really spoken. In the case of so pious a people as the Egyptian, whose chief interest throughout life was the worship of the gods, it was only natural that in dreams as when awake they should cling to communion with the higher powers, and believe themselves to enter into personal communication with their deities and thus to receive counsel and reply in difficulty.

According to the opinion of the Egyptians, god sent dreams might come to a man anywhere. Thus Thothmosis IV. was taking his siesta out hunting when Râ Harmakhis appeared to him and commanded him to clear away the sand from the Great Sphinx, in the shadow of which he was sleeping. We have also a record later by some thousand years of how a dream opportunely commanded King Nût Amen of Ethiopia to march into Egypt. But to make sure of a prophetic dream it was safer to sleep within a temple known to be the seat of an oracle, such as that of Serapis at Memphis. This oracle is often mentioned in Ptolemaic writings, and there are still in existence notes made by the anchorites who dwelt there of the dreams vouchsafed to them.[1] As a rule these dreams could be interpreted by the dreamers, but sometimes the meaning was dark and recourse was had to the professional interpreters of whom we find mention in Genesis xli. 8. Their calling lasted late in Egyptian history, and a Greek stela refers to one of these officials as still established in the Serapeum at Memphis. The belief in prophetic dreams, and in dreams by which cures for diseases were made known, was not confined to Egypt; it prevailed, for instance, in connexion

---

[1] Cf. WIEDEMANN, *Herodot's Zweites Buch*, p. 344.

with the temple of Asklepios at Epidaurus; but Egypt
was its main centre, and even towards the end of the
fourth century A.D. the poet Claudian speaks of oracular
dreams as "Egyptian."[1]

The dreams were sent by the gods at their pleasure,
and as a general thing men simply besought the gods
for them. If this proved of no avail recourse might be
had to magic, and the gods could be compelled to send
not only such dreams as they might approve of but
certain dreams specified by the applicant. Many of the
directions for thus coercing them have come down to us,
and the following formula found in a Greek Gnostic
Papyrus from the Leyden Museum is based throughout
on Egyptian ideas, notwithstanding the comparative
lateness of its date.[2]

"Nostrum of Agathokles for producing Dreams.

"Take a cat, black all over, and which has been killed;
prepare a writing tablet, and write the following with a
solution of myrrh, and the dream which thou desirest to
be sent, and put it in the mouth of the cat. [The text
to be transcribed runs:] Keimi, keimi, I am the Great
One in whose mouth rests Mommom, Thoth, Nanumbre,
Karikha, Kenyro, Paarmiathon, the sacred Iau ieê ieu aêoi
who is above the heaven, Amekheumeu, Nennana, Sennana,

---

[1] CLAUDIAN, *Entr.*, i. 312.

[2] *Papyri Graeci Musei Lugduni-Batavi*, edited by LEEMANS,
ii., p. 16: cf. DIETERICH, *Papyrus Magica*, Leipzig, 1888, p. 800
(from *Fleckeisen's Jahrbücher für klassische Philologie*).

Ablanathanalba, Akramm khamaria brasiua lampsor ciceiciei aôêêô theuris ô. . . . Put thyself in connexion with N. N. in this matter (as to the substance of the dream named). But if it is (?) necessary, then secure (bring?) for me N. N. hither by thy power ; lord of the whole world, fiery god, put thyself in connexion with N. N. Tharthar thamara thatha mommom thanabotha apranu bamalea khr[a]thna basuleth rombru tharael albana brokhrex abranazukhel! Hear me, for I shall speak the great name, Thoth! whom each god honours and each demon fears, by whose command every messenger performs his mission. Thy name answers to the seven (vowels) a, e, ê, i, o, y, ô, iauôêeaô oueê ôia. I named thy glorious name, the name for all needs. Put thyself in connexion with N. N., Hidden One, God, with respect to this name, which Apollobex also used."

As by means of this formula the magician could compel the god to send a certain dream to a certain person, in the same way he could cause the sending of a prophetic dream, or obtain for himself the answer to any stated question : some slight variation of formula made all the difference, but all the formulas were very much alike. They are preceded by a brief description of the preliminary proceedings, and special directions are given as to the material upon which the words are to be written, whether the manuscript is to be placed in any particular spot or destroyed, or whether a simple repetition of the words will suffice. Then follows the formula itself, which, apart from prescribing the desired action of the divinity, contains little beyond invocations. An observation is generally appended to the effect that the formula had once been employed successfully by a god, as in the example above given, where the god in question is named Apollobex. "Apollobex" is compounded of the Greek "Apollo," corresponding to the Egyptian solar Horus, and of the syllable "bex," probably derived from the Egyptian *bak*, "a hawk." Hence the name denotes Horus the hawk, that is the son of Isis in the form of a sparrow hawk, who appears in other texts also as a god well versed in magic. In the invocation proper there are few genuine divine names, such as the name Thoth in the above; generally it is a string of syllables apparently utterly destitute of meaning, but which sounded mysterious and incomprehensible and was on that account credited with all the greater significance. Like the Ancient Egyptians, the Gnostics attached much value to such combinations, and they have always been in favour with magicians. The succession of syllables was supposed to convey the hidden name of a god, and after they had been pronounced the god was bound to do the will of the magician who had spoken them. It was long believed that the knowledge of these essential names lay chiefly with the Egyptians, and Synesius of Cyrene, who lived about 400 A.D., remarks in one of his writings [1] composed while he was still a heathen, that he had heard that "the Egyptians knew how to employ a certain method against the gods and a certain sorcery, so that as often as they pleased they mumbled a few incomprehensible words, and so drew to themselves all that was divine, which is apt to follow certain drawings." And because

[1] *Calvitiae encomion*, cap. 10.

of this frequent intercourse with their gods their outward forms also were familiar to the Egyptians.

Nonsensical as these invocations now sound, they were not originally without meaning ; for the most part they consisted of versions of the names and titles of gods of foreign nations. Writers on ancient magic, as for instance Origen, state emphatically that it was considered of the utmost importance to invoke a god by his right name. Thus the word "Sabaoth" borrowed from the Jewish sacred writings was thought to be of exceptional efficacy ; but if "Lord of Power" or "Lord of Hosts" was substituted for it, the power of the spell was gone. This lay, therefore, not in the sense of the words, but in their sound, and any attempt at translating them not only made the invocation inoperative, but was attended with the gravest peril ; for, in Egypt as elsewhere, the demons were believed to obey the commands of the sorcerer only on compulsion, and always to be on the watch for any opportunity which might place it in their power to destroy him. Most of this apparent gibberish, therefore, originally meant something, although this is difficult to prove in detail. However careful the attempt to reproduce foreign words, it was never quite successful, and as time went on the right pronunciation was forgotten more and more, for the oral tradition of unintelligible sounds never could be accurate, and the transcription of magical texts seems to have been singularly careless. As an instance of this debasement we may take the word "Paarmiathon." This is apparently Egyptian, and a corruption of *pa Her m átḥû*, "the Horus in the marsh," a common designation of Horus the son of

Isis, who had dwelt during his youth in the marshes of the Delta.[1]

Magic played an extensive part in Egyptian medicine. The Egyptians were not great physicians; their methods were purely empirical and their remedies of very doubtful value, but the riskiness of their practice arose chiefly from their utter inability to diagnose because of their ignorance of anatomy. That the popular respect for the human body was great we may gather from the fact that the Paraskhistai who opened the body for embalmment were persecuted and stoned as having committed a sinful although necessary deed. The prescribed operations in preparing a body for embalmment were never departed from, and taught but little anatomy, so that until Greek times the Egyptians had only the most imperfect and inaccurate ideas of the human organism. They understood nothing about most internal diseases, and especially nothing about diseases of the brain, never suspecting them to be the result of organic changes, but assuming them to be caused by demons who had entered into the sick. Under these circumstances medicines might be used to cause the disappearance of symptoms, but the cure was the expulsion of the demon. Hence the Egyptian physician must also practise magic.

According to late accounts, his functions were comparatively simple, for the human body had been divided into thirty-six parts, each presided over by a certain demon, and it sufficed to invoke the demon of the part affected in order to bring about its cure—a view of matters

[1] See pp. 210, 214.

fundamentally Egyptian. In the Book of the Dead[1] we find that different divinities were responsible for the well-being of the bodies of the blessed ; thus Nû had charge of the hair, Râ of the face, Hathor of the eyes, Apûat of the ears, Anubis of the lips, while Thoth was guardian of all parts of the body together. This doctrine was subsequently applied to the living body, with the difference that for the great gods named in the Book of the Dead there were substituted as gods of healing the presiding deities of the thirty-six decani, the thirty-six divisions of the Egyptian zodiac, as we learn from the names given to them by Celsus and preserved by Origen.[2] In earlier times it was not so easy to determine which god was to be invoked, for the selection depended not only on the part affected but also on the illness and symptoms and remedies to be used, etc.

Several Egyptian medical papyri which have come down to us contain formulas to be spoken against the demons of disease as well as prescriptions for the remedies to be used in specified cases of illness. In papyri of older date these conjurations are comparatively rare, but the further the art of medicine advanced, or rather receded, the more numerous they became. Take, for example, the following formula to be spoken while preparing certain drugs ; it dates from about the year 1700 B.C. and is from a medical papyrus in the Leipzig collection.[3] " May Isis deliver, deliver ; Horus was delivered by Isis from all ill that was inflicted upon him by his brother Set when he slew his

---

[1] See Chapter XLII.　　　[3] *Pap. Ebers*, i. 12 *et seq.*
[2] *Con. Celsum*, viii. 58.

father Osiris. O Isis, mistress of sorceries, deliver me, set me free from all bad, evil, red things,[1] from the power of illness coming from god or goddess, from death male and female, from plague male and female that taketh hold upon me, even as thou didst set free, even as thou didst deliver thy son Horus! [Do this] because I enter into the fire and rise forth from the water, and fall not into the snare on that day (*i.e.* because I possess magic power), etc. Oh save me from the power of all bad, evil, red things, from the power of illness coming from god or goddess, from death male and female!"

The above formula might be used at the preparation of any drug; others were intended for use only in certain illnesses. Thus, for inflammations there was a remedy compounded with the milk of a woman who had borne a man child, and over this was to be said:[2] "O my son Horus! it burns on the hills; no water is there, no helper is there; bring water over the flood (*i.e.* the water of the inundation) to put out the fire." These words refer to the myth of a universal conflagration, to which the texts often, but only incidentally, refer, and of which even Plato had heard;[3] and as Horus had on that occasion extinguished the flames, so he was to subdue the burning of the inflammation.

It might even be the proper thing to threaten a god who refused his aid. Thus, in one conjuration,[4] a woman in

---

[1] Red being the colour of Set, red things were equivalent to evil things.

[2] *Pap. Ebers*, pl. lxix., l. 3, *et seq.*

[3] PLATO, *Timaeus*, 22.

[4] Magical papyrus, discussed by PLEYTE, *Études Égypt.*, pp. 176 *et seq.*

labour declares herself to be Isis, and summons the gods to her help. Should these refuse to come, " Then shall ye be destroyed, ye nine gods ; the heaven shall no longer exist, the earth shall no longer exist, the five days over and above the year shall cease to be, offerings shall no more be made to the gods, the lords of Heliopolis. The firmament of the South shall fall, and disaster shall break forth from the sky of the North. Lamentations shall resound from the graves, the midday sun shall no longer shine, the Nile shall not bestow its waters of inundation at the appointed time." Such formulas were used until Roman times, and philosophers, as for instance Porphyry,[1] still found occasion to mock at the presumption of magicians who threatened to destroy the heavens and the earth if their will was not accomplished.

It was not always enough to speak the formulas once ; even their repeated recitation might not be successful, and in that case recourse must be had to other expedients : secret passes were made, various rites were performed, the formulas were written upon papyrus, which the sick person had to swallow, etc., etc. But amulets were in general found to be most efficacious, and the personal intervention of a god called up, if necessary, by prayers or sorcery. In an inscription originally written in honour of the god Khûnsû of Thebes, about 1000 B.C., we have a story which shows how such a cure by means of the divine touch might be brought about ; the following is an abstract of it.[2]

---

[1] In EUSEBIUS, *Praep. ev.*, v. 10.

[2] LEDRAIN, *Mon. Égypt. de la Bibl. Nat.*, pls. 36-44 : cf. DE ROUGÉ, *Étude sur une Stèle Égypt.*, in the *Journal Asiat.*, 1856-8.

FIG. 70.—SHRINES OF THE TWO KHÛNSÛS, THE KING BETWEEN THEM.
(PRISSE, "MONUMENTS," PL. XXIV.)
From the Bekhten Stela.

Once an Egyptian king went to Asia to take tribute. The prince of Bekhten brought him his daughter as a gift, and the king loved her and raised her to be his wife. Long years after, when the king of Egypt had returned and was holding a feast in Thebes, there came thither a messenger from Bekhten, who said to him : " I come to thee, O prince, my lord, because of Bentresht, who is thy sister in law through the royal wife.   A plague hath entered into her members.   Let thy majesty send a learned scribe that he may see her."   The king despatched the very learned royal scribe Thothemheb ; but when he came to Bekhten he found Bentresht in the condition of one possessed by a demon, and that he himself was not strong enough to oppose the demon.   Then the prince of Bekhten sent again unto Pharaoh and said : " O prince, my lord ! let a god come (to fight the demon)."   And Pharaoh went to Khûnsû the Fair-resting One in Thebes, and said : " O thou my beauteous lord ! again I come unto thee because of the daughter of the prince of Bekhten."   Then Khûnsû the Fair-resting One in Thebes was brought to Khûnsû the Carrier out of Plans, the great god who overcomes the wicked (*i.e.* the form of Khûnsû known as the "Fair-resting One in Thebes," which always remained in the temple and which devised plans, was taken to the other form of the god which was known as the "Carrier out of Plans," and which executed the designs of the former). The king spoke before Khûnsû the Fair-resting One : "My beauteous lord, oh turn thy face hither to Khûnsû the Carrier out of Plans that he may go to Bekhten !" Then the god nodded twice. And the king said : "Let thy talisman be with him when I cause him to go to Bekhten to save the daughter of the prince of Bekhten." Then Khûnsû the Fair-resting One nodded twice. He invested Khûnsû the Carrier out of Plans four times with his amulet.

So Pharaoh sent the god to Bekhten, where he was received in state. Then the god went to the place where Bentresht was ; he invested with his amulet the daughter of the prince of Bekhten, and immediately she was well. But the demon that had been in her said before Khûnsû the Carrier out of Plans : "Approach in peace, thou great god, overthrower of the wicked ; Bekhten is thy city, its inhabitants are thy slaves, I myself am thy servant ! I will go to the place whence I came that I may satisfy thy heart in relation to the matter on account of which thou art come hither. But let thy Majesty command that a feast shall be established for me and for the prince of Bekhten." Then the god bowed twice to his priest, in consent, and said : "Let the prince of Bekhten make a great offering to this demon." While the god Khûnsu was negotiating with the demon, the prince of Bekhten and

his soldiers stood by in great fear. The offering was
made, and the demon went forth in peace to the place
whither he would go, at the command of the god Khûnsû
the Carrier out of Plans.

The prince of Bekhten rejoiced greatly, and thought
within himself that he would do well to keep in Bekhten
the god who had thus evinced his power, that he might
in emergency make use of him again ; and he withheld
him from returning to Thebes for three years and nine
months. But when this time had gone by, one day when
the prince was resting on his couch he saw the god coming
forth from his chapel in the form of a golden sparrow
hawk, and fly away through the high heavens towards
Egypt. On awakening he felt ill, and thereupon called
to him the priest of the god, and sent them back to
Thebes laden with rich presents. "Now when Khûnsû
the Carrier out of Plans had come into the temple of
Khûnsû the Fair-resting One, he gave unto him the gifts
which he had received from the prince of Bekhten, and
kept back none of them for himself."

Magic availed not only against illness, but also against
accidents and perils from without, and especially against
dangerous animals. Of these there were many in Egypt,
and even at the time of the XIIth Dynasty herdsmen knew
formulas for frightening away the crocodiles which lay in
wait in the shallows to fall upon the cattle.[1] The magical
papyrus of the Harris collection, which dates from the
New Kingdom, also contains conjurations by means of
which men could protect themselves from amphibious

[1] L. D., vi., pl. 112, ll. 156 *et seq*.

animals. All that was needed was to call out:[1] " I am the Chosen One of millions, who goeth forth from Dûat, whose name is not known. If my name is spoken on the bank of the river, the river is dried up ; if my name is spoken on the land, it begetteth fire. I am Shû, the image of Râ, which hath its seat in his eye (*âza.t*, the sun disk). When a water monster openeth its mouth, when it moveth its legs, then I cause the earth to fall into the flood (?), the South to become the North, and the earth to turn round." Hearing these words the crocodile thought the speaker the god whom he announced himself to be, and speedily dived below. The crocodile in particular was supposed to stand in dread of the gods and all belonging to them : to attack, for instance, no one who might be in a papyrus bark in the Delta, because Isis had once made use of one when there.

Still more fearsome to the Egyptians than the crocodiles were snakes, from which they were always threatened with sudden death, and which even in the world to come were a continual peril. The formulas for use against them were many, and a long series are given in pyramid texts of the VIth Dynasty.[2] These were chiefly intended for use in the next world, but might also be used here. A man must say : " The snake curleth itself, it curleth itself round the calf. O hippopotamus that wentest forth out of the nome of the earth, thou atest what went forth from thee ! Snake, thou who descendest, lie down, go

---

[1] *Harris Magical Papyrus*, edited by CHABAS, Chalon-sur-Saone, 1860, pl. vii., ll. 1-4.

[2] See, *e.g.*, *Pyramid of Unas*, ll. 300-340.

back ! The god Ḥen-pe-sezet is in the water ; the snake is overthrown, thou beholdest the god Râ." Or else : " Fall, body which came forth from the earth ! Flame which came forth from the celestial ocean, fall ! go back !" The second of these formulas simply contains the conjuration of the snake to force it to retreat, but the first is full of mythological allusions which we cannot understand.

Formulas against all kinds of hurtful creatures, such as scorpions or hippopotami, may be classed with those against crocodiles and snakes. Some of them might even undo the hurt which had been done ; thus we have the formula by means of which Isis called her son Horus back to life after he had been killed by a scorpion, and instructions are appended as to the manner in which the formula is to be used for a man in like case.[1]

In the next world a correct knowledge of magic words and formulas was absolutely essential. There no door would open to him who knew not its name ; no demon would allow the passage of the dead who did not call upon him correctly, nor would any god come to his help unless invoked by the right name ; no food could be had so long as the exactly prescribed prayers were not uttered with the true intonations. But the dead who knew these formulas and who knew how to speak them correctly at the proper moment, who was *maâ kherû*, "right speaking," might rest assured of immortality and of eternal blessedness. Hence there was added to the names of the dead, and even occasionally to those of living persons, this epithet, in order to characterize them as

[1] *Metternich Stela* : cf. *Aeg. Zeit.*, 1879, pp. 1 *et seq.*

rightly prepared and perfect for entering into eternity, there to have dominion over both gods and men.[1] The number of the magic formulas was incalculable ; still they accumulated as the world to come was pictured in greater complication and refinement of detail, and such was their potency that they inevitably constrained the demons to the aid of those who knew them. At the words, "O door ! I know thy name, which is so-and-so," straightway the door sprang open. So too it was with every divinity : the secret name of a god was scarcely uttered before he was at the disposal of the dead who invoked him, and whom he was bound to help to the full extent of his power and capacity. The firm belief cherished by the Egyptians as to the efficacy of formulas and magic in the next world prevented any doubt as to the possibility of practising sorcery here. Sorcerers were in demand on every hand, and well understood how to fortify the faith of their clients by the display of conjuring tricks : in the Bible we have an allusion to feats of this kind performed before Pharaoh in opposition to Moses and Aaron.

Hitherto we have considered Egyptian magic only on what we may call its good side, as being helpful to man in life, in sickness, in affliction, and also after death ; but far greater was the harm feared from it than any pretended good hoped for. The power of the sorcerer was prodigious.

---

[1] Cf. MASPERO, *Études de Myth.*, i., pp. 93 *et seq.* ; ii., pp. 373 *et seq.* Sometimes it appears as if the Egyptians had used the epithet *mad kherû* in a more passive sense. Thus it is applied to a person who had been declared by the godhead to speak right, to be *mad kherû*, and therefore worthy of immortality, as, for instance, the judgment before Osiris.

Thus in the Ptolemaic Story of Setna[1] two formulas are mentioned, and "if a man recite the first he will enchant the heaven, the earth, the Underworld, the mountains, and the waters; he will know the birds of the sky and all reptiles; he will see the fishes of the deep, for a divine power will cause them to come to the surface of the water. And if a man read the second formula, then, although he lay in the grave, he shall take again the form which he had on earth; he shall see the Sun god rising in the sky, and his divine cycle; he shall see the Moon god in his true form which he takes at his appearing." It was not indeed easy to get possession of such formulas; those above mentioned lay in a golden box, which was in a silver box, which was in an ivory and ebony box, which was in a wooden box, which was in a bronze box, which was in an iron box. Round that was coiled a deathless snake, and there was a swarm of snakes and scorpions and all manner of creeping things which must be vanquished before a man could secure the formulas for his own. But, as the Story of Setna shows, this was not considered an impossible thing to do; and if the possession of the formulas brought Setna to grief, it was not because of their intrinsic nature, but because he had been guilty of wrong doing, and had thus put himself in the power of the spirits which he thought to have controlled.

According to the texts, the magicians of Egypt were guilty of turning their science to the injury of their fellow men. It is related that a man was sentenced to death for

---

[1] For the *Story of Setna* see *Egyptian Tales*, W. M. FLINDERS PETRIE, London, 1895.

trying to harm Pharaoh himself by means of magic, and in the papyri we have repeated instances of hurtful formulas. The sending of dreams, as described above, might be the means of producing most unpleasant effects ; but, worse still, a woman at a distance might be compelled by means of intricate rites to fall so desperately in love that she no longer ate or drank, no longer anointed herself or sat down, and took no thought for anything about her until she came to the man whom she loved. Love charms have been familiar to many nations. Theocritus, in his second idyll, gives a highly poetical description of how such sorcery was practised by the Hellenes in Alexandrian times. In Roman times it was considered necessary solemnly to forbid it. Paulus the jurist decreed that any one guilty of having presented a love philtre should be sent to the mines if he belonged to the lower classes, and if to the upper should be banished to an island, as a warning to others ; but if he had thereby caused the death of either man or woman he should be executed. During the Middle Ages, too, belief in love spells and charms and philtres was rife, yet after all it is to the Egyptians that the doubtful credit belongs of having been the first to systematize such practices.

Magic could not only cause very disagreeable inconvenience, but it might also bring about death : there is a set of directions for visiting your enemy with shivering and fever—probably ague—until he is undone ; in another place we are told how a man may be made to die of insomnia, and there is much more of the same kind. Absurd as the pretensions of the magicians may seem,

the multitude thoroughly believed in them, and great was
the fear of sorcerers and of sorcery. In Egypt magical
doctrines were not mere popular superstitions ; they were
part of the religion of the land, which was largely based
on magic, and always intimately connected with it.

CHAPTER XI.

AMULETS.

IN Egyptian texts of all periods amulets and their uses are prominent. They are represented in the scenes as borne in the hands or worn on the bodies of all sorts and conditions of men, and even of gods; and as minor Egyptian antiquities they abound. Some of these objects were regarded as amulets simply on account of their ideographic value as hieroglyphs. Others were closely connected with doctrines sometimes formulated to explain the shape of the amulets, and sometimes representing forms of belief otherwise rarely mentioned in the texts, but which must nevertheless have prevailed extensively, judging both by the diffusion of the amulets themselves and by the frequent allusions to them. Any sketch of the Egyptian religion must therefore necessarily contain some account of these objects.

1. The commonest and most important of all Egyptian amulets is in the shape of a scarabaeus; generally it is modelled with the wings closed, but in later times it also represented the beetle with wings outspread. The insect is the *Ateuchus sacer*, common in Mediterranean countries and especially in Egypt. The female *Ateuchus* lays her egg in a cake of dung, rolls this in

the dust and makes it smooth and round so that it will keep moist and serve as food for her young ; and finally she deposits it in a hole which she has scooped out in the ground, and covers it with earth. This habit had not escaped the observation of the Egyptians, although they had failed to understand it, for scientific knowledge of natural history was very slight among all peoples of antiquity. The Egyptian supposed the scarabaeus to be male, that it was itself born anew from the egg which it alone had made, and thus lived an eternal life. The idea of the phoenix as arising from its own ashes was a similar one; and as the phoenix subsequently became a symbol of human immortality, so was it also with the scarabaeus : the scarabaeus came forth reanimate from within its egg, and so the human soul, *i.e.* the *ba*, would emerge from its mummy into new life, and, winged like the scarabaeus, fly upwards to heaven and the sun.

Thus the scarabaeus became a symbol of the resurrection, like butterflies and flowers in later times ; but the Egyptians were confirmed in the use of such symbolism by their devotion to the verbal suggestions of their own language. The Egyptian name of the beetle was *kheper*, a word which also means "to become," "to come into being"; so the picture of the scarabaeus became the ideographic sign for that verb, especially when used in the sense of renewed life after death. And it was believed that for the man who was buried with a scarab upon him this immortality was already to some extent secured, or that at least the gods might be constrained to grant it.

Besides being guarantees of immortality, scarabs served

a second purpose, in common with another class of amulets consisting of conventional images of the jar in which the heart of the dead was usually placed when taken out of the body at embalmment, ♉. But since to the Egyptian the heart was the seat of life, it was evident that, as many of the religious texts imply and declare, there could be no resurrection of the dead who were without heart. Hence a distinct doctrine was gradually formulated as to the part played by the heart in the next world and how it was to be recovered by its owner. This taught that after death the heart led an independent existence, journeying alone through the Underworld until it met the deceased in the Hall of Judgment.

The doctrine was simple in itself, but to the Egyptian it presented great difficulty; for during the time intervening between death and judgment the Osiris was supposed to be without heart, and yet to be alive. The expedient was therefore devised of providing the mummy with a provisional heart for this intermediate period by means of an inscribed amulet of stone or earthenware, either of heart-jar shape or in the form of a large scarab, both being pledges of immortality. The inscription on these scarabs[1] related to the significance of the heart, and in it the dead desires that his heart may be with him when he assumes his different forms in the Underworld, that it may not give evidence against him in the Hall of Judgment, but may take his part at the momentous weighing scene. For the heart, as he emphatically asserts, is a

---

[1] BIRCH, *Aeg. Zeitschr.*, 1866 and 1867: cf. *Book of the Dead*, chaps. xxvi.—xxx., lxiv., ll. 34-6.

distinct personality within him : it is the god Khnûm, the creator, strengthening and making sound his limbs. It is also independent, able to find its own way, and to open the path to the gods both for the dead and for his name. In conclusion, the deceased assumes that his wishes are already granted ; his heart has been favourable to him, there is joy at the Judgment, and he lives, *i.e.* he is pronounced worthy of immortality.

This formula and its explanatory texts teach the curious doctrine that it is not the heart which sins, but only its fleshly envelope. The heart was and still remained pure, and in the Underworld accused its earthly covering of any impurities contracted. Only if the latter was pure did it return to its place ; otherwise it probably dwelt in a place set apart as the Abode of Hearts, and so devoted its former possessor to destruction. Like all amulets, the heart scarab was only of temporary efficacy ; once the judgment had taken place it was powerless to prevent destruction.

2. Generally there are found with any carefully interred mummy one or two examples of an amulet in the form of a knot, ⚱, and made of gold, red stone, or glazed ware : this amulet is called *tet*. According to the texts with which it is sometimes inscribed,[1] it represents the blood of Isis, which, together with her conjurations and formulas, protected the dead and destroyed all that was harmful to him. If such an object was placed with a man in his grave it enabled him to become one of the

---

[1] *Book of the Dead*, chap. clvi. : cf. MASPERO, *Mém. sur quelques Pap. du Louvre*, pp. 1 *et seq.*

followers of Osiris; the doors of the Underworld and the ways of heaven and of earth were open to him, and a corn-field was granted to him in the Fields of Aalû.   The amulet was most efficacious when made of carnelian and hung about the neck of the dead; but, judging from the various positions in which it is found on mummies, no particular weight seems to have been attached to the latter direction.

3. The sign ☥ is found as an amulet; this too represents a knot.   Since *ânkh* was the name of the knot and also a word meaning "life," the picture of it served as the ideogram for the letter.   It has nothing whatever to do with a cross; the name of *crux ansata* has no more relation to its origin or nature than the countless conjectures as to its hidden mean-ing made before the decipherment of the hieroglyphics and even at the present day.   The sign was placed in the hands of gods and

FIG. 71.—PERSONIFIED ÁNKH.
(L. D. III. 207, *b.*)
Khûnsû Temple, Karnak, XXth
Dynasty.

kings to show that they were living; and in some cases they are represented as using it to "give life," as the Egyptians called it, by touching with the symbol the mouth of the being to whom they are imparting their gift.   In very early-times an independent existence had been ascribed to the *ânkh*; there is an inscription on an altar dedicated to King Pepi of the VIth Dynasty[1] which names the *ânkh* and the symbol of stability (*ded*), together with joy, day, the year, and eternity, as beings

[1] Now in Turin.   Published by BONOMI and BIRCH in the *Trans-*

to receive divine honours. In scenes we may also find a sort of pictorial personification of the sign, furnished with arms and legs.

4. The *ded* amulet, ⌸, has been much misunderstood. It has been taken for a fourfold altar, a stand on which sculptors put down their tools, a representation of the universe showing four superimposed worlds, a disbranched tree trunk, and more especially for a Nilometer ; but none of these identifications has been proved. The inscriptions show that the Egyptians themselves considered that the symbol stood for the backbone of the god Osiris, that part of his body which was kept as a sacred relic in the city of Busiris in Lower Egypt. The backbone gives stability and firmness ; and the setting up of the backbone of Osiris was one of the most important functions at the restoration of his body after its dismemberment. This was annually celebrated at Busiris on the 30th Khoiak, at the end of that part of the Egyptian year devoted to the Osirian festivals, and was kept with strange rites ; *e.g.* the priests of the different sanctuaries fought together with fists and cudgels. This was probably the same feast as that described by Herodotus[1]

actions of the Soc. Bibl. Arch., iii., pp. 110 *et seq.* An attempt has lately been made to show that a long series of monuments inscribed with names of sovereigns of the Old Kingdom—this monument included—are forgeries of the end of the New Empire. I must confess that in by far the greater number of instances this attempt seems to me to have failed : in the case of this altar there seems no reasonable motive why any Egyptian should have taken the trouble to forge either the altar itself, the king's name upon it, or the list of divinities.

[1] Cf. WIEDEMANN, *Herodot's Zweites Buch*, pp. 265-6.

as celebrated at Papremis, another city of the Delta, and which was supposed to show how once the followers of Set had opposed the restoration of Osiris.

The *ded* amulet was a memorial of the resurrection of Osiris, and by virtue of its name it acquired a further significance. *Ded* means "firm," "established," and this quality or condition was greatly desired by the Egyptians for their dead. Chapter CLV. in the Book of the Dead is devoted to this amulet. The picture of the symbol is given, and the deceased speaks: "Thy back (backbone) is thine, thou who art of the still heart (Osiris); it is granted in thy place. I give unto thee thy needful humour (*mū*). I bring unto thee the *ded*, whereupon thou rejoicest. These are the words to speak over a gilded *ded* made from the heart of a sycomore and placed on the neck of the glorified one. Then he shall enter through the door of Dûat. This shall be done in his place on that day on which begins the year of the followers of Osiris (*i.e.* on the first day of the god's new life). If a man knows this chapter he is a perfect glorified one in the Underworld, who shall not be turned back at the gate of Amenti, to whom shall be given bread, cakes, quantities of flesh on the altars of Râ (Variant: of Osiris the Good Being); right are his (the deceased's) words (*mað kherû*) against his enemies in the Underworld, in true wise." As the text shows, this amulet also procured for the dead entrance in the Underworld, and sufficed to provide him with needful food there. The Egyptians, however, judged it more prudent not to trust to one amulet alone, but rather to be buried with many, so that in case any one failed in its object others might take its place.

5. The significance of the papyrus column ╽ [1] as an amulet was chiefly owing to its ideographic value: its name was *úaz*, a word which means "to be green," "to sprout up." Here, as in many other languages, a metaphor derived from plant life became transferred to the life of the soul. A Ptolemaic relief shows plants growing out of the body of Osiris; this represents the new life of the dead as evolved from his own body: "growing green" becomes a paraphrase for "resurrection." Chapter CLIX. of the Book of the Dead was devoted to this amulet, and was to be spoken over a little felspar model on which the words were inscribed, and which was to be hung round the neck of the deceased. It begins with the invocation: "O thou who goest forth on that day from the house of the god, great-speaking mistress of potent magic formulas, who comest forth by the gate of the palace and seizest the magic formulas of her father!" this being evidently an allusion to the legend of Râ and Isis, and the magic power which Isis had guilefully acquired from him.

6. The *úsekh* amulet was supposed to ensure freedom of movement after death. In derivation the word *úsekh* means "to be wide"; it is specially employed in connexion with the formula, "Thy legs are wide"— *i.e.* thou movest freely.[2] This is the attribute symbolized by the amulet, which was a gold necklace and was placed on the neck of the "glorified one." According to Chapter CLVIII. of the Book of the Dead, the words

[1] Cf. p. 219.

[2] Cf. the name of the first judge in the hall of Osiris, "He whose legs are wide coming from Heliopolis" (*Book of the Dead*, chap. cxxv., l. 14).

inscribed on it should be : "My father, my brother, my mother, and thou, Isis, I am freed from my mummy wrappings and I see. I am one of those who are freed from their mummy wrappings and who see the god Seb." As in most similar Egyptian texts, the deceased assumes that his prayer is fulfilled, for this could not fail to be the case if he had spoken the correct formula in the right way.

7. The amulet representing the human eye, with indications of the lines and modellings about it, was in Egyptian named *ůza.t.* Some of these amulets represented the right ⟨eye⟩, and others the left eye ⟨eye⟩ of the god Râ. But as the right represented the sun and the left the moon, Râ is in this connexion considered as the god of the light giving heavenly bodies rather than as the Sun god only. The eye of day was usually called the eye of Horus, and was regarded as the source of all things good. Many useful and agreeable products, such as wine oil, and honey, were said to come from it, and were ultimately confounded with it ; sometimes they were said to come from its tears. The eye of day, and also the eye of night, were again and again in peril from the attacks of Set, and in solar or lunar eclipse often seemed to have been conquered by him. But the eye always in the end came out victorious, and hence it was that the dead were placed under its protection, in the hope that they too would triumph over the powers of darkness and of death. Besides, the word *ůza* means "flourishing," "healthy," and as an ideogram the amulet had also this significance. It was bound on the knuckles, neck, or

breast of the mummy, or placed within the abdomen. The material of which it was to be made is not prescribed, and it is found in gold, lapis lazuli, felspar, wood, and glazed ware : next to the scarab it is the commonest of all Egyptian amulets.

8. One series of amulets was connected with somewhat different ideas : they represented the insignia of kingship, especially the kingship of Osiris. In the first place there were *net* ⬦, the red crown of Lower Egypt ; *hez* ⬦, the white crown of Upper Egypt ; and ⬦, the *pshent*, which was a combination of the two, and by assuming which Pharaoh proclaimed himself lord over the whole land. In the second place there were sceptres : the amulet of the royal sceptre, *tis* ⬦, which gave dominion over heaven and earth ; *hek* ⬦, the shepherd's crook, also used as the ideogram of the word *hek*, "to rule"; and *nekhekh* ⬦, the scourge. The *hek* and *nekhekh* symbolized the twofold power of the king : to restrain and moderate, and to incite to progress. These and other similar amulets were given to the dead with the idea that he would not merely continue the same kind of life which he had led here, but that he would become an Osiris, a ruler of the Underworld. The necessary badges of his dominion were therefore placed ready to his hand, and their intrinsic magic efficacy was a further guarantee that he would surely attain to the power which they symbolized.

9. The amulet ⬦ represents the so-called "cartouche," or "royal oval," which enclosed the names of the kings and of the kings of the gods, so that even in writing

such names should be obviously distinguished. This amulet stood for the name of the dead ; for the Egyptians regarded the name not only as part of a man, but also as part of his immortal ego : no being could exist without a name. Hence it was a man's supreme wish that his name might live, for if his name continued that which it expressed would also live on. This was the main object of the careful reiteration of the name in inscriptions on the walls of temples, stelae, and other monuments : that it might be spoken and kept alive by the readers. Even in Pyramid times a formula had been compounded, which remained in use to the end of Egyptian history, constraining the gods to cause the name of the dead to flourish.[1] But it was also needful to protect the name, since to know the true name of any being was to be master of the owner and of his powers. No risk was involved if the name were inscribed upon something in itself sacred, for the sacredness of the object protected the name also ; but if it were written on anything not so protected, such as the amulet in question, he who obtained possession of the latter had power over the name, and power therefore over the owner of the name. Thus, most of these amulets were uninscribed : so long as there was nothing on them to steal, a demon had no profit in possessing himself of them. This doctrine of names did not, however, remain in force throughout the whole duration of the Egyptian monarchy : under

---

[1] LIEBLEIN, *Le Livre Égyptien, Que mon nom fleurisse*, Leipzig, 1895 : cf. WIEDEMANN, *Le Livre des Morts*, in *Le Muséon*, xv., pp. 40 *et seq.*

Amenophis III., for instance, names were freely inscribed on these talismans.

10. The *menâ.t* (⌘) was worn hung at the back of the neck, serving as a kind of counterpoise to the necklace ; it was worn by certain goddesses, and also by Ptah. It served a symbolic as well as a practical purpose ; the sight of the *menât* drove away care, even as the sight and sound of the sistrum brought peace and joy to the heart. It was also a sign of divine protection, and as such we see it presented by goddesses to the king ; as such too it was laid with the dead, especially in Saite times.[1] Generally it was made in glazed ware.

11. The following amulets should here be mentioned and briefly described. Their wide diffusion testifies to the esteem in which they were held ; but their exact significance is undetermined. The rarer amulets we shall not consider.

, *nefer*, represents originally a heart and trachea ; afterwards it appears to have been taken for a stringed instrument. It is the ideogram for "beautiful," "good," and as an amulet was meant to secure these qualities to the dead.

, *sam*, signifies "union. This amulet was supposed to secure union with the earth in "good" and orthodox burial, and also union with the gods, a pantheistic deification.

, *neh*, the figure of a right angle. The sign seems to have the meaning of its phonetic value *neh*, "protection," *i.e.* divine protection to the soul.

---

[1] For this amulet see LEFÉBURE, *Proc. Soc. Bibl. Arch.*, xiii., pp. 333 *et seq.*

khekh, *sekhekh*, represents a level, to which, however, the plummet is usually lacking. It symbolized the justice and moderation hoped for on behalf of the dead.

khti, the image of the sun rising on the hilly horizon, and the symbol of the god Râ Harmakhis. The dead man provided with this amulet was assured of union with the sun ; he might rise with the sun in the morning and sink with it to rest at night : in short, he would be as a god in the next world.

12. Statuettes of gods or figures of their insignia were laid with the dead in their coffins and abound in Egyptian tombs ; generally they are of glazed ware and furnished with a ring for suspension. Necklaces of these alone, or in combination with other amulets, were hung round the necks of mummies. By taking with him the statuette of any god the deceased placed himself under the special protection of that deity, who would help him according to its power in the world to come : Osiris would uphold him at the Last Judgment ; Isis and Nephthys would recite potent formulas in singing his funeral lament ; Khnûm would help him to build up his new body, etc. The greater the number and variety of such statuettes a man took with him, the more certain might he feel that, where the power of one god for his help and protection ceased, it would be supplemented by that of another.

The same purpose might be served by drawing pictures of the gods in question on mummy wrappings or on the coffin ; pictures or statuettes alike were supposed to be changed into the real gods, who in the Underworld hastened to the service of the dead as soon as he invoked them by the correct formulas.

13. Other counterfeits placed with the dead might in the same way be changed into corresponding realities in the next world : an expedient which greatly reduced the cost of funerals. These votive objects were, in the first place, tiny models of useful articles, such as shirt like garments finished off with a fringe round the bottom, ⵎ ; this was generally made in stone. There were also stone or earthenware models of seals, ☉, and of head rests, ⵣ, which the Ancient Egyptian, like the present Soudanese, placed under his head to preserve the arrangement of his hair during sleep ; and of tools, etc., of all kinds. Food also was thus symbolically represented, a custom to which Herodotus alludes when he tells how poor Egyptians, at the feast of the full moon, made votive swine of dough to take the place of real swine as offerings.[1] Funerary offerings, however, were often made, not of perishable bread, but of stone or of glazed ware, and by virtue of magic formulas these produced the foods which they represented, at the desire of the dead. The process might even be carried so far that not only, for instance, one ox but thousands of oxen might be made from the one image. Generally images of oxen bound down for slaughter were made of red earthenware. There were also tiny models of different kinds of fruits and many of loaves of bread, ⵀ. These so called "funerary cones" have been the subject of many false explanations. Almost invariably they are of unbaked clay, the name

---

[1] ii. 47.

of the dead for whom they were intended being written on the flat base to prevent any misappropriation of the supply. And there were models of libation vases ⍭ for the Nile water, which they kept fresh and cool, besides many other things of the kind. Sometimes several offerings were combined in the shape of a little altar piled with provisions for the use of the dead; one of

FIG. 72.—HYPOCEPHALUS IN THE BRITISH MUSEUM. (DRAWN BY W. H. RYLANDS, ESQ.)

these little altars, now in my possession, is scarcely $\frac{3}{8}$ in. wide by $\frac{5}{8}$ in. long, and displays two libation vases, four loaves of different forms, and two fruits. Other similar altars are still more richly furnished.

14. Finally, there is an amulet differing essentially from all which we have hitherto considered, and known as a hypocephalus because usually it is found under the head

of the mummy. The hypocephalus[1] is generally a disk
of stuccoed linen ; sometimes it is found in bronze. One
side is blank, but the upper side, that upon which the
head rested, is covered with figures and inscriptions, which
do not seem to have been strictly prescribed but rather
to have varied in detail acccording to taste. On the
whole, however, the purport of the texts is much the
same, and a description of the hypocephalus figured in
the accompanying illustration may stand for a general
description of all such objects.[2]

A line of inscription runs round the disk and reads :
" O thou shrine in *Hat benben*, Exalted One, Exalted
One ! Glorious One, Glorious One! Husband [of thy mother],
great, living God ! Chief of the gods, come thou to the
Osiris Hor (name of the owner of this hypocephalus),
maâ kherû. Grant that there be warmth under his head,
for he is one of thy followers." A central band of figures
crosses the field of the disk ; the central figure is a
squatting god with four rams' heads, two turning one
way and two another, and crowned. This god is Amen ;
the four heads represent the four winds, and show that
he is lord of the winds and of the four quarters of the
world. On either side of him stand three cynocephali,
each wearing the solar disk. These are the spirits of
the East and of the West, of sunset and sunrise, doing

---

[1] It may be remarked that the Mormon religion is largely founded
on a fantastic interpretation of such a hypocephalus.

[2] Published, *Proc. Soc. Bibl. Arch.*, vi., p. 52 : cf. *l.c.*, pp. 37, 106,
126, 129, 170, 185 ; vii., p. 213 ; PLEYTE, *Chapitres Supplémentaires
du Livre des Morts*, 162-163, pp. 60 *et seq.*; LEEMANS in *Mém. du
Congr. des Orientalistes* at Leyden, iv. 3, pp. 91 *et seq.*

homage to Amen, who is also Amen Râ, the god of the Sun.

Directly over the figure of Amen is the figure of a god with two human heads, of which one is turned to the right and the other to the left. This also is Amen, striding from West to East, lighting and looking upon the whole world. On his head he wears the plumes of Amen, the sun disk, and the usual ram's horns. The head of a jackal grows from either shoulder, emblematic of the two forms of Anubis as Opener of the path of the North and Opener of the path of the South, and on the god's sceptre Anubis, in the form of a jackal, is carried as his guide. To his right is an inscription: "Thou (Amen) art in the eight souls of thy gods," *i.e.* thou appearest in all the divine manifestations which thou animatest. Beneath the inscription the Sun god, Râ, sits in his bark, in the form of a sparrow hawk with outspread wings. On the other side of Amen are two barks, one drawn above the other ; on the middle of the upper boat is perched the soul (*ba*) of the deceased, the name of Isis being inscribed on one side of it and the name of Nephthys on the other, in allusion to the deceased as an Osiris, bewailed and protected by the two divine sisters. At one end of the lower boat squats the hawk headed Râ ; at the opposite end is written the word *ba*, " soul " (of the deceased) ; between them is a scarabaeus coming towards Râ : that is, the soul of the deceased in the form of a scarabaeus, of the god Khepera, approaches the Sun to become one with him and with the universe.

Turning the disk upside down, on the other side of

the central band, below an inscription referring to the inundation of the Nile, we find a scene with a cow in the middle. This is the MEIIÛRT, or Hathor cow, upon whose thighs, as we are told in a very ancient text,[1] the sun of yesterday was born, other inscriptions explaining that by this is meant not the sun of the previous day, but the night sun which had been born on the evening of that day, for this cow was one of the forms supposed to dwell in the western sky. Mehûrt, or rather the *ûzat* which is born of her, is the sun, or the moon, and therefore behind the cow is drawn a female figure with an *ûzat* eye for a head. In front of the cow stand the four funerary genii which have charge of the viscera of the dead, while behind the *ûzat* headed figure is a scene of adoration. Here an ithyphallic snake god figured with arms and legs, the cosmic deity NEIIEBKA, is adoring a winged god who is seated upon a throne, crowned with the solar disk and bearing a scourge. This is intended for Amen Min, *i.e.* for Amen as the god of procreation.

The fundamental idea of these scenes and inscriptions is pantheistic : they express a belief in an all embracing power of nature, especially as manifest in the Sun. This deity was the source of the gods, and they were manifestations of him ; this was the power which protected the dead, and their hope it was to be merged in him. None the less this universal god had his abode in Heliopolis, in the sanctuary of the temple of the Sun, and to Heliopolis therefore the doctrine must be traced. These Heliopolitan

---

[1] *Book of the Dead*, chap. xvii., l. 29 : cf. LEPSIUS, *Aelteste Texte*, pl. ii., l. 24 ; pl. xxxii., l. 36.

views, however, found expression on the hypocephalus,
not as a confession of faith on the part of its owner,
but only because he hoped to induce Amen Râ in his
pantheistic form to grant him the warmth needful even to
the dead.

The texts which most clearly set forth this pantheistic
tendency, expressed principally in late Egyptian texts, are
found on the walls of the temple at El Khargeh, which was
built during the Persian rule. Here we have a long hymn
placed in the mouths of eight gods which have been considered erroneously as gods of the elements ; and it is from
this that the following passages are taken [1] :—

" The gods salute his Majesty as their lord, who revealeth
himself in all that is, and whose name is in all, in the hills
as in the river. Amen is in all things. This venerable
god was from the beginning, the earth was according to his
plans ; he is Ptah, the greatest among the gods. . . . The
heaven is upon his head, the water containeth thy secret.
All beings praise thee when thou settest at evening in the
Underworld (Dûat). Thou awakenest Osiris by the glory
of thy rays. They who rest in their graves hail thee. . . .
Thou art lord, thine is the dominion. Lord of heaven, the
earth is subject to thy will. The gods are in thine hand
and mankind lieth at thy feet. What god is like unto thee ?
The land of Memphis openeth to thee as Ptah ; like Amen
thou hast made thy throne in Ankh-ta-ûi (Memphis).
Thy soul is the support of both heavens. Thy form went

---

[1] Published by BRUGSCH, *Reise nach der Oase Khargeh*, pls. 25-
27 : cf. BIRCH, *Trans. Soc. Bibl. Arch.*, v., pp. 293 *et seq.* ; RENOUF,
Lectures on the Origin of Religion, pp. 231 *et seq.*

forth at first ; thou shinest as Amen, Râ, and Ptah. . . . Shû, Tefnût, Nût, and Khûnsû are thy forms in thy sanctuary under the forms of Min who lifteth his feathers on high. . . . Thou art Ptah, thou appearest as the Nile. Thou art the old, thou art the young. Thou givest life to the earth by thy flood ; thou art the heaven, thou art the earth ; thou art Dûat, thou art the air, and all that in them is."

Such ideas of the entering of the god into all things, or rather of the entering of all things into the god, were of great antiquity in Egypt: in the Pyramid texts we find the same views applied to the deified dead and elaborately set forth in very crude concrete terms.[1] There we read that "the sky weeps, the archers (the constellations) flee away, the bones of the guardian of the gods tremble and their subjects flee, when they see the dead king whose soul appeareth as a god, who liveth on his fathers and feedeth on his mothers ; he is the lord of magic wisdom, whose name his own mother knoweth not." He devours men, and lives on the gods whom he hunts with the assistance of several demons ; he eats their magic formulas and consumes their magic power ; the great gods serve him for breakfast, the medium gods for his noonday meal, the little ones for supper ; the old gods, male and female, he uses for his oven, *i.e.* for fuel. He eats the crown of Upper and Lower Egypt that he may be lord of the whole land.

These pantheistic views found their way into the Book

---

[1] *Pyramid of Unas*, ll. 496 *et seq.*; *Pyramid of Teta*, ll. 319 *et seq.*

of the Dead. Chapter CLXII.,[1] "The chapter of giving warmth under the head of a glorified one," is devoted to the hypocephalus and is characterized by a long series of passages of similar import to those given above.

"Hail to thee, mighty lion (sacred animal of Râ), Exalted One with the two feathers, Lord of the Diadem, thou who wieldest the scourge. Thou art lord of virility growing in shining rays, to the splendour of which there is no limit. Thou art the lord of many bright coloured forms, who embraceth them in his *âaat* (the sun) for his children (mankind). Thou protectest those who are separated from the circle of the Ennead of the gods (? probably beings of the Underworld). Thou runner, striding far forth with his legs. Thou art the god of salvation, coming to him who calleth upon him, saving the wretched from the hand of his oppressor.

"Come at my call. I am the cow (Mehûrt). Thy name is in my mouth; I will speak it: *Penhakahakaher* is thy name, *Aûlâûaâkresaank-Lebatî* is thy name, *Khaib-mâu-serâu* ("shadow of the lion of the ram") is thy name, *Khalsatâ* is thy name.

"I praise thy name, I the cow. Hearken unto my prayer on this day; give warmth under the head of Râ. Protect him in Dûat, renewing him in Heliopolis. Grant that he may be even as one who is upon earth. He is thy soul. Forget not his name.

"Come unto the Osiris N. N. Grant that there be warmth under his head. Oh! he is the soul of the great

---

[1] Cf. PLEYTE, *Chapitres Supplémentaires du Livre des Morts*, chaps. 162-3, pp. 6 *et seq.*

corpse which rested in Heliopolis, (Râ,) the Radiant One, He who becometh, the Great One (or the Ancient One) is his name. *Barekatàthaña* is his name. Come! Grant that he may be like unto one of thy followers. Oh! he is thyself.

"[These are the] words for a young cow which is made out of beautiful gold and placed on the neck of a glorified one, and which are written upon a new papyrus leaf which is placed under his head. Henceforth there is much warmth in all his forms, even as it was upon earth. This is a very great talisman which was made by the cow for her son Râ at his setting. Then was his throne surrounded by comrades, to protect him from the fire (?) ; he was renewed in the Underworld, nor was he shut out by any gate of Dûat, conformably to order (the result being inevitable for one who wore this amulet).

FIG. 73.—THE MEḤÛRT COW. VIG-NETTE OF CHAP. CLXII. OF BOOK OF THE DEAD. (LEPS., 'TODT.")
Ptolemaic.

"Words which thou hast to speak when thou placest this goddess (the cow) on the neck of a glorified one : 'O Hidden One (*Amen*) among beings, Amen, who dwellest in heaven, mayest thou turn thy face hither towards the corpse of thy son (the deceased) ; restore him to health in the Underworld.'

"This book is a great secret. Let it not be seen of any eye. It is a sin to know it, to hide it, to make it, this book of the Lady of the Temple (the cow) whose name is hidden." A Leyden text has an appendix to the effect that the writing was made by the cow (Isis, as identified with Mehûrt) for her son Horus, and concludes with the invocation : " O Osiris, and ye dwellers in the Underworld, may you protect the Osiris N. N., may his well being be your well being, and inversely ! "

It is obvious from this text that the fusion of the Râ myth with the Osirian myth was complete. Amen, who is as Râ, is called to the help of the dead because the god too had suffered death ; the same plea which was formerly addressed to Osiris. Just as in the Osirian faith it was held that the most potent amulets had first proved their efficacy in the case of Osiris himself, so it was held that the hypocephalus had first been used for the dead Râ.

The Leyden text still further connects the hypocephalus with the Osirian myth by stating that the amulet was used by Isis for Horus, who appears in the later versions of the myth as a dead god restored to life. Notwithstanding the fundamental pantheism of this formula, it is full of traces of the effort to preserve the distinct individualities and fates of different gods from absorption in the universal deity. To this end the gods are explained as equivalents of that deity, which is shorn of its all embracing nature and imagined in the form of a man in order that to it also a life history may be attributed. The above text is thus an interesting example of the absurdities in which the Egyptians were necessarily landed whenever they attempted to express deep philosophic thought in terms of their religion. It was inevitable : far from resigning any article of their ancient faith, they invariably sought to turn every single characteristic of it to account, and in the ensuing absurdities lay the germs of the decay and death of the national religion. The thoughtful Egyptian must have recognized its impossibilities ; he must have admitted to himself that gods such as he was taught to worship could in nowise be co-existent ; he must have known that his religion was not true.

When Christian evangelists came into the Valley of the Nile, apparently the people in general gave up their heathen faith without struggle. Until the third century A.D. mention was indeed made of the ancient gods on the walls of temples and in inscriptions ; but these were official documents of the heathen authorities : to the people, and especially to the upper classes, their gods no longer appealed. In the course of a few decades Christian doctrines had penetrated deeply into the consciousness of the nation. Among all the translations of the books of the Bible the Coptic translation is the oldest ; and Coptic—the spoken language of the country from the first century A.D.—was the daughter tongue of Ancient Egyptian. The Coptic version was no learned book intended only for a restricted circle of adherents to the new faith ; it was a popular work issued almost contemporaneously in different dialects of the country. Full of the courage of faith the Christians by the Nile endured the storm of persecution which broke over them under Diocletian, and with burning zeal took part in the fierce strife concerning dogmas which rent the Christian world of the fourth century. Isolated at length through rigid adherence to doctrine, to this day the Coptic Church stands aloof from the rest of Christendom.

INDEX.

K

Ka, the, 87, **240-2**.
—— of Shû, the, 87.
—— the king's, 176.
Ka (god), 146.
Kambyses, 137, 200.
Karnak, 125, 127.
Kebehsenûf, funerary genius, 248.
—— one of the souls of Nekheb, 163.
Kedesh, **152-3**.
Kek (darkness), 233.
Kekt, 233.
Khâ (sunrise), 30.
Kha (corpse), 234.
Khafrâ, 29.
Khaib, the, 242.
khekh amulet, 296.
khens, 124.
kheper, 31, 285.
Khepera, 24, **31**, 32, 44, 45, 51, 55, 113, 197, 300.
—— in Dûat, 92, 93.
Khepersh helmet, 113.
Kheraû (Bes), 160.
Kherheb, the, 139, **236-7**.
Kheta treaty, 150, 151.
Khoiak, feasts in, 135, 212, 215, 289.
—— 10th, 264.
Khnûm, Khnef (Khnûmis), 105, **128-9**, 287.
Khnûm Râ, 13, 43.
Khnûm, sacred animal of, 119, 128-9.
Khnûmû, the, 137.
Khû (glorified dead), 48 *et pass.*, **242**.
khû amulet, 296.
Khûenaten (Amenophis IV.), 36-9, 43.
Khûfû, 53.
Khûnsû, 104, 107, **124-5**, 225, 303.
—— Carrier out of Plans, 124, 275 *et pass.*

Khûnsû, Fair-resting One in Thebes, 124, 275 *et pass.*
—— Her, 125.
—— month of, 261.
—— nefer hetep Shû, 33.
—— Râ, 125.
—— Shû, 125.
—— Thoth, 124.
King, the, as incarnate deity, 175-6.
—— in temple, 203.
—— the son of the god, 53, 175, 183-4.
Kom Ombo, 124-5.
—— triad of, 104.
Krokodilopolis, 192.
Kronos, as Seb, 207, 208, 231.

L

Labyrinth, the, crocodile cemetery in, 193.
" Lady of the Bark," 87.
—— of the Temple," 305.
Lake of necropolis, 230.
—— of temple, 204.
" Land of Life," 49, 50.
—— of Rest," 49.
—— of the Deep," 67.
Latin, 170.
Latopolis, 33.
Legend or myth of Isis and Osiris, 206-218.
—— —— of Râ and Isis, **54-8**, 214, 291.
—— —— of the Destruction of Mankind, **58-68**, 138, 231.
—— —— Winged Sun Disk, **69-79**.
Leto (Ûazit), 141, 214.
Letopolis, 27, 28, 117.
Libanius, 145.
Libyan deities, 140, 148-9, 159.
—— influence, 36.
Libyans, the, 111, 112.
Light and darkness, 78-9.

R

râ, 14.

Râ, 14, **25-7**, 30, 33, 36, 44, 52 *et pass.*, 83 *et pass.*

—— and Isis, 54-8.

—— and Osiris, 43-4, 91-3, 94, 101-2, 212, 214-5, 218, 306.

—— and Sebak, 143.

—— and the dead, 88-9, 91.

—— as Pharaoh, 52, 91.

—— barks of, 23-4 *et pass.*

—— fusion of, with other gods, 17, **43**, 108, 306. *See* Amen *and* Osiris.

—— hymns to, 44.

—— in Dûat, 84 *et seq.*

—— in his Aten, 35.

—— name and nature of, 14-15.

—— old age of, 55, 58.

—— sacred name of, 56-8.

Râ, Son of," or "Son of the Sun," 53.

—— *See* Amen Râ.

Râ Harmakhis, 17, 32, 42, 49, 69, 197, 266, 296.

Râ Harmakhis Aten, 39.

Ram of Amen Râ, 86 *et pass.*, 118-20.

—— of Khnûm, 119, 128-9.

—— of Min, 127.

Râmâka (Hatshepsût), birth of, 162-3.

Rameses II., 81, 134, 146, 150-2, 198.

—— III., 18, 54, 124, 146, 152.

Râ-neb-maâ (Amenophis IV.), 36.

Râ.t taûi, **15-16**, 30, 125.

Relics of Osiris, 216-17.

ren, 241. *See* Name.

Rennût, 146.

Renpt, 169-70.

Reptiles, formulas against, 64-7.

Rert, 169.

Resef, 146.

Resef (Phoenician), 152.

Reshpû, **152.**

Rhea as Nût, 207.

S

Sa, 87.

Sacred Ways, 204-5.

Safekht, 156, 226.

Sâhû, the, **242**, 243.

Sais, 93, 199.

—— festivals of, 141.

—— triad of, 140.

sam, 295.

—— amulet, 295.

Samhûd, 122.

Saqqarah, god of the necropolis of, 136.

Satit, 105, **130.**

Saturn (planet), 30.

Scarabaeus, the, 284-5.

—— and deities, 31, 88, 92, 146, 300.

Scarabs, 284-7.

Scribes, carelessness of Egyptian, 64, 84.

Seb (Keb), 59, 64, 106, 107, 134, **230-1.**

Sebak, **143-5**, 223. *See* Sûkhos.

Sebennytos, 30.

Sehel, 131.

Seked, 74.

Seker (Sokaris), 134.

Sekhem, the, 112 (note), 242-3.

Sekhet, 60, 61, 132, **137-8**, 264.

—— crown, 113, 114.

Sekhmet (Sekhet), 87.

Sekti, 60.

—— bark, 24, 47, 48, 51, 88, 135.

Selene in Plutarch's Osirian legend, 207.

Semitic deities and influence, 25, 149-55, 223.

Sepd, 160, **164-7.**

Sepulchral texts, 83.

Printed by Hazell, Watson, & Viney, Ld., London and Aylesbury.